Manufacturing Green Prosperity

Recent Titles in
New Trends and Ideas in American Politics

Importing Democracy: Ideas from around the World to Reform and
Revitalize American Politics and Government
Raymond A. Smith

Manufacturing Green Prosperity

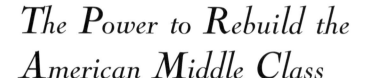

The Power to Rebuild the American Middle Class

JON RYNN

FOREWORD BY ROBERT E. PAASWELL

New Trends and Ideas in American Politics
Raymond A. Smith, Series Editor

 PRAEGER

AN IMPRINT OF ABC-CLIO, LLC
Santa Barbara, California • Denver, Colorado • Oxford, England

Library of Congress Cataloging-in-Publication Data

Rynn, Jon.
    Manufacturing green prosperity : the power to rebuild the American middle class / Jon Rynn; foreword by Robert E. Paaswell.
        p. cm. — (New trends and ideas in american politics)
    Includes bibliographical references and index.
    ISBN 978-0-313-38476-9 (hbk. : alk. paper) — ISBN 978-0-313-38477-6 (ebook) 1. Economic development—Environmental aspects—United States. 2. Manufacturing industries—Environmental aspects—United States. 3. Sustainable development—United States. 4. Environmental policy—Economic aspects—United States. I. Title.
    HC110.E5R96   2010
    338.973'07—dc22   2010007935

ISBN: 978-0-313-38476-9
EISBN: 978-0-313-38477-6

14   13   12   11   10   1   2   3   4   5

This book is also available on the World Wide Web as an eBook.
Visit www.abc-clio.com for details.

Praeger
An Imprint of ABC-CLIO, LLC

ABC-CLIO, LLC
130 Cremona Drive, P.O. Box 1911
Santa Barbara, California 93116-1911

This book is printed on acid-free paper ∞

Manufactured in the United States of America

To Sharon, my wonderful wife, and to Joshua and Ryan, my amazing sons, who inspire me to write and motivate me to create a better world

Contents

Series Foreword

Change is perennial within the American system of politics and government: the electoral calendar, the ebb and flow of presidential administrations, shifts along generational lines, and long-term patterns of partisan realignment—to name a few of the rhythms and cycles to be found in the political sphere. And so, one year's innovative thinking can become the next year's conventional wisdom, and then the following year's stale orthodoxy. This book series, *New Trends and Ideas in American Politics*, focuses on the most important new currents that are shaping, and are shaped by, U.S. politics and government.

The early 21st century is a particularly important time to focus on a proactive approach to the participatory processes, governmental institutions, socioeconomic forces, and global contexts that determine the conduct of politics and the creation of public policy in the United States. The long demographic dominance of the Baby Boom generation has begun to recede as the Boomers age, even as society becomes ever more open and diverse along lines of race, ethnicity, gender, and sexuality. From the waning of the worship of "the market," to the disasters of the Bush era, to the unprecedented presidential election of 2008, to the steady emergence of a more multipolar and ever-less-certain global context, Americans are faced with new challenges that demand not simply new policies and procedures but entirely new paradigms. At the same time, emerging vistas in biotechnology and information technology promise to reshape human society, the global ecological system, and even humankind itself.

New Trends and Ideas in American Politics casts a wide net, with volumes in the series unified mostly by novel, sometimes even counter-intuitive, perspectives that propose new policies and approaches for Americans to govern themselves, to relate to the rest of the world, and to safeguard the future for posterity. This is no small task, yet throughout its history, the United States has proven itself capable of initiating creative, productive periods of reform and renewal. Indeed, in one of the most strikingly regular and recurrent features of American history, intense periods of political change have occurred about every 30 to 40 years, including the founding in the 1790s, the Jacksonian age of the 1830s, Reconstruction in the 1860s and 1870s, the Progressive Era of the early 20th century, the New Deal of the 1930s, and the upheavals of the 1960s.

By this reckoning, the United States is overdue for another such fertile period of political reform; indeed, all the elements of a major political realignment are already in place: the Reagan Revolution has run its course, its political coalition fragmented beyond recognition; government is proving itself unable to tackle issues from health care to the environment to globalization, yet seems frozen in place; and citizen engagement is on the rise, as seen in such measures as exceptionally high voter turnout in 2004 and 2008 and proliferation of citizen discussion in political blogs and at "tea parties" tinged with near-revolutionary zeal. Discerning the patterns in this welter of change will be among the chief tasks of *New Trends and Ideas in American Politics*.

In this volume, *Manufacturing Green Prosperity*, Jon Rynn offers an important new voice at the intersection of two major debates: the meaning and impact of the decline of the U.S. industrial sector and how to respond to the increasingly urgent need for environmental protection, eco-conscious technology, and green jobs. Rynn argues that, contrary to conventional wisdom, a strong manufacturing base is absolutely necessary if the United States is to remain a prosperous country. A green infrastructure of transportation, energy, and urban life can both rebuild and be built by the manufacturing industries.

Rynn contends that the more the United States can democratize its economy by increasing employees' skills and decision-making power, the greener and wealthier it will be. With the analysis of a scholar and the passion of an activist, he makes the case that the abandonment of manufacturing will not advance the United States to the status of a post-industrial country but rather return it to being

a pre-industrial one, leading to downward mobility for future gener-
ations. In *Manufacturing Green Prosperity*, Rynn offers a different way
forward.

Raymond A. Smith
Series Editor

Foreword

When I moved to Buffalo, New York, in 1964, the local and national economies were flourishing. And why not? Our auto manufacturers were turning out 8 million cars each year, feeding them to an ever more prosperous population. Housing was on a growth surge that seemed never-ending, as were all of the manufactured items that go into houses and display the new American lifestyle. Buffalo, indeed all the rust belt cities—Detroit, Cleveland, even Gary, Indiana—contributed significantly to this exuberant economy. In Buffalo and Niagara Falls, Bethlehem Steel, Dunlop Tire, and primary chemical producers had major plants, each of which supported thousands of workers and their families, as well as the places where those families shopped and played. This region could be labeled a geographer's dream. It had (and has) excellent transportation by every mode—highway, rail, air, water—giving it a locational advantage. It had cheap hydropower energy and abundant water. It had—and still has—a solid housing stock. And it had that most critical economic component: a highly skilled, well trained, educated labor force.

When I left Buffalo in 1982, the city population, which was greater than 500,000 in 1964, had shrunk to 300,000. The younger skilled workers and their families had moved out. Steel plants, tire plants, and their suppliers had gone; the suburb of Lackawanna, New York, once a symbol of black smoke manufacturing, had become a ghost town. The grain elevators were empty. What happened? What mistakes were made by these metropolises on the Great Lakes?

Jon Rynn has given us a clear picture on the fundamentals of economic failure. His overarching approach of defining ecosystems leads the reader to conclude that Buffalo, and indeed, Detroit, Cleveland, and Gary, did nothing wrong. In fact, grasping at subsequent economic development strategies in the 1980s and 1990s, national and local, did little to alleviate the problems of declining employment, underutilization of a skilled labor force, and population out-migration; in fact, by providing assistance but not understanding regional economics, these strategies only exacerbated the problem.

These local problems were being repeated, albeit in different form, nationally. The country was undergoing a fundamental shift during the 1980s, from strong manufacturing base to a service- and finance-based economy. The engineers and entrepreneurs who built our great industrial and postindustrial society were replaced with accountants and lawyers who looked only at the bottom line. Simply, during this period, we exported our manufacturing know-how and entrepreneurial edge to Asia and Eastern Europe; we are still paying a great price for that. And those younger workers who left Buffalo, Detroit, and Cleveland? There were fewer manufacturing jobs to go to; retraining, often for lower paying jobs, put bread on their tables. Now, we are in the last chapter of the shift from manufacturing to service. This chapter has not ended well as the country is searching, in 2010, for the newest generation of employment generators.

But Rynn tells us that there is some hope. Achieving that hope must come through a paradigm shift. The paradigm shift arises from the fact that the 21st century must address and solve problems of dislocation created, ironically enough, by the wealth of the 20th century. We have the tools to remain productive and to create a high quality of life for our citizens. Nevertheless, the paradigm shift must embody values that integrate environmental awareness and equity instead of wealth generation for its own sake. His example of transportation, my own discipline, is a showcase for how the new paradigm calls together environmental awareness, the role of manufacturing, and economic multipliers with innovations in energy. What we have learned from the 20th century is that apparent social gifts (for instance, the personal car) have large-scale unintended consequences. Organizing our resources and energy supplies and rethinking capital investment through major shifts in national budgeting can achieve new sources of economic strength and sustain a high quality of life.

Rynn refers to this as the "Green Transformation"; this also arises from new approaches to regional and urban planning being discussed throughout the nation.

What remains to be done? The difficulty in paradigm shifts is to prod institutional change. The institutions that budget, plan, and build our infrastructure and would support new industry are still laboring under rules, regulations, and organizational structures and operating philosophies designed to meet 20th-century needs. The paradigm shift will start in our schools and places of higher education, in community groups and citizens panels. As these workers and others have impact on the agencies and firms that employ them or on the governments that set their missions, shifts will occur.

The bottom line is that we must reindustrialize—sooner rather than later. This is at the heart of Rynn's work. In contrast to Buffalo, the next generation of investments is being made in Albany, New York. The nanotech complex brings together academics and industry in a multibillion-dollar complex that addresses high-tech solutions to problems in health and the environment. A major research and development complex, nanotech combines the best of computer designers and engineers and physical and biological scientists to develop state-of-the-art, cutting-edge, prototype products and processes that represent this century's entrepreneurial contributions. It employs thousands, involves many suppliers, and has had a very great, positive impact on Albany and its surrounding communities. It is only one happy ending for New York state, but it points the way toward meeting the paradigm shift so elegantly envisioned by Rynn.

Robert E. Paaswell
Interim President and Distinguished Professor of
Civil Engineering (on leave), The City College of New York
15 April 2010

Acknowledgments

This book would not have been possible without the friendship of Seymour Melman, who was a Professor of Industrial Engineering at Columbia University until he passed away in 2004. Through countless dinners and conversations, I learned a wealth of knowledge and insight from one of the great economists of our time. He is very much missed.

Toward the end of his life, Seymour sought to bring subway manufacturing back to the United States, and through that effort I had the good fortune to come to know Robert "Buz" Paaswell, Interim President of the City College of New York; Mike Locker of Locker Associates; and Jonathan Feldman, Professor at Stockholm University. I have gained much from their wisdom.

I owe a debt of gratitude to David Roberts, senior staff writer and blogger extraordinaire at the Web site Grist.org, who helped launch me into the blogosphere and beyond. I am also very grateful to have Ray Smith as my editor, and to be associated with Robert Hutchison at Praeger Publishers.

I am indebted to Howard Lentner, my dissertation advisor at the City University of New York, and the other professors in the political science department who were very helpful and friendly during my time there: Wentworth Ofuatey-Kodjoe, Lenny Markovitz, Thomas Halper, John Bowman, Christa Altenstetter, Asher Arian, William Tabb, and Francis Fox Piven.

I would like to thank the Institute for Policy Studies for their support, including financial support from a Seymour Melman

Fellowship grant. Marcus Raskin, Miriam Pemberton, and John Cavanagh have encouraged me and helped me to pursue many intellectual projects, including this one.

There are numerous friends who have helped me in many ways on this and other projects: Marshall Auerback, Bryn Barnard, Mitch Berman, Tom Boucher, Brian D'Agostino, Patrick Deer, Jeff Dumas, Ted Glick, Jim Haughton, Gar Lipow, Mike McCullough, Chris Sanders, Elizabeth Savage, Chuck Spinney, and Colin Wright. Also, my supportive family of David, Margie, Glenda, my father, Nathan Rynn, and my mother, Ruth Rynn. And of course, I relied on the love, support, and patience of my wife, Sharon, and my sons, Joshua and Ryan. Thanks to all.

CHAPTER 1

Introduction: An Overview

We live in the best of times, times in which science and technology have made incredible advances, the international political system is the most peaceful it has ever been, and democracy steadily advances. But we also live in the worst of times, times in which the U.S. economy and middle class have gone into long-term decline, global warming, if not stopped, could fundamentally alter life, critical ecosystems are being destroyed, and the end of the era of cheap oil has arrived. We seem to possess the means to solve our global, systemic problems; yet we are having a hard time setting a path that will lead us to a sustainable future.

BEST OR WORST?

Computers and new communications technologies seem to be changing our lives almost every day. Scientists are continuously exploring new ways of understanding the world, including the universe, terrestrial ecosystems, and the inner workings of the cell and the human body. Engineers constantly create technological change, including better vehicles, better buildings, and better gadgets. Cutting-edge factories are miracles of productivity and output.

Despite the horrors of 9/11, this may be the most peaceful moment in world history, at least among the planet's most powerful nations. No one seriously thinks that war could break out among the United States, Europe, China, India, or even Russia or other

large countries such as Brazil. Before 1991 and the breakup of the
Soviet Union, the threat of nuclear and conventional superpower
war hung over our collective heads; the 20th century had been the
most violent, including two world wars; the 19th century was one
long string of international and colonial wars, and so on, back for
thousands of years.

With the important exception of China, most countries in the
world are at least nominally democratic, a first in world history.
From 1776, when the United States was born as a white-male-property-
owning democracy, until now, a world in which India and Russia are
democracies, along with Latin America and most of eastern Asia, the
peoples of the world have never had such a large voice in the conduct
of their own affairs.

And yet, even with all of this technological, international, and
national good news, the world stands at the precipice of environmental collapse, and the people of the United States, in particular,
risk slipping into a sharply lower standard of living. Even as scientists are able to unravel the complexities of ecosystems, those ecosystems are being wiped out. The engineering marvels of the global
energy system are leading to changes in the climate that will melt
the glaciers needed for many of the world's rivers, wipe out cities
that are close to sea level, and turn lush agricultural areas into deserts.
The global transportation infrastructure and much of the world's
buildings were constructed on the assumption that oil will continue
to be found for a very long time, even though global production has
peaked. Although medical advances are made in the United States,
millions of people can't even get medical help.

Even though the Cold War no longer exists, the enormous U.S.
military still does, soaking up money and engineers, embroiling the
United States in unwinnable and unwise wars such as in Iraq and
Afghanistan. Human beings seem to have moved from making war on
each other to making war on the planet, stripping it of various minerals, leveling huge forests, and turning oceans into wet deserts. Even
though there are fewer global wars, there is more global poverty.

Although people can elect their political leaders, they can't elect
their economic ones. In the United States, large corporations have
just about taken over the federal government; hundreds of chief executive officers (CEOs) have more power than millions of voters.
Globally, financial and corporate decisions affect whole communities
that have no say over how their economies are affected. In the United

States, millions of people and thousands of communities had no choice but to see their factories closed and their jobs lost.

On the one hand, we have the technological means to solve the myriad problems we face, we have the democratic means to achieve those ends, and the international situation is conducive to a peaceful, cooperative resolution of these crises. On the other hand, we face a daunting set of interconnected problems that are global in nature, that provide wealth and power to those already wealthy and powerful, and that require the development of a new global consciousness.

A SYSTEMS PERSPECTIVE

This book is written with the assumption that we live in a world full of tough problems, but that it is possible to build a better global civilization. To handle the complexity of these times, *Manufacturing Green Prosperity* will offer a new framework for understanding the political, economic, and ecological systems that are at the heart of what we call civilization. In particular, an entirely new kind of economics will be presented with the following characteristics: an economics in which production, and manufacturing in particular, is acknowledged to be at the center of economic life; one that presents a realistic picture of the need for the government to design and finance much of the structure of the broader economic system; and one that incorporates an understanding that, for an economy to operate in the very long run, it must be a good steward of the environment on which it depends.

Once we have a usable framework in hand, we can more easily understand the interactions of the various parts of our society and ecosystems. We can more clearly perceive the direction that the system as a whole is headed, and then we can better understand what kinds of solutions are needed. We will need to change some of the fundamental structures of our global systems, not just fix things around the edges. When changes are big, we need a road map of where we are and where we are going.

In this book, I will use the concept of a *system* to mentally organize the complexity of national and global systems. The term has been used for many things over the years,[1] so I will be very specific about my definition of the term. Generally, a system contains both the elements that compose it and a *structure*, that is, a description of how the pieces fit together. For instance, a drawing is composed of lines and dots that are positioned according to a particular structure; one kind of structure of lines might lead to a drawing of a face. With the same elements, a different structure might lead to a drawing of a window.

How do you know what elements make up a system and how they are structured? You create different models and see which one is better at explaining the complex system under consideration. In the domain of economics, the conventional, neoclassical model is the one that is most used, and it has many important problems. It cannot differentiate among different sectors of the economy, such as manufacturing and finance; there is no concept of a "function" in neoclassical economics, that is, every firm is assumed to exist as a separate, nearly identical entity in a competitive market.

What if we thought of the economy as an ecosystem, like a forest, made up of essential pieces or niches, all of which are dependent on each other? We can model a society as being composed of several systems: first, an economic system, which in turn would include a production system—machinery, which then produces manufactured goods, agriculture, construction, most services, and the physical infrastructure, including transportation, energy, and urban systems—and a distribution/exchange system—finance, retail/wholesale, marketing; second, a political system composed of the government, citizenry, and the territory of the country; and third, the various ecosystems, such as forests, oceans, water, air, grasslands, and climate. Each element of a system is itself another system. Throughout this book I will go into greater and greater detail about some of these systems, particularly the production system, and also show how these various systems form the structure of a wider system (see Figure 1.1).

Most importantly, all of these systems are interconnected. Changes in one system lead to changes in others, often reverberating back to the originator of the change. For instance, because of innovations in manufacturing, at the beginning of the 20th century the potential for automobile manufacturing increased rapidly, and because of advances in petroleum exploration, mining, and processing, enough gasoline was supplied to fill the gas tanks of all of the new automobiles. The transportation system was profoundly changed by the automobile, and oil therefore became an important part of the energy system. Eventually, cities were depleted by new suburbs. Pollution from oil affects both health and the climate, and as oil becomes more and more scarce, the entire oil-drenched parts of our

Figure 1.1 A political ecological economy as a system

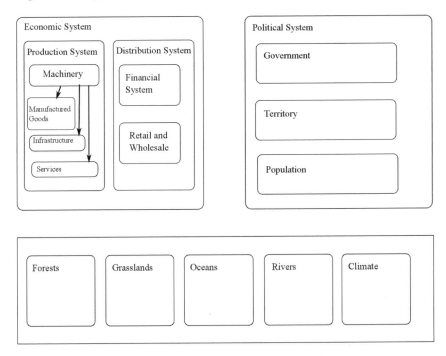

civilization will face decline and a restructuring. The automobile's very success will lead to its decline.

Because of the structure of the agricultural system, it has also risen and will soon decline. Over the millennia, societies have eroded and in various ways destroyed their soil, thereby making the production of food very difficult, if not impossible. Currently, the U.S. government subsidizes corn production, which is intensively produced, depleting soil and water, leading to the overuse of artificial fertilizers that pollute water and oceans, leading to algal blooms that kill large stretches of the ocean. Meanwhile, agriculture has become dependent on the aforementioned peaking oil, both for planting and harvesting the food as well as for transporting it the long distances it must now travel to the spread-out suburbs. The subsidized corn is used for feed for unhealthy livestock "factory" farms, which turn natural fertilizer (cow poop) into a terrible pollution problem. This form of agriculture is also responsible for about one-sixth of global greenhouse emissions. Industrial agriculture is destroying the ecological processes on which it depends.

Changing any one part of the society, involves changing myriad different parts as well. It's like a spider's web—pull on one part and the other parts move.

A SPIDER'S WEB OF PROBLEMS AND SOLUTIONS

Since the parts of the society are all interconnected, the solutions to their problems are interconnected. It will be difficult to solve one set of problems without solving another set at the same time. Solving one set of problems means restructuring one system, which is a critical part of other systems' functioning.

For instance, the economy of the United States is not creating enough jobs, and the middle class looks to be in long-run trouble. What to do? According to the argument I will make in this book, the basis of any large economy is its manufacturing sector, and in particular, its machinery industries. These have been declining in the United States for many reasons: the federal government has supported military industrial production, which has made military producers less able to compete in civilian markets; the government has also helped companies to close civilian factories and open them up abroad; improvements in transportation, particularly large cargo ships and trucking logistics, have made it possible for companies to easily import goods produced abroad; and financial manipulation has become a faster way to make profits than the laborious task of innovating and producing real goods.

The market alone cannot rectify this situation, because trying to make a profit in a market is a relatively short-term, narrow process of planning, whereas what we need is a long-term, systemic redesign. But the logic of the conventional, dominant framework for understanding the processes of an economy lead to the conclusion that the market is to be trusted over the government. The framework for understanding must be changed; then we can get on with the task of actually fixing the problem. Manufacturing can be rebuilt in a particularly effective way if the government simultaneously rebuilds several parts of society, in particular, the transportation, energy, and urban systems. By buying the output of domestic factories making vehicles, energy generators, and buildings, and by providing financing for firms to expand, government can fix three problems at once: a declining industrial base, a crumbling infrastructure, and a disappearing middle class.

In the process of rebuilding the infrastructure, governments could intelligently design those systems to be ecologically sustainable as well. The word *sustainable*, like the word *system*, has many meanings (as can the term *intelligent design*). Here I wish to use the word *sustainable* to mean indefinite, that is, a system is ecologically sustainable if it can operate in its current state for thousands of years; a sustainable economy would have to pass the same test. This is quite a tall order, but it is achievable, and should be the goal of any morally defensible society. Why would we design a society that will collapse at some point in the future?

By discussing the problem of a declining economy, we took up the problem of manufacturing, which led us to the problem of a crumbling infrastructure, which led to the possibility of making the infrastructure and society sustainable. If we look at these issues separately, the solutions not only become harder, the solutions might exacerbate the problems of other systems. For instance, we could just blithely assume that oil will continue forever, and focus our manufacturing program on a resuscitation of a petroleum-based automobile industry; meanwhile, we could try to rebuild the roads, which require massive amounts of petroleum-based asphalt; and the pollution from cars might exacerbate problems of pollution and global warming. If oil becomes too expensive, the car industry will collapse anyway, asphalt for repairing the new roads will become too expensive, and we might make pollution worse by desperately looking for solutions like using dirtier, more expensive oils like tar sands or coal-to-oil technologies, or destroying more agricultural areas by growing corn ethanol.

On the other hand, we could focus on electrified trains. Trains can use electricity, and electricity can be generated with renewable, that is, sustainable technologies, such as wind and solar energy. Instead of roads, trains use steel rails; steel is very easy to recycle, and steel also uses electricity for its manufacture.

But to use trains, the urban structure needs to be changed. Trains are not very efficient if everybody is spread out in suburbs, and the stores are spread out in malls and giant big boxes; in dense cities like New York City, trains such as subways are the most efficient powered vehicles known, but subways don't work nearly as well in spread-out urban areas such as Los Angeles. So to stop using oil we need to move toward the use of trains; however, to fully embrace trains we need to move toward denser, more diverse urban structures.

Like manufacturing and transportation, the problems of the health system are connected to many different sectors. Most famously, there is a large conglomeration of power called the health insurance industry, which controls the federal government's health policies, and directs unto itself a significant percentage of the resources needed for the health sector. This is a political economic problem: as power concentrates in an industry, like health care, the process of concentration increases in speed, and soon only a few behemoths remain standing. Since corporations are essentially dictatorships, a few CEOs have the power to control governmental policy, because they can much more easily organize among themselves than hundreds of millions of health service users. They grab governmental power, which hands over yet more power, and we see the expense of the health sector increase even as millions more people are denied health care services.

This process of power leading to more power is an example of a *positive feedback loop*. In a positive feedback loop, the increase of something leads to a greater probability that something will increase even more—like a snowball rolling down a snow-covered mountain. On the other hand, in a *negative feedback loop*, an increase of something leads eventually to less of that something, as when a thermostat detects that a room is too hot and turns off a heating system.

Although the health system is shaped by the positive feedback loop of the constantly increasing power of the health insurance companies, many of the causes of ill health emanate from the other systems we have been discussing. For instance, automobile accidents cause about 40,000 deaths per year, and hundreds of thousands of injuries; coal plants for generating electricity probably contribute a similar amount of death and destruction. If transportation was based on trains using cleanly generated electricity, the health system would not be burdened with two major causes of ill health. If agriculture was restructured to not use pesticides, artificial fertilizers, and live-stock factories, and if corn was not subsidized to make processed foods and drinks so inexpensive, the health system could shrink to an even smaller size. If people lived in walkable communities instead of their having to drive everywhere, the resulting exercise would lead to the population's better overall health. And of course, if there was a universal health care system, tens of thousands of deaths and ill-nesses would be avoided.

Thus there is a positive feedback loop, or a self-reinforcing synergy, among the various subsystems of the system we call society. It is actually easier to solve all of the various problems of society at the same time then to solve them piecemeal. Just as the whole can be greater than the sum of its parts, so fixing the whole would be easier than fixing its parts separately.

The transformation of a system from one structure to another is a long-term process, whether that transformation leads to an unsustainable system or whether the transformation moves society in a sustainable direction.

For instance, the late Professor Seymour Melman wrote a book in 1965 called *Our Depleted Society*[2]—depletion referring to manufacturing, a process that did not become evident until the turn of the millennium and still seems to have escaped the notice of much of the economics profession. The oil engineer M. King Hubbert predicted in 1956 that a peak in global oil supply would occur in about the year 2000; nobody believed him (they didn't believe his simultaneous prediction that U.S. oil production would peak around 1971, which it did).[3] It has taken decades to destroy most of the ocean's top predators and to reduce the world's forests to dangerous levels. We have been working for a couple of centuries on dumping pollution into the air and water, and emitting the greenhouse gases now threatening the long-term survival of civilization.

The design and construction of new, economically and ecologically sustainable energy, transportation, urban, manufacturing, and agricultural systems will be a long-term project as well. This program of economic reconstruction will consist of an enormous, upfront cornucopia of capital. Ironically, even though we live in a "capitalist" system, the concept of capital is not clearly understood.

CAPITAL, THE POWER TO CREATE WEALTH

According to the way I will use the term, capital is the power to create wealth in a society. It is not the wealth itself that people use and consume, but the *generators* of that wealth.

Almost 200 years ago, the German economist Freidrich List wrote:

The causes of wealth are something totally different from wealth itself. A person may possess wealth, i.e. exchangeable value; if, however, he does not possess the power of producing objects of more value than he consumes, he will become poorer. A person may be poor; if he, however, possesses the power of producing a larger amount of valuable articles than he consumes, he becomes rich . . . *The power of producing wealth* is therefore infinitely more important than *wealth itself* . . . This is still more the case with entire nations (who cannot live out of mere rentals) than with private individuals.[4]

Further, "the forces of production are the tree on which wealth grows, and . . . the tree which bears the fruit is of greater value than the fruit itself."[5] If capital, the power to create wealth, is not maintained, is consumed, or is in any way destroyed, then eventually wealth itself will disappear.

There are three types of capital that are necessary in order to build a wealthy society: physical capital, human capital, and natural capital. Financial capital only reflects the other three, and has no power to actually create new wealth.

Physical capital, for the most part, is the machinery that is used to create goods and services, and the infrastructure that enables the use of those goods and services. The rise and decline of Great Powers, the most important nations in any given epoch, is caused by the rise and decline of their physical capital sectors. In the 20th century, the three or four countries that were the Great Powers at any particular time produced about 80% of global industrial machinery output.

More important than physical capital, however, is the human capital that knows how to put the physical capital together. During World War II, Japanese and German factories were devastated, but enough engineers survived the war that those countries were able to eventually become the top machinery makers in the world. On the other hand, when factories are closed down, the human capital of the skilled workers and operational managers can be lost. When companies fire workers, engineers and skilled production workers lose the knowledge that those employees have of the enterprise's operations. Their wealth of experience is a form of human capital. Germany and Japan, which in their own ways make it difficult to fire employees, have reaped the benefits of the long-term development of human capital and now have the world's best machinery industries. Their engineers and skilled production workers make up an anchor for their middle classes, while in the United States the middle class is slipping away.

Underlying all other capital is natural capital, that is, ecosystems and resources.[6] Food comes from ecosystems, whether from hunting and gathering or from agriculture and gardening. Throughout history, societies that have depleted their natural capital—particularly, soil and water—have collapsed. The same could still happen today. Currently, we are busy destroying the natural capital of the oceans, which if intelligently managed, could easily provide much of the protein humans want. Other ecosystems, such as forests, provide services, like water management, prevention of soil erosion, and even generation of rainfall, as well as the genetic material for most of our food. Ecosystems also include the resources that we use, which are limited in nature, particularly fossil fuels.

Markets can create economic booms when investors become exuberant about new kinds of physical capital, like railroads, cars, or computers. Private firms can also liquidate their physical capital, allowing it to deteriorate, in order to milk factories for profit until they go bust. Governments have always played a critical role in building infrastructure; it is the hallmark of a declining civilization when their infrastructure is allowed to run down, as ours is now.

Governments are depended on to provide most of the human capital needed for the economy in the form of education. Business enterprises create an enormous amount of human capital as well, as people "learn by doing," as the economist Kenneth Arrow put it, but businesses will also throw that human capital away if they are allowed to pursue the lowest wages across the globe, as ours have done.

Markets are just plain catastrophic when it comes to preserving natural capital. Mining is the extreme example; you are digging something out of the ground that cannot be regenerated, and you might destroy an ecosystem or two in the process. Destroying an ecosystem to generate output is an example of destroying or liquidating capital by turning it into short-term output, for example, by clear-cutting a forest and turning it into timber or sweeping everything from a particular area in the sea in the course of fishing. Often the natural capital could be harvested sustainably, that is, by taking only as much as would not decrease the capacity of the ecosystem to produce; but instead, societies often try to maximize output in the short run, and destroy the capital from which wealth comes. They kill the goose that lays the golden eggs.

All three market-based capital problems could be at least partly solved if most firms were employee-owned-and-operated. Because democratically run firms would not shut themselves down, but instead would do everything possible to keep a factory or office open, then human capital would remain within the firm. The physical capital would be maintained, because it would be the key to the long-term future of the owner-employees. Employees come from the area in which they work; therefore, they would probably be more sensitive to the problem of destroying their natural environment as well.

SUSTAINABLE DESIGN

The market cannot design a *sustainable* interdependent set of infra-structures and industries. The government as currently constituted cannot either, because the government has been, to a large extent, captured by "the market." The market is essentially controlled by about 1,000 very powerful corporations, each managed by an omnip-otent dictator called a CEO. So essentially, the government is serv-ing the needs of 1,000 CEOs, not 200 million voters. And yet, it is up to the voters to remedy this situation; the democratic means exist for creating a citizen-controlled government, as opposed to a market-controlled one.

Assuming that we could have a citizen-controlled government, why would we then have a better chance to have a sustainable soci-ety? Much of the work of economic reconstruction will require large amounts of capital at the beginning, and generally governments have been the ones that can create, raise, or guarantee this capital, along with a hefty assist from the private sector.

After the initial continental systems of capital have been built, the general cost level of everyday necessities for most people will go down, and the standard of living will go up—but only if the syner-gies available when designing all of these systems simultaneously are captured.

To claim that the government must step in and design the basic structure of society certainly flies in the face of the last 30 years of the Reagan Revolution, which tried to sell the idea that the govern-ment can do no good (except when fighting wars). We see where this faith has left us; we also see that we face a set of crises that are not amenable to market-based solutions. We need a post-Reagan eco-nomics. What would a sustainable design of our infrastructure sys-tems look like?

The transportation, energy, and urban systems would ideally be designed as a set of interconnected systems. If buildings within cities were close enough together to enable the use of electrified mass transit, then we could wean ourselves away from oil and make the transportation system electric. In order to be ecologically sustainable, that electricity would have to be generated by renewable sources: an Interstate Wind System, solar panels installed on most buildings, and geothermal energy. In order to take advantage of the fact that wind is always blowing somewhere, we would need an Interstate Smart Transmission system. To minimize the use of electricity and natural gas, we would want to make buildings self-sufficient, at least in terms of heating and cooling, by giving most of them energy retrofits, geothermal heat pumps under them, and solar hot water and photovoltaic systems on top.

With a dependable system of renewable electricity, and denser, walkable communities, we could provide for relatively small, slow, short-distance all-electric cars and trucks, which along with electrified Interstate Freight Rail and Interstate High-speed Rail Systems, would eliminate most of the need for oil for cars, trucks, and planes. If farms and factories were close to cities, the freight system could be even smaller and less energy-intensive. Agriculture that rebuilds the soil, doesn't use pesticides and artificial fertilizers, and uses recycled organic material from a close-by set of cities and towns, and a manufacturing system that uses recycled materials, doesn't pollute, and creates goods that are easy to recycle, would make the entire production system eminently sustainable for the foreseeable future.

All of these systems need a thriving and competent manufacturing sector to build the necessary machinery and infrastructure. Manufacturing does not take care of itself, any more than any other part of the economy, and historically governments have been very motivated to ensure that the manufacturing base should be as competent as possible. In the case of the United States, rebuilding the manufacturing economy would require providing a stable market for private firms, so that they could plan on a steady supply of orders, and could confidently hire and train skilled workers and engineers. By planning for the construction of all of the various systems that I have outlined above, all of the parts of a manufacturing sector should be able to rebuild and grow.

Most of the government spending for a program of economic reconstruction should require that only domestic producers could participate; this means that foreign producers in the U.S. would qualify, because now many types of industry have disappeared from the United States. The government could require foreign firms to hire locally, or even engage in joint ventures with U.S. firms, or to work with new, employee-owned, and employee-controlled firms. As in Scandinavia, policies could be put into place to insure a high wage and salary level. Firm owners use more machinery in order to offset higher wages if the firms cannot move overseas, and this focus on using more machinery leads to more innovation and productivity, which in turn helps to rebuild the middle class.

Building a green economy is a golden opportunity to rebuild the manufacturing sector. Since so much capital needs to be provided up front, a citizen-controlled government should design and finance a long-range program of economic reconstruction, not the big banks and wealthy global investors.

The role of the financial system is to recycle wealth into the best possible investment. I have just outlined the best possible use of wealth in our society, the reconstruction of the economy to be sustainable. This means that in the medium term, most investment capital should be funneled through citizen-controlled government to reconstruct the society—that would imply the need for much heavier taxes on wealthy individuals and companies, and for a public banking system that could create the money needed for reconstruction. Ideally, national debt payments could be eliminated by replacing the debt with new money printed by the government, not the Federal Reserve, the way Lincoln financed the Civil War with greenbacks. Logically, the huge military-industrial complex should be converted into an infrastructure-industrial complex, since the long-term national security of a country is dependent on a sustainable infrastructure and economy.

At this point, the perceptive reader might be asking, "How could this possibly happen in our current political environment?" The answer is that, in the current political environment, this can't happen. The first step in changing the political environment, however, is to have a vision of where to go and how to get there. Part of that vision has to include an understanding of how the economy, infrastructures, ecosystems, and political system are all interconnected; that understanding will be the task of this book.

AN ECOSYSTEMS PERSPECTIVE

As I argued earlier, using the concept of a system is very useful for understanding complexity. Every theory, including mainstream economics, is based on some conception of what a system is. A theory, or paradigm, is a kind of system, at the heart of which is a model of a system.

A system contains elements, which may themselves be systems, and a system has a structure, a way in which the elements are ordered relative to each other. The model of an economic system in neoclassical economics doesn't have a structure, because a large number of identical firms are modeled as interacting in the same way, like a ball of gas or water. In ecosystems, there is much more structure, because each part, or niche, of the ecosystem fills a function; in a body, each organ also fills a function, but in an ecosystem, much as in an economy, the structure is much "looser," that is, there is not nearly the kind of coordination that there is in a body.

It would be better to choose a model of a system for an economic theory that is not too tightly interconnected, as in a body, and not too loose, as in a ball of gas, but that is more like an ecosystem—just right. Economies are more coordinated than a truly wild ecosystem—governments can and always have tried to shape and design their economies. A closer analogy, then, for an economy would be an ecosystem, like a national park that is closely managed by the National Park Service. Usually, the park ecosystem runs pretty much by itself—certainly the vast majority of actions take place without human interference. But when something is out of whack, does not fit together, or is making the system as a whole malfunction, then the Park Service steps in and makes some changes.

An economic system is part of a larger system, a political-economic system. The other subsystem, the political system, has its own dynamics. A domestic political system can be beset by a positive feedback loop; that is, those who have power tend to have the capability to gain even more power, which eventually results in dictatorship. In addition, the government can, because of its growing power, suck all of the economic resources out of the economy, particularly as it attempts to increase its means of expanding power militarily. Only a democratically structured political system can break these cycles, although democracy does not guarantee a positive outcome.

The production system stands at the center of the economy, and is the underlying cause of economic growth and the rise and decline of nations as well as of ecological collapse. The production system is itself made up of three levels, which are also systems. At the outermost level we have the production of goods and services, as well as the infrastructure. But what makes these goods and services? For the most part, machinery is used to make the goods and services we use. The second level is therefore what I will call the "production machinery" level. But what makes this production machinery?

At the center of the production system is a self-reproducing system, which I will call the "reproduction machinery" system, composed of a set of machinery which collectively reproduces itself. While in natural systems, organisms (like rabbits) have sex to reproduce, in the human production system, a certain set of machinery does the same thing. For instance, there is a set of machines called machine tools that shape and cut metal to make the parts for machines—including more machine tools. They also make the parts for other kinds of reproduction machinery, such as steel-making machinery, which makes the steel for more steel-making machinery, which also make the steel for more machine tools.

Part of the task of societal transformation will be to change the main reproduction machinery used for electricity generation, turbines, to wind turbines and solar panels, which will provide the energy for their own reproduction as well as the energy to run the other kinds of reproduction machinery, and the electricity for the production machinery used in factories, as well as the electricity used for consumer goods and services.

Changes in these most fundamental reproduction machinery technologies give birth to whole new eras—as we are witnessing with the introduction of semiconductor-making equipment, whose advances in technology have driven the computer and communications revolutions. In turn, changes in one kind of reproduction machinery reverberate to all the other kinds of reproduction machinery. For instance, changes in semiconductors accelerate technological change in the machine tool industry, just as changes in particular kinds of machine tools, such as grinders for optical equipment, make more powerful semiconductors possible.

We can further divide the reproduction machinery system into five separate niches—the machine tools are examples of "structure-forming" production, steel-making machinery is used for "material-making" production, the turbines (wind or steam) are for "energy-conversion" production, assembly lines are examples of "goods-moving" machinery, and the semiconductor-making equipment is for "information-processing" production (see Figure 1.2).

Figure 1.2 Reproduction underlies economic growth

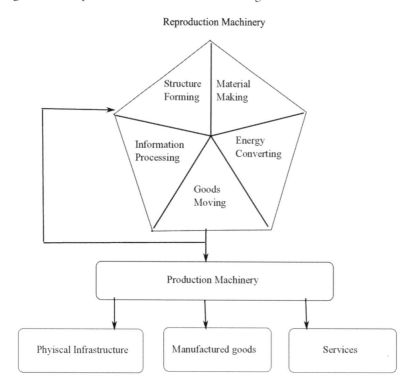

Thus, sitting at the center of the production system, reproduction machinery makes possible the positive feedback loops that both accelerate technological change, and also create the kinds of exponential (that is, constantly increasing) growth that we have been experiencing, particularly since the advent of the Industrial Revolution.

In other words, there are two kinds of economic growth: quantity-based and quality-based. We can spit out more and more machinery, and make more and more things, because reproduction machinery gives us the capability to do so. If those produced things—manufactured goods—use new raw material every time they are made, and pollute and spew carbon dioxide into the atmosphere, then quantity-based growth will be a source of more wealth for the society, but also is self-limiting because we will run out of the resources that are constantly being used up, as well as fundamentally changing the ecosystems that we're pouring waste into (such as in the case of global warming). A quantity-based economic system will rise and lead to its own decline.

The other source of economic growth consists of increases in quality, as when a semiconductor becomes more powerful or a machine tool becomes more precise, or even when we can produce more electricity with fuel-less energy-converting technology, such as wind power.

The inner two levels of the production system—production machinery and reproduction machinery—are the key elements of the manufacturing sector. Without them, the rest of the economy, and indeed, modern society, is impossible. They serve the specific functions of creating the means of production. They cannot be eliminated and the rest of the economy, such as services, is directly affected by technological changes in machinery. In fact, the most important technological changes are the changes in machinery technologies.

Services, for the most part, are what we do with machinery and manufactured goods. That is why 80 percent of world trade is in goods; it is difficult to trade something that is an action. The vast majority of the service economy is dependent on machinery. Then indirectly, the financial system is dependent on machinery to create the goods and services which then become the economic surplus that the financial system recycles back into the production system—or keeps for itself, as happens more and more, since the financial system can control the flow of those surplus resources.

The government also uses those goods and services to support its vast bureaucracy of employees, which then ideally manage the economic system in such a way that the economic system can expand, again ideally, in a sustainable way. The government often uses vast amounts of the goods and services produced by the machinery sectors to build military equipment, as the United States is doing today and the former Soviet Union fatally did after World War II.

The entire point of a military establishment is to destroy. But ironically, to destroy something you have to create the means of destruction, using, in particular, reproduction machinery. This is why machine tools, steel plants, and electrical generation have been the priority of any country trying to build an independent military capability. The United States, with the largest military establishment in world history, is losing the capacity to build its own military equipment; in other words, the United States is declining in its long-term capability to be a "Great Power."

In the short term, international power depends on military power, that is, the amount of destruction machinery at hand. But in the long term, since destruction machinery is produced by production and reproduction machinery, international power is based on civilian machinery. This is why the United States, which had a tiny military just before World War II, created the largest military system in world history during four years in World War II, because of its huge reserves of physical, human, and natural capital.

The military subsystem of the political system, and the financial subsystem of the economic system, both of which are completely dependent on the production system for their existence, do everything they can to rob that production system of resources so that they can expand their own power, thus leading eventually to their own downfall.

The financial system is particularly dangerous because of the speed with which its power can be extended, particularly in the era of high-speed computers. By contrast, a firm that controls factories controls something that takes much longer to use for the purposes of the projection of power.

In general, if a government or industry can increase their power by consuming, or *liquidating* capital, and thereby gain a short-term advantage over those who are *maintaining* their capital, the liquidators can use their short-term advantage to overwhelm the long-term maintainers. All societies contain this contradiction, and all societies, if they are to survive, must overcome it.

YES, WE CAN BUILD A SUSTAINABLE WORLD

The production system has a certain structure—it is made up of stages of production, from reproduction machinery to production machinery to final goods and services. The reproduction machinery subsystem is full of positive feedback loops, both in production and in technological innovation. The production machinery industries depend on reproduction machinery innovations to propel their own advances, as well as developing some of their own, which can then be used to create better goods and services. All of these parts of the production system are interconnected, and all of them should be in close proximity to each other to maximize the speed with which innovations and production occur if we want to maximize economic growth. Therefore, a production system needs to be situated in a territory within which there is free trade among the various parts, the territory should be *large* enough to encompass a full suite of industries, and the territory should be *small* enough that the various parts are in close enough proximity that innovation and production are maximized. This means that a "natural" production system is continental, or in the case of the supercontinent of Asia, subcontinental in size—but not global.

If economies need to be continental, then for the poorer parts of the world to develop, they need to form economic unions, just as the Europeans have done. We are entering the era when a continental political economy must be spanned by large, sophisticated, sustainable infrastructural networks and policies. The basic structure of the production system cannot be left to the market, even though within each particular industry, the market will dominate. Government policy should ensure economic sustainability as well as ecological sustainability. The infrastructure systems cannot be built without a strong manufacturing base, and a strong, sustainable manufacturing base requires a strong, sustainable infrastructure.

The care and feeding of a continent-wide, manufacturing-centered economic system, along with the green transformation of energy, transportation, building, and agricultural systems, would expand and lay the foundations for the long-term maintenance of the physical, human, and natural capital of society. The motto of every world region should be, "unify, democratize, industrialize—for the long-term."

How might all of this be paid for? The U.S. economy is very concentrated right now, and with that concentration goes extraordinary political power, which is used to prevent the government from using the resources currently controlled by those with economic power to reconstruct the society.

Mountains of finance capital and government subsidies are currently controlled by several sectors: the military, currently running close to $1 trillion in yearly expense[7]; the health insurance industry; the oil, coal, and natural gas industries; much of the for-profit utility industry; the large amounts of taxes that the richest few percent of the population should be paying; the large amounts of taxes that the large corporations used to pay but don't pay anymore; much of the financial industry; the real estate industry; and the industrial agricultural complex.

It is because of these large concentrations of power that Al Gore can correctly state that, in the case of global warming, "The maximum that seems politically feasible still falls far short of the minimum that would be effective in solving the crisis."[8] Going further, Wackernagel, Rees, and Testemale state, "In today's materialistic, growth-bound world, the politically acceptable is ecologically disastrous while the ecologically necessary is politically impossible."[9]

Although the current political situation may seem frustrating or even hopeless, we don't know for certain what is politically possible, in the long term. Why not *first* investigate what is "ecologically necessary" and economically essential, and *then* adopt a long-range strategy to make that plan of action politically possible? Hope is a rather vague concept; why not have the audacity to design a sustainable civilization?

PART ONE

A PRODUCTION-CENTERED ECONOMIC PARADIGM

As the economist John Maynard Keynes once said, "even the most practical man of affairs is usually in the thrall of the ideas of some long-dead economist," and that certainly applies to our era. Economic ideas can be very powerful, and none are more powerful than the various myths about manufacturing that are the subject of Chapter 2. Fortunately, sometimes a splash of reality can wake people from thralldom. A look at how the economy actually operates, at a comprehensible level of detail, particularly as concerns services and trade, should dispel some of the misconceptions about production and manufacturing.

It is not enough, however, to simply cast aspersions on the reigning philosophy. If one doesn't offer an alternative, then even the most ardent skeptic will have nowhere else to go, except to continue to wrestle with mainstream economics, like a dog chewing on an old bone. Chapter 3 attempts to explain an alternative theory of economics. This requires understanding how systems work. If the economy and society are modeled as systems, the chances are increased of being able to comprehend these very complex processes, which increases the chances that even the skeptic can throw away that old bone.

The most important phenomenon to explain in economics is the process of economic growth. Although people have wanted to know how to increase economic growth throughout most of history, we now also have to understand how to grow without destroying life on the planet. Can we have growth that doesn't require huge increases in the quantity of goods? Can we grow sustainably, that is, can we grow as if the human race was going to be around for millions of years? Chapter 4 attempts to grapple with these questions.

CHAPTER 2

Myths of Manufacturing

The conventional wisdom of the last few decades has been that manufacturing is not a necessary part of a wealthy nation. This attitude toward manufacturing is enmeshed in a series of carefully constructed myths. Services exist in a world that is separate from manufacturing; we live in a "post-industrial" world, that is, one in which we don't have to do much, if any, manufacturing in the United States. This leads to the myth that we can import whatever manufactured goods that we want. Somehow, they will just flow to us forever because all anyone needs are dollars, not goods and services. Most of the world thinks that they can grow their economy by selling to the United States. After all, in the magical world of the 21st century, the United States has proceeded through various "stages," emerging from the primordial agricultural society, to the intermediate step of manufacturing, finally appearing in the guise of a services-based society. Finally, the mythical base of middle-class employment is almost exclusively in services, since manufacturing jobs are never coming back.

In reality, both services and manufacturing are indispensable for a wealthy economy. Services are, to a great extent, those activities that people do to use manufactured goods. The two sectors, manufacturing and services, therefore depend on each other, and their interdependence leads to positive feedback loops of innovation and growth. The base of the middle class is both services *and* manufacturing, and the decline of manufacturing is leading to the decline of the middle class.

Part of the reason that these myths can be propagated is that the economy is discussed as if it were an abstract set of ideas, not a complex system of interdependent, functionally different parts. Mainstream, or neoclassical economics is based on its own set of myths, which I will explore in the course of this book, but critical to the neoclassical outlook is the idea that every part of the economy is basically the same and can be understood as a competitive industry operating in the short term. As an antidote to that sort of thinking, let's look at the economy more as a naturalist or ecologist looks at ecosystems: by examining what is going on in an actually existing economy. The first part of the economic ecosystem we need to understand is the services sector, which, it turns out, is a diverse, varied system of its own, dependent on manufacturing.

THE SERVICES MYTH

Let's start by looking at a table of the various services, including their size in terms of value-added, that is, the percentage of the economy they constitute. "Value-added" is the best way to compare sectors of the economy. Often, when people want to emphasize the importance of an economic sector, they will use the total industry output statistic, which shows not what the particular sector produces by itself, but what that sector *plus* all of the other sectors produced for that sector. For instance, the value-added for motor vehicles (mostly cars) in 2007 was $98 billion, yet the total output was $477 billion.[1] In other words, all the other industries added $379 billion to the motor vehicle output, while the vehicle industry itself added $98 billion. The advantage of using "value-added" as a measure is that, if you add up all of the value-added output for all industries, you come up with the gross domestic product, that is, the total output for the economy. In other words, you don't double count the various industries, and you get a more accurate reading of the various pieces of the economy.

I've also included the trade balances in Table 2.1, that is, the statistic which indicates whether a particular service sector has more exports than imports (a positive figure), or whether the sector has more imports than exports (a negative figure).

I have actually tried to minimize the number of categories; the first thing to notice in Table 2.1 is that there are quite a few

Table 2.1 Services Are a Very Diverse Set of Industries

Service	GDP	% of GDP	Trade Balance (billions)
Wholesale and Retail	1,415,845	12.87%	N/A
Transportation Services	319,284	2.90%	−18
TV, Radio, & Publishing	169,357	1.54%	0
Movies and Music	41,195	0.37%	10
Telecommunications	200,879	1.83%	0.8
Legal	160,587	1.46%	2.5
Accounting	69,450	0.63%	0
Engineering Services	106,458	0.97%	1.9
Software, Computer Services	208,958	1.90%	5.9
Management Services	267,927	2.43%	0.5
Scientific R&D	51,422	0.47%	4
Advertising	57,435	0.52%	−0.4
Other Professional Services	94,736	0.86%	N/A
Health Care	89,342	6.26%	2.1
Educational Services	94,511	0.86%	11
Arts, Entertainment, & Recreation	106,597	0.97%	−0.05
Hotels and Restaurants	383,057	3.48%	8
Employment Services	84,491	0.77%	N/A
Building Services (e.g., Janitors)	38,725	0.35%	N/A
Business Support (Call Centers)	107,412	0.98%	N/A
Travel, Security, Other Administrative services	54,276	0.49%	N/A
Repair and Maintenance	106,389	0.97%	4.3
Personal and Laundry Services	57,474	0.52%	N/A
Organizations & Social Assistance	166,527	1.51%	N/A
Finance	626,886	5.70%	13
Insurance	256,010	2.33%	−21
Real Estate and Leasing	1,367,399	12.43%	5.4
Trade in other services, not elsewhere categorized	0	0	7
Nonsoftware Royalties	0	0	24
Total Services	**7,302,630**	**66.36%**	**61**

Source: Percentages are from *Survey of Current Business*, January 2005, "Annual Industry Accounts," Table 1, and trade figures are from *Survey of Current Business*, October 2004, "U.S. International Services," Table 1. To calculate the value-added percentages for several small service subsectors, the data on revenue was used to calculate the percentage that a certain sub-subsector was of a subsector, and that percentage was applied to the subsector's value-added.

different kinds of services. Some services distribute the goods and services that the production sector creates, that is, they are part of what I call the *distribution system*. Retail services sell the goods that are the output of the manufacturing sector, and wholesale services store and distribute those goods; together they comprise 12.3 percent, or about one-eighth, of the economy. This includes Walmart and the other big-box stores, the small mom-and-pop stores that still exist, as well as larger warehousing centers. This sector is almost completely dependent on trucks and shipping, both of which are considered services.

Real estate constitutes fully one-eighth of the economy, almost exactly the same as the entire manufacturing sector. Real estate's function is to redistribute buildings, which have to be produced by construction workers using construction equipment, using materials output by the manufacturing sector.

So just distributing goods, services, and real estate comprises one-quarter of the economy, twice as much as manufacturing. Finance and insurance generate 7.5 percent of economic activity; finance, insurance, real estate, retail and wholesale, took up almost one-third of the economy. By contrast, in 1970, finance and insurance constituted 4.1 percent and manufacturing, 22.7 percent. Finance and insurance recycle surplus resources that translate into money that the rest of the economy generates. They generate nothing of tangible use themselves; they are completely dependent on others to generate that which they then use.

There are other parts of the distribution system. Advertising comes in at about one-half of 1 percent, as does accounting. Advertising might be ubiquitous, but it is actually of little direct economic importance (except in New York City). I'll also add in one-third of transportation's 3 percent for freight transportation, that is, trucks and ships. Adding this all up yields a little over one-third of all economic activity just for distribution of goods and some services. This doesn't even count the finance, marketing, and accounting departments of companies within the production system.

One kind of service has the function of directly interacting with government: legal services, at about 1.5 percent (one could count part of accounting here, perhaps). Then there is government itself, at about 12.9 percent of value-added. So distributive and government services together equal about half of the economy. Government is almost totally dependent on taxes, borrowing, and printing money; however, much of government spending is used to make military equipment. So one half of the economy—manufacturing (one-eighth, although dropping all the time) and the nondistributive services (three-eighths)—provide the wealth that enables the other half of the economy—the distribution system (three-eighths) and the government (one-eighth)—to operate.

Most of the rest of the services involve the use of manufactured equipment to help people. Health consumes 6.3 percent of gross domestic product (GDP); it uses massive amounts of equipment and drugs. The two-thirds of transportation that I didn't put under distribution is used to move people in nonprivate vehicles, such as planes, trains, and transit, and constitutes 2 percent of the economy. Hotels and restaurants, at 3.5 percent of GDP, use buildings and food machinery to provide a service. Telecommunications services, at about 2 percent of the economy, use sophisticated telecommunications equipment to move voice, video, and cable. Personal and laundry services (0.5 percent), such as haircuts, use various instruments and machinery as well. So at least 14 percent of the economy is taken up with using machinery to provide services.

Some services should probably be considered industrial, because machinery is their focus. Repair and maintenance of machinery, 1 percent, fits this definition, as could most engineering services, another 1 percent.

Then there are the entertainment sectors: TV, radio, publishing, movies, and music, at about 2 percent, and the rest of art, recreation, and other entertainment comes in at 1 percent. Most of the public would probably guess that these industries constitute at least one-quarter of the economy, because they focus so much attention on themselves, and they are certainly interesting to most people, but their contribution to the entire economy is quite small. Most of these small industries rely on telecommunications networks and various other, mostly electronic, technologies. Just as planes are used to move people from one place to another, TV and movie cameras, editing, and music studios move information and entertainment to people.

This "movement" takes place using flows of information. Because software, which takes up 2 percent of the economy, is the action of making changes to instructions for a piece of hardware, a computer, there might be some justification for considering software industrial. After all, the first hardware computers were hard-wired to calculate certain equations; by changing gears and other metal mechanisms, you could calculate a different equation. Now, of course, we can type in the changes in the form of pieces of software. In turn, software is used for all kinds of economic sectors, so it is probably safe to categorize software with the other services in which machines are used to provide a service.

Educational services, whether nongovernmental (about 1 percent) or governmental (1 percent from federal sources,[2] 3 percent from local sources for primary and secondary education,[3] and 0.5 percent from local higher education financing[4]), also require various kinds of media and information technologies, although here we see some straight person-to-person transfer of knowledge, some of it not mediated by technology. Organizations and social services (1.5 percent) may use various technologies, but are closer to being "pure" services. Scientific research and development, at 0.5 percent, usually involves some form of equipment.

There are various other services, such as management consulting at 2.5 percent of GDP, that are used in all industries, as well as miscellaneous services totaling 3.5 percent, which are numerous and involve a mix of machinery and people-to-people services. Most services either use machinery to provide the service, or are somewhat industrial in the sense of working directly on machinery; only small parts of particular categories of services are not focused on machinery of some kind. The conclusion is clear: services need machines.

Even the one-third of the economy that composes distributive services needs machines. The financial industry was revolutionized by computers and communications—it could not have taken down the global economy in 2008 without them! Then there is retail and wholesale, which Walmart and other big-box stores and chains have taken very far into the computer age by focusing on supply chains, that is, the complex task of making and moving goods all over the planet.

Once we break down the service categories, we can see how important manufacturing is even in the service industries. However, when we look at trade, we can see that the dependence is even stronger.

THE TRADE MYTH

Fully 80 percent of world trade among regions is in goods, and only 20 percent is in services. That is, if you take a region such as

North America, Europe, or Africa as a unit, then the vast majority of trade among these regions is in goods, not services. As the World Trade Organization (WTO) documents, "While the services sector generates approximately two-thirds of the total world value added, its share in total trade remains below 19 percent" in 2007.[5] As seen in Table 2.2, the United States is the only region or country with such a huge imbalance. The other closest deficit is Europe, whose deficit is almost the same as its deficit with China, while the United States is in deficit with every region.

In 2008, the United States imported over $2.1 trillion of goods, and exported almost $1.3 trillion, yielding a trade deficit, or imports in excess of exports, of $840 billion. Yet the United States exported only $550 billion worth of services, while importing $405 billion,[6] yielding a trade surplus in services, or exports in excess of imports, of $144 billion; this surplus in services equals only 17 percent of the trade deficit in goods. Services constituted only 30 percent of all exports and 16 percent of all imports. If we look at all trade by

Table 2.2 U.S. and World Trade Deficits

Country/Region	Trade Surplus with United States, (in Dollars)	Trade Balance with the World (in Dollars)	Percentage of U.S. Trade Deficit
China	285	262	33%
Japan	87	92	10%
Rest of Asia	66	220	8%
Europe	117	−254	14%
Canada	69	29	8%
Mexico	77	24	9%
Rest of Latin America	35	48	4%
Former USSR	16	112	2%
Middle East	34	273	4%
Africa	72	74	8%

Note: The United States has a trade deficit in merchandise of $858 billion in 2007, and is in deficit to all parts of the world. Only Europe has a large trade deficit besides the U.S., of $254 billion, 219 billion of that from China.

Sources: WTO, International Trade Statistics, 2007, Table I.13 for U.S. trade, U.S. total; Europe trade with China, Table I.14; for the former Soviet Union, Africa, Middle East, South and Central America total, Table I.4; Mexico, Table I.9. Rest of Asia total is estimate based on above tables and Table II.30.

adding up imports and exports, we find that services constituted 22 percent of all trade for the United States, close to the world average.

Table 2.1 shows, in the rightmost column, the trade surplus or deficit of the service categories. We see from table 2.1 that even in allegedly "post-industrial" sectors, like finance, which has a trade surplus of $13 billion or software of $6 billion, there is not nearly enough trade going on to make up for the $840 billion shortfall in goods. In fact, there are also some service sectors that have a large deficit for the United States, such as insurance at $21 billion or transportation services at $18 billion (not surprising considering the number of cargo ships sailing our way). Movies have a surplus of only $10 billion; *The Sopranos* cannot save the U.S. economy.

Most services cannot be packaged up and sent abroad, because most services involve, in one way or another, actually using a manufactured good, and you can't export or import that experience. The main way in which services are "exchanged" is through tourism, in which the person physically moves to the place where the service takes place. Except for small nations that are particularly well-endowed with tourist destinations, no country can survive on tourism—nor should one want to, because tourism-centered economies can experience wild swings depending on the global economic conditions.

A large nation such as the United States cannot exchange the goods it needs for services alone. *It must exchange goods for goods*, in the long term. In the short and medium term, as long as the rest of the world accepts U.S. dollars in return for goods, the United States can keep giving the rest of the world currency instead of goods. But either the international community will decide that they will never get much back for their dollars, or the mountain of dollars outside the United States will become so large, that the dollar will plummet in value. When that happens, the $2.1 trillion in imported goods will require many more dollars to purchase, and the trade deficit could actually get worse.

Most economists assume that if the dollar goes down, U.S. exports will become more competitive in terms of price, and so exports will go up, imports will go down, and the trade deficit will start to narrow. This assumes that the United States can easily increase its manufacturing to take advantage of a cheaper dollar; it also assumes that U.S. manufacturers can replace more expensive imports with homemade varieties of goods. But both of these assumption are based on the further assumption that U.S. manufacturing is competent enough to compete with even more expensive foreign goods, and that the United States can easily ramp up production, if needed.

Since 2006, however, the Japanese Yen has generally become more expensive,[7] even as the U.S. trade deficit with Japan has increased.[8] Since 2000 a similar counterintuitive phenomenon has taken place with Europe: even as the Euro increased vis-a-vis the dollar,[9] the deficit with Europe, except for the recession/depression year of 2008, went up.[10] A lower dollar will not necessarily lower the trade deficit.

Well, the story goes, we're losing out to China and other lower-wage countries. But in reality, higher wages can lead to trade deficits too. As of 2007, as we see in Table 2.2, about 32 percent of the goods trade deficit of the United States was with countries that pay the same or higher wages: $117 billion with Europe, $69 billion with Canada, and $87 billion with Japan. At 32 percent, this is just under the 33 percent of the U.S. trade deficit that is accounted for by China. We never hear that we need to raise wages to compete with our developed trading partners.

German manufacturing workers were compensated 44 percent higher than U.S. manufacturing workers in 2006, and that figure increased from 15 percent in 2000, probably reflecting the rise of the Euro; Workers in the part of Europe that uses the Euro receive 23 percent higher wages. For Japan, the Yen fell between 2000 and 2006, resulting in a decrease in compensation from 12 percent higher than Americans to 15 percent below.[11]

The percentage of goods that the United States consumes from abroad, instead of from U.S. producers, continues to grow. In 1998, 25 percent of U.S. consumption of manufactured goods was imported; by 2007, that number had jumped to 37 percent.[12] For industrial machinery, the consumption of imports jumped from 35 percent to 57 percent[13] in the same years.

So countries with either higher wages or comparable wages in manufacturing are outcompeting U.S. manufacturing firms in the international market. It is possible to trade goods for goods, using high-priced labor, as Japan and Germany show, and as the United States was able to do until about the 1980s. But it will not be possible over the long run to trade services for goods. We are thus in a trade bubble, just as we were in a dot com bubble and then a subprime bubble.

Much of U.S. trade is with regions such as Europe and Japan that pay higher or similar wages (depending on the exchange rate).

Europe and Japan have roughly comparable wealth per person[14] and larger manufacturing sectors. Does that mean that they are not as advanced as the United States, or simply that a large and thriving manufacturing sector is necessary to be wealthy, unless the country is the United States? After all, only one country in the world can prop itself up by providing the international reserve and exchange currency.

The United States is wealthy now exactly because it was so dominant in manufacturing for most of the 20th century. Because of that dominance, the dollar became the international reserve currency and exchange medium of choice, and because of the exalted status of the dollar, the United States has so far avoided the worst of its abandonment of manufacturing-centered policies.

STAGES OF GROWTH MYTH

The myths that services and trade can be separated from manufacturing have a foundation in the larger historical myth that there are stages of growth that countries go through, from hunting and gathering, to agriculture, to industry, to services. In reality, this sequence is completely wrong. First of all, many hunting and gathering societies, such as the Native Americans, had a much better grasp of the ecological necessities of life, and were able to live, sustainably, in thriving ecosystems for millennia. On the other hand, it is unclear how much longer the current particular variant of civilization is going to last.

As for the rest of the sequence, manufacturing, agriculture, and services have always been intermixed. Not only did human beings never exist who were not completely dependent on tool-making, not even the *previous* species, Homo erectus, lived without tools. Homo sapiens always invested at least some time in the "service" of the arts, as the prehistoric caves, such as Lascaux, attest; and that was before agriculture.

However, most stage theorists argue that societies moved from a predominance of labor being invested in agriculture, to the majority being involved in manufacturing, to most people working as "service" workers. The implication is that agriculture is less advanced, associated with peasants; then comes the huge soul-deadening assembly lines of manufacturing; then the quiet, air-conditioned life of the service worker. Each stage involves more and more knowledge, until we come to the final "knowledge worker," in Robert Reich's terminology. There are several problems with this image.

First, agriculture has always been knowledge intensive, and has involved the tool-making expertise of urban artisans, then guild members, then engineers designing machines. In addition, agricultural advances, which have always been important to societies, involve a sophisticated understanding of ecology and chemistry. The Incan methods of raised gardening and the use of a charcoal-type soil additive, terra preta, may even now have important implications for mitigating global warming[15]; the central Americans discovered how to make corn, chocolate, and tobacco, among other foods.

In Europe, important advances in productivity took place as a result of changes in the design of plows, a kind of tool; also societies figured out how to keep some land without crops, that is, stay fallow, while cycling various crops on the same piece of land to raise its fertility, as in growing nitrogen-fixing legumes. These were all important steps in the advancement of agriculture.

When chemists applied their new ideas to agriculture as they learned about the nature of soil and the production of artificial fertilizers and pesticides, a revolution in productivity occurred. For centuries people have been breeding different varieties of plants for various uses, and in the 20th century various strains of grains were developed that ushered in the "green revolution."

Just because agriculture only employs about 1 percent of the American population now does not mean it is "lower" than other sectors. It is exactly because so many knowledge workers are involved in agriculture that so few people need to be involved. However, it may be the case that it will be necessary to drastically increase the number of people devoted to gardening and farming so that we do not destroy the soil and water that makes agriculture possible. Will this mean that agriculture will rise to a higher stage because more people are employed there? Does the number of people employed in a sector tell us which sector is more advanced? Or, since agriculture is at the lowest stage, does that mean that a society that employs more people in growing food will be a less advanced society?

No, an increase in labor in agriculture will simply mean that human beings are finally attempting to feed billions of people without destroying the biosphere. An expansion of organic farming could even lead to an expansion of the middle class, because the skill and knowledge level of the new farmers/gardeners will have to be high. All stages of an economy are important and crucial; the functions of the various sectors are critical to understand, not the number of people involved or how much money they happen to make in any particular economic era.

Through the latter half of the 19th and first half of the 20th centuries, people in developed countries moved from the farm, where productivity increases were phenomenal. Productivity in manufacturing increased at the same time, because the increases in productivity in both manufacturing and agriculture occurred for the same reason: machinery improved. Millions of people went from the fields to the factories; millions also moved to services. Services were burgeoning because of the activities that used all of the new goods rolling off of the assembly lines, and because machinery, such as office equipment and electricity-generating equipment, led to new jobs in new service industries.

Manufacturing was always a very knowledge-intensive activity. In fact, it may be argued that humans have big brains and dextrous hands exactly to create and use tools, a form of manufacturing. Perhaps speech developed mainly to communicate and discuss the process of making tools.

Jane Jacobs argues that cities formed before agriculture.[16] That is, tool and artifact making, along with commerce for various kinds of materials for use in manufacturing, created the cultural interchange that resulted in agriculture. Thus, one form of knowledge intensity, cities and manufacturing, gave rise to another form of knowledge, agriculture.

THE POST-INDUSTRIAL MYTH

To argue that manufacturing has been superseded by the service economy involves some interesting problems of dating. When exactly did this switch take place? Daniel Bell published *The Coming of Post-Industrial Society* in 1976.[17] He argued that there was a shift from manufacturing to services in more advanced societies. Many societies were 90 percent farmers before they became industrial; were most people employed in manufacturing at some point in time, only to move to services?

Except for rather short periods in specific cities, no society ever even surpassed using 50 percent of its workers in manufacturing; for most societies; one-third of employment in manufacturing seems to be the maximum.

In fact, according to *The Historical Statistics of the United States*, perhaps the only time there were more manufacturing workers than service workers was around 1850![18] The first year when manufacturing was separated from construction in the statistics was 1870, when there were 2 million manufacturing workers and almost 3 million service employees. Agriculture employed about 6 million. By 1920, there were about 11 million farmers and 11 million manufacturing workers, and over 14 million service workers. Already by 1940, there were over 23 million service workers, and still about 11 million manufacturing workers, with agriculture down to 9 million. By 1970[19] the numbers for both manufacturing and services had basically doubled, while agricultural employment had plummeted to less than 4 million.[20]

Thus, by the time Daniel Bell celebrated post-industrialism, the ratio of manufacturing to service workers had been holding very steady for 30 years—about one-quarter of workers were in manufacturing and a little less than two-thirds in services. In 2007, there were about 2 million agricultural workers, 16 million manufacturing workers, about 11 million in construction, and the rest, about 113 million, in services[21]—three-quarters of the working population, compared to only 11 percent for manufacturing. In 1970, very few manufactured goods were consumed in the United States that were manufactured abroad; currently, about 37 percent are, with over half of machinery made abroad. So it makes sense that from 1970 to 2007 the percentage of U.S. workers in manufacturing would change from about 24 percent to about 11 percent; half of the workers who used to be employed manufacturing for domestic consumption are now in services. Is this an advance or a decline? Should a society that has an industrialized agricultural system have about one-quarter of its workers in manufacturing and about two-thirds in services, including government? This certainly seems to be approximately the number that one finds in leading countries such as Germany and Japan.

The Japanese and German manufacturing sectors are larger than the U.S. sectors: in 1995, the Japanese, German, and U.S. sectors were 22.4 percent, 22.6 percent, and 17.6 percent; by 2005, the shares were 20.2 percent, 23.2 percent, and 13.4 percent, respectively, according to the Organisation for Economic Co-operation and Development (OECD).[22]

As we saw in the discussion of services above, manufactured goods are used by the service industries to generate services. It is exactly because manufacturing is so efficient that it is able to generate more jobs in the services industries than in its own industries. The same leveraging process operates within manufacturing; the machinery industries, which provide the basic machinery to build all output, generate at most 3 percent of GDP. Yet they directly help in the creation of the 12 percent of the GDP that comprises manufacturing, which in turn is used—along with imported manufactured goods—to generate the rest of the economy.

How can an economy change into a "post-industrial" one, when its actual consumption patterns between manufacturing and services have been pretty similar since 1947? In 1947, personal consumption of goods from the United States was 40.7 percent, and from imports, 2.4 percent. By 1970, the figures were 30.7 percent and 5.4 percent, respectively. In 2007, only 23.9 percent of goods were consumed from domestic sources and 14.1 percent from imports. Consumption of goods went from 43 percent in 1947 to 36.1 percent in 1970 to 38 percent in 2007;[23] hardly an earth-shattering shift. Clearly, we're not post-industrial when it comes to consumption—have you been in a mall lately?—but when it comes to production, since many of the things made in the mall come from abroad.

But how can we consume something that we can't trade for? As I showed above, we can't trade services for goods, in the long term. If we want to consume things, we need to make things, either to directly consume or to trade for and consume indirectly. In other words, we have to produce the goods that we consume. "*Post*-industrial" ultimately means "*pre*-industrial," that is, *poor*.

THE MYTH OF THE NEVER-RETURNING JOBS

Even if it can be shown that manufacturing is necessary for an economy, the conventional wisdom responds, "but the jobs aren't coming back." Apparently discussion of the phenomenal changes of the past century comes to a screeching halt when the idea of rebuilding the manufacturing sector rears its head. We put a man on the moon, wiped out polio, built thousands of miles of roads and millions of acres of suburbs, we talk on computers and compute on phones, but we can't have millions more manufacturing jobs, even though the country will sink into poverty without them. And the alleged reason for this seems to be that low-wage countries will beat us, particularly China.

If wages were the most important determinant of manufacturing prowess, then China would never have lost its leadership from 1,000 years ago, because they always had a surfeit of people. In fact, according to the historian John Darwin, by the late 1700s, "A technological transformation would be needed before European producers could overcome the historic advantage of their Asian competitors: the much lower costs of production in their artisan industries."[24] If Europeans needed to use better machinery two hundreds years ago to compete against lower wages, shouldn't the U.S. be concentrating on making better machinery now?

By the logic of wages-determine-all, China would have been number one all along, and America would have been an also-ran. Because in the 20th century almost the exact opposite took place—American wages were the highest in the world while American manufacturing was the most competitive in the world—there must be something wrong with the focus on low wages. As Eamonn Fingleton points out, in the course of praising what he calls "hard" industries:

> The whole trend of wages over the last fifty years underlines the importance of pivotal production technologies in the world income league table. In the 1950s, when the most advanced production techniques were typically deployed only within the United States, American manufacturing workers were the world's highest-paid, earning about six to eight times as much as their counterparts even in Japan and Germany. By the 1980s, however, Japan and Germany had caught up in production technologies. Wages in these nations duly passed American levels and have stayed ahead ever since.[25]

The problem with the low-wage approach is that it is the capability and reliability of the machinery, not the cost of the workers, that is the most important factor in manufacturing competence. The Chinese realize this, which is why they have been training up their workers and engineers, even to the point of insisting that foreign manufacturers train Chinese workers and own the factories jointly. The idea is to advance up the ladder of technological competence, as the Japanese did when they moved from being the butt of jokes about their toys in the 1960s to becoming the symbols of reliability and design that they are now.

The low-cost idea, like many ideas in neoclassical economics, assumes that the technologies of production already exist, and that the technology doesn't change. Therefore, the reasoning goes, we just have to worry about costs, like workers on an assembly line. But a wealthy nation innovates and changes more than a poor nation, and it does so by empowering its scientists, engineers, and skilled production workers. It does so by paying the workers so much that the managers are motivated to continuously improve the power of the machinery so as to minimize the number of workers hired. This process actually increases the number of workers hired overall, because the newly gained wealth is used to hire more workers—if the factories can't move abroad.

If workers should be as badly paid as possible, it is a short step to the idea that manufacturing work is miserable and not worth saving. There is a relentless portrayal of manufacturing as consisting of huge assembly lines full of people doing deadening, physical work. Manufacturing work is portrayed as dull, dirty, and dreary. In reality the most important physical work in manufacturing is done by highly sophisticated, skilled production workers who make the components outside of the assembly line. In partnership with skilled production workers, engineers design the machinery that is used to create goods and organize how humans will use the machines to create goods. Managers on the factory floor must monitor this entire process. The considerable and important technological progress that takes place in manufacturing comes out of the heads and experience of engineers and skilled production workers who are intimately involved with the manufacturing process.

CONCLUSION

The popular conception of manufacturing seems almost like the fantastic images that medieval painters imagined the world outside Europe to be—full of bizarre beings, many scary and many ridiculously powerful, evoking strange cultures and strange people. But when Marco Polo and others finally went out into the real world, and when scientists explored the actual ecosystems that were "out there," they discovered how approachable and rational the world really was.

We seem to be in the same position in relation to economies that the European medieval painters were in relation to Asia. We need to take a look at all of the sectors of the economy, both service and industrial, and see how they actually fit together. We need to see what gets traded and why. Surprisingly, neoclassical economists sing the praises of trade but don't seem to understand some basic ideas, such as a nation can't trade services for goods.

In fact, neoclassical economics is the theoretical bulwark for many of the misconceptions that arise about manufacturing. The biggest misconception of all may be that neoclassical economics has a theory of economic growth and an understanding of how technological societies change and create mutually self-reinforcing, virtuous networks. In the next chapter, I will explain how a different way of looking at the world will help us to understand how the economy really works.

CHAPTER 3

The Economy as an Ecosystem

One day in the late 1970s, while I was a student at the University of California, Berkeley, I went to hear a talk from the great philosopher of science, Thomas Kuhn. While I was sitting outside the hall waiting for the lecture to begin, I looked up at one of the geekiest individuals I had ever seen, in a bowler hat and thick glasses, seemingly looking down at me. We looked at each other, both with a faint scent of disgust, I in my jeans, tee shirt, and long hair, he with short hair and a suit.

The next time I saw the individual, he was being introduced as Thomas Kuhn, and I was treated to a wonderful, personal lecture about how he had come to the field of the philosophy of science. Perhaps strangest of all, he described what he called an epiphany, or perhaps even a different state of consciousness. He related how he had been struggling with the thought of Aristotle, whom he had been studying in a course on the history of physics (he was at the time in the PhD program in physics). Nothing quite made sense, as he related, until finally in one magical instant he understood how Aristotle was thinking, in terms of a complete system, as a holism, or, as he was later to immortalize, as a paradigm. "My jaw dropped," I remember him saying, as I tried to imagine this so-very-gray-flannel person dropping his jaw, eyes wide open.

This insight drove him to drop his physics work and obtain a doctorate in philosophy instead. What he had experienced was a *paradigm shift*, moving from one worldview to another, in a flash of understanding. The important concept he discovered was that sometimes comprehension involves experiencing an entire set of ideas as one, interconnected web of ideas—not just as a series of analytical lessons.

Kuhn has been criticized for not giving one, concise definition of a paradigm,[1] but I always liked the way he explained it in that lecture. A *paradigm* is a linked set of ideas that serve to reinforce each other. Pull one idea out—perhaps it has been thoroughly discredited, an "anomaly" in Kuhn's wording—and the structure of the paradigm still holds up, because the other links in the web hold it together.

Pull enough links out, and the paradigm is in danger of collapse. The paradigm collapses only, as Kuhn explains, if there is a paradigm available that can better explain the paradigm's domain of reality. This is Kuhn's second great insight, after the idea of the paradigm itself: a theory, or paradigm, is not destroyed by criticism, although criticism lays the groundwork by weakening the old paradigm. A paradigm is *only* superseded by the introduction of a new, better paradigm. Thus is made a scientific revolution.[2]

The subject of Kuhn's thesis was the Copernican revolution, in which the process he describes is perhaps most clearly exposed. Copernicus advocated the idea that the Sun is at the center of the solar system, not the Earth, as was claimed by the then prevailing astronomical paradigm, the Ptolemaic system. To keep the Ptolemaic system at least somewhat synchronous with reality, Ptolemaic astronomers had invented many complex "circles within circles" in the heavens that sort of took care of various anomalies that had been discovered with the use of the telescope.

Negative observations did not overturn Ptolemaic astronomy; data plus a new theory did the trick (and quite a bit of literally putting one's body on the line). Similarly, conservatism, neoclassical economics, Reaganism, or any other economic, social, or political philosophy, will not be overthrown by pointing out the large and gaping holes in the theory, they will only be replaced if a better theory, or paradigm, is available.

WHAT IS A SYSTEM?

Is it possible to define a paradigm rigorously? A starting point comes from Kuhn: a paradigm is a set of interconnected ideas that reinforce each other, and that explain a particular domain of reality.

Another way of looking at a paradigm is to look at it as a system. But then, what is a system?

The simplest way to think about a system is as a set of elements and a structure that defines the way in which those elements relate to each other. The difficult part to master is the structure—that is what made Kuhn's jaw drop—the experience of taking what looked like a mush of disparate ideas from Aristotle and putting them together in a meaningful way.

The gestalt psychologists in the 1920s and 1930s advanced the understanding of the idea of a structure when they emphasized the totality (gestalt, approximately, in German) of a sensation. For instance, a face is not recognized by analyzing the nose, eyes, and mouth, although that is certainly part of the process, but by recognizing the position of the eyes, nose, mouth, and other features, together. A Rorschach test is useful because the human mind, constantly trying to perceive structure, displays some of its hidden tendencies in trying to make structure out of a splotch of ink when there really isn't any there.

Kenneth Waltz, the most important theoretician of international relations in the post-World War II period, based his theory of international relations[3] on a carefully constructed theory of systems. He drew on concepts from psychology, anthropology, biology, economics, political science, and his own synthesis of concepts—his own structure of the structure of systems. He emphasizes the structure of the international system, and thus his theory is called "structural realism," since it is also based on a view of international relations called realism, which emphasizes the allegedly "realistic" view that war is always a possibility in international affairs.

Waltz's theory about systems is actually designed as a general theory, although he only uses the theory for political science. Most systems have some kind of ordering—for instance, in music, there is an ordering in time, as when the notes are played, as well as an ordering of the musical scale, as well as an ordering based on which instruments play when (one could also include more subtle orderings like phrasing). In international politics, we have none of this, at least, not in Waltz's theory: since there is no overarching authority, international systems are anarchic, they have no ordering.

Actually, in older forms of international political theory, associated with a more geopolitical way of thinking, the actual geographic ordering of nations was deemed to be an important part of the

international system. Of course, the United States worries more
about what goes on in its own "backyard," as in Mexico or Cuba,
then, say, in China's "backyard." Waltz is trying to model reality in
the simplest possible way to be able to discern important processes
that are obscured when more of reality is included in a theory.

In other words, a theory needs to *not* model some parts of reality
to be useful. No theory reflects absolute truth, theories should be
judged according to how useful they are in *explaining* a particular domain of reality. Simplification is essential; all theories leave something out, because if you don't leave something out, you wind up
with an exhaustive description of reality, and you can't make out the
patterns that are hopefully there and that allow you to make your
way through the fog of complex systems.

Waltz assumes that the international system has no ordering, is
anarchic, and that the relative position of various countries geographically doesn't make enough of a difference to be worth including in his
theory. A similar simplification occurs in his second criterion for
a system structure, the functional differentiation among the elements
of a system. As he points out, in a domestic political system, we have an
executive, legislative, and judicial branch, which fill those functions. In a
human body, we have the various functions that the heart, stomach,
and other organs and subsystems fulfill. But in an international system,
because each nation has to basically fulfill all of its own functions and
can't depend on its neighbor because the international system is anarchic, there is no functional differentiation among states.

Waltz's conception of an international system shares some similar-
ities with the neoclassical economic paradigm. The market is conceived as basically anarchic, with no functional differentiation among
its parts. By contrast, I will argue that the economy should be explic-
itly modeled as a system with functionally differentiated parts, which
absolutely need outside, that is, governmental help to ensure that all
the parts operate adequately in relation to the other parts. If the international system is a set of functionally similar entities set within an
anarchic system, what patterns could we possibly see? Waltz adds a
third criterion of a structure, the relative distribution of capabilities,
which differentiates the various units, that is, the nations. According
to Waltz, there is really a dividing line between "Great Powers," as
they have often been called, and lesser or smaller nations that can't do
much to influence international affairs.

TO FEEDBACK OR NOT TO FEEDBACK

Using Waltz's simplified model of the international system, we can see that there are a couple of main processes at work; there is a positive feedback loop, a process by which those who have power obtain more power; and there is a negative feedback loop, that is, those who have power are cut down to size, or prevented from getting more.[4] The first process, which is the accumulation of power, engenders the second, which Waltz (and many others) have called the balance of power. Without the balance of power to prevent the accumulation of power, there would be one globe-spanning empire; for instance, the United States and United Kingdom teamed up with the Union of Soviet Socialist Republics (USSR) to defeat Hitler, even though the United Kingdom and United States had previously been enemies of the USSR and would return to being enemies after beating Germany. They practiced a balance of power strategy to prevent Germany from attaining global supremacy.

Economic systems also exhibit a process of the accumulation of power. A once competitive market, as in cars, turns into an oligopoly, as in the case of the Big 3 automakers; at one point it looked like General Motors would become a monopoly and take over the entire industry.

Waltz stresses the negative feedback process in international relations, the balance of power, as a way to stabilize the system. In fact, he simplifies his discussion of a system so far that he winds up arguing that a bipolar system, that is, one with two Great Powers, is more stable than a system with more than two. People found it difficult to accept this hypothesis when the world became unipolar; he argued that he meant that a bipolar system is more peaceful, not longer lasting.

Most social sciences, and even sciences, tend to focus more on negative feedback processes than positive feedback ones; neoclassical economics steers clear of positive feedback as if it were toxic—which it is, for neoclassical economics. There has been some scientific work that focuses on the subject of positive feedback, and the cutting edge of mechanical physics has been led by the work of such thinkers as Ilya Prigogine,[5] who developed the field of nonlinear systems, or in more popular terminology, chaos theory.

Climate science has also had to use the idea of positive feedback, as in the concept of albedo, or the reflectivity of certain parts of the

Earth's surface. In particular, when the Arctic, or other areas covered by glaciers or ice, starts to melt, the melted areas become dark and soak up more heat, which causes even warmer conditions, which causes more melting, and more dark spots, and more warming, until the entire area has melted. This reveals another aspect of positive feedback loops—they always end up in some sort of "stable" state. The system appears to be "locked-in." For instance, if the Arctic melted, it would be extremely difficult to make it ice up again.

One field that has always been comfortable with positive feedback loops (at least relatively) is ecological and evolutionary biology. Clearly, biologists have to understand reproduction and the changes that take place as a result of the generation of "variation," Darwin's term for the raw material of evolution.

However, the kind of positive feedback loop that explains biological growth of populations is different from the positive feedback loop that leads to the accumulation of power. I will differentiate between two kinds of systems: those that generate, and those that control or distribute. Ecologists discuss ecosystems, which are mainly concerned with generation of new life, and which include processes of positive feedback that lead to growth. The dynamics that Waltz discusses vis-à-vis the international system, and the ones that economists discuss vis-à-vis a particular industry, are systems of control. Control can be accumulated, at the extreme by one unit in a system; within a country, this is called dictatorship. When control is dispersed equally, at the other extreme, we call this pure democracy.

The part of the economy that economists aren't very good at modeling, the production system, grows as a result of a similar positive feedback loop as occurs in ecosystems, that is, by generating output. An economy's growth is constrained by the need for all parts of the system to grow in some roughly equal relation to each other, and in particular, by the need to use ecosystems sustainably.

Thus there are four combinations of feedback processes and kinds of systems: a system of control has a positive feedback process that leads to the accumulation of power, and a negative feedback process that leads to a balance of power; a system of generation has a positive feedback process that leads to growth, and a negative feedback process that leads to the need for balanced growth and a constraint of limits.

A HIERARCHY OF HIERARCHIES

One other aspect of systems implied by Waltz is the possibility that the individual elements that make up systems are themselves systems. Waltz discusses the domestic political system, which is a nation, and makes up one unit of the larger international political system. However, one of his arguments is that by making the explanation of the system at the international level so spare, it is possible to ignore the inner workings of the domestic political system. In other words, a hierarchy of systems allows for much of the complexity of systems to be retained, while enabling a person to concentrate on one particular level at a time. If you want to explore other parts of the system, you either go down one level—for example, in biology, from the level of the body to the level of the organs—or up one level, back to the level of the individual. Thus a biology textbook will move from the cellular level, to the level of internal organs, to the level of the individual organism, to the ecosystem (which may also involve several levels).[6]

The definition of a system is itself a system of sorts, made up of various elements arranged in a specific way. A model of a system is composed of elements, which may themselves be systems, and of a structure. The structure is composed of an ordering, possibly a functional differentiation, a distribution of capabilities, and depending on these parts of the structure, particular negative and positive feedback processes. The system applies to a particular domain of reality, for example physics or economics.

The model of a system is itself not testable in a scientific or logical sense, but we can *use* the model of the system to generate *hypotheses*, and then we can test the hypotheses to determine if the model of the system is useful for explaining a particular domain of reality. The model of the system for a particular domain of reality, plus the hypotheses that the model generates, is what I will define as a paradigm.

THE NEOCLASSICAL PARADIGM

Neoclassical economics was built as a variation of the paradigm of statistical mechanics in physics, although the two are not exactly the same. Many of the early theorists were engineers or physicists; Leon

Walras, the founder of the theory of general equilibrium analysis, kept a copy of a statistical mechanical textbook by his bed, and was himself an engineer; Irving Fisher, one of the great economists of the pre-World War II period, was trained in physics and constructed a hydraulic model of the economy at Yale that still works. Many economists today have extensive training in physics, and use physics as a source of new ideas.[7]

Neoclassical economics started out as a paradigm by trying to explain the short-term behavior of a specific industry that is competitive (that is, no firm can set the price of its goods). Each firm is considered to be basically identical, as are the industries that the firms inhabit. As for how an industry relates to another industry, it is assumed that the entire economy is bound together as a set of points of investment opportunity, and that investment will flow where the return to investment is highest. This flow will reflect the best use of investment capital; in other words, returns on investments will reflect their true value to the economy. Other than this mechanism, there is no concept that there might be a functional differentiation or relationship among the various parts of the economy.

Thus the neoclassical system is composed of identical elements—firms—that are not themselves a system. There are theories of the firm, but since the firm is basically an organized dictatorship in most manifestations, the theory of the firm has not engendered too much attention.

There is very little structure in the neoclassical model, because there is no ordering among the firms (the industry is anarchic) and no functional differentiation; ideally, the relative distribution of capabilities, or power, among the firms is fairly equal, although oligopoly and monopoly can form where the distribution becomes uneven. The subfield of industrial structure acknowledges the idea of "increasing returns," that is, that as a firm becomes bigger, it may become more profitable, mainly for technological reasons; however, this phenomenon also does not play a central role in the neoclassical paradigm.

Negative feedback loops predominate in the neoclassical model, bringing the system back into stability, and positive feedback loops do not exist, with the partial exception of oligopoly. The neoclassical system really covers the domain of economic distribution, not production. Environmentalists sometimes accuse economists of being focused on production, but actually, production is not very interesting in the neoclassical view and is not well studied.

If the economy self-stabilizes, partly because capital and income flows to its optimal destination, then a hypothesis generated by the neoclassical paradigm is that the government has very little, if any, role, in overseeing the level of investment in any particular industry. I will argue that on the contrary, the government must shape the general structure of the economy, because the market can't do it. Neoclassical economics is really an economics of a very narrow domain of reality—the short-term behavior of a competitive industry, not the long-term processes of a production system.

What we desperately need now is a national and global coordination of plans to overcome the massive economic and ecological crises that humanity faces together. Such an effort would be aided by the existence of an economic paradigm that tries to explain long-term processes of production.

THE ECOSYSTEM PARADIGM

Instead of using statistical mechanics as a foundation for an economic paradigm, we should use ecological studies for our reference point (including evolutionary biology). The main unit of analysis in ecology is the niche, which means the part of an ecosystem that a particular organism, or set of organisms, lives in; that is, the niche specifies the resources and organisms that various organisms use and create. Each ecosystem might have a different set of niches; even if two ecosystems have similar niches, the niches will often be occupied by different organisms because evolution is unpredictable and yields different species, even in similar circumstances. For instance, in a forest, each plant has a different niche depending on how tall it is, and how much sunlight it can capture; different organisms might have different niches depending on what kinds of leaves they can eat, or whether they can occupy certain parts of trees to capture insects and other plant eaters; there may be some large, ground-based plant eaters, and then some large, ground-based carnivores that eat the ground-based plant eaters. There will also be whole sets of fungi, microbes, and small animals that decompose dead plants and animals. Each ecosystem might have a completely different set of species occupying each of these niches.

All of these niches can also be categorized as being part of a larger, or trophic, level; that is, most ecosystems have plants that are the main producers (production trophic level), herbivores that eat the producers (primary consumers trophic level), and carnivores that eat the herbivores that eat the plants (secondary consumers trophic level). Another way to think of an ecosystem is as a food web, made of several food chains, which traces who eats whom and who gets their nourishment from which niche.

Each of these elements, niches, is made up of a population of an organism or organisms, which grow or decline according to particular positive and negative feedback loops, depending on their environments; that is, they reproduce to grow the population, and may decline because of lack of resources or destruction, as in being eaten. Ecologists have used various dimensions to order these niches, and using trophic levels is one way of doing so.

Most importantly for our purposes, each niche in an ecosystem serves a function; the trees produce leaves, the caterpillars eat the leaves, the birds eat the caterpillars thus preserving the leaves, the fungi eat the dead organisms, thereby creating soil, which the plants mine for nutrition. Although some niches wax and wane, each one is important to the functioning of the ecosystem as a whole. Without a niche, or a specific species that fills a niche or part of a niche, the ecosystem will be much more vulnerable to disruption, at best, and, at worst might be destroyed. For instance, a keystone species[8] is one whose removal will mean that the entire ecosystem may be transformed; if all the trees in a rain forest are cut down, the whole ecosystem collapses and turns into something else entirely.

In just the same way, an economy is made up of a set of functional niches, and the disappearance of a niche—or the equivalent of an entire trophic level—is disastrous. In particular, the manufacturing and machinery sectors are like the plants in an ecosystem—everything else depends on them. An economy that loses, or never builds, its manufacturing sector, is like an ecosystem with no plants—a desert.

STAGES OF PRODUCTION

The definition of an ecosystem includes nonliving physical aspects, not just the organisms. The climate, rivers, mountains, oceans—all are part of the ecosystem. So the biotic community of organisms, as a system, interacts with the physical environment as a system to create a higher level, the ecosystem. We now know that the biological part of this larger system actually changed the physical part, as when micro-organisms created the oxygen that we breathe today, which in turn has a profound effect on geological processes.

In much the same way, the economic system is part of a larger system, a political-economic system, and that larger social system is part of the larger ecosystem that encompasses it. By building up a hierarchy of systems, we can describe and understand a very complex system (Earth).

I've argued that neoclassical economics doesn't actually explain the functioning of the economy as a whole; it concentrates on the short-term behavior of a competitive industry and then generalizes to the whole economy. It's sort of a "what's good for one industry is good for the economy" kind of view, or alternatively, "if you've seen one industry, you've seen them all."

Many economic textbooks define the economy in a useful way—the "production and distribution of goods and services." Let's bisect the "economic system" into a "distribution system" (of goods and services) and "production system" (of goods and services). Each in turn is composed of subsystems. On the distribution side, as detailed in Chapter 2 on myths of manufacturing, we have retailing and wholesaling, including the transportation services associated with them. The other major part of the distribution system is the financial system—recycling investment capital, either into retail and wholesale, or into production—or not so productively, back into the financial system itself.

On the production side, things are more complex. Think of the production system as three concentric circles, that is, one circle in the middle, surrounded by another circle, and those circles surrounded by a bigger one. On the outside circle, called the *final consumption system*, all the goods and services that are used by people, including buildings and infrastructure, are produced. Most of the production of goods takes place in factories, using machinery that I'll call "production machinery." Much construction is done using construction machinery, another kind of production machinery, outside of factories. Production that takes place outside of the factory includes agriculture, which uses agricultural machinery; mining, which uses mining equipment; and utilities, which use electrical, natural gas, and water-management equipment.

Most of what we do involves the use of machinery of one sort or the other (I'll use the word "machine" interchangeably with the word "equipment"). Even service industry offices are filled with office equipment such as computers, copying machines, and telephones, not to mention all the cars, trucks, elevators, and lights. Restaurants use many kinds of machinery, such as cooking equipment, and they use food that has gone through food processing machinery and been transported by trucks, gathered by agricultural machinery, and fumigated by pesticides made with chemical processing equipment. Even in the home, all of the remote devices, TVs, and kitchen equipment are forms of machinery. The machinery that makes the final consumer goods and services are themselves all made with a whole different set of machinery-making machinery.

The machinery that makes machinery I will refer to as *reproduction machinery*. Reproduction machinery not only makes all of the production machinery, but makes all of the reproduction machinery. This is a vast oversimplification—you could conceivably keep going back further and further to determine which machinery made the previous set of machinery, and so on. But as I stated earlier, it is a characteristic of theory that reality is simplified, so that we can discern important patterns of reality. Dividing production into three levels seems like a good way to explain the process of modern production, while hiding much of the detail.

So we have an ordering of the elements of the production system, in a series of three stages—stages of production. At the first level, reproduction machinery makes more reproduction machinery. The reproduction machinery that is not being used to make more reproduction machinery is then used as the means of production in the next level, the production machinery stage. Here, the construction, agricultural, mining, textile, telecommunications, computer data servers, and other equipment is made that will be used in the third stage, the final production stage, where all the final goods and services and infrastructure are made. This output of this final stage constitutes the wealth of a society, and the production machinery creates that wealth. Reproduction machinery, the source of economic growth, is not itself wealth, because people cannot use it in their daily lives, but it creates the means of producing wealth.

CATEGORIES OF PRODUCTION

These levels represent different functions within the economy—producing machinery, producing nonmachinery goods—but we can also identify other kinds of functional subsystems, or niches, in this economic ecosystem that I am describing. Again, the problem is to reduce a complex system, the economy, into enough categories to describe the systems, but not too many to overload understanding. Since we have the concept of hierarchy available to us, we can put some categories within others; we can create a taxonomy.

We have stages of production, from reproduction machinery to production machinery to final production; we can also devise a set of *categories* of production, and divide each of the stages by those categories, to form a matrix of niches, all of which are necessary for a production system to function properly. How do we choose a few categories out of the massive complexity of a modern economy?

Depending on the epoch, different kinds of technologies are declared by various thinkers to be the penultimate, revolutionary, more-important-than-anything-ever-was-or-could-possibly-be technology. Currently, because of problems with oil prices and the emissions of carbon dioxide from fossil fuels, energy is often proclaimed to be the basis for all of human society. Just 10 years ago, we were being informed that information was the key to all—the Internet was changing everything because information was everything. And indeed, information has also always been important, which is why writing was such an important discovery, for instance.

About a century ago, history as a process of ever-better materials was all the rage, as was a fascination with all things mass production. We had gone through a Stone Age, Bronze Age, Iron Age, and now we were witnessing the power of the Steel Age (Superman was the Man of Steel, and Stalin means steel). Mass production was possible because of improvements in machine tools, which allowed for parts to be made of such exacting similarity, that an uneducated assembly line worker could pick up a part and repetitively insert it into a predetermined place, monotonously, for thousands of hours per year. We are in the Age of the Automobile, or Plane, just as 100 years ago we were in the Age of the Railroad.

Looking over these proclamations of the-one-most-important technology, it appears that it is possible to put together a "metaphysics" of production, to try to account for four or five categories of production that have, at one time or another, been claimed to have precedence in technological change, but in reality have all been important all of the time.

First, within production we need the ability to make a particular material; steel has been the premier material for the last century or so, but wood has always been and is now very important, as are certain minerals (think of glass and cement), and other metals, and chemicals. The key to these materials and their use is not the materials themselves, but the capacity to make or transform them; for instance, the history of steel is the history of steel-making machinery, which is at the core of our ability to make materials. There are other important processes such as turning bauxite into aluminum or sand into pure silicon—all part of the category of *material-making* production. Food can be considered part of the material-making category of a production system.

Second, possessing an unshaped blob of material, one can then fashion a shape or an entire piece of material that can be used with a machine or to make a machine. Machine tools and other structure-forming equipment are used to fashion parts out of materials. The cutting tools that were human beings' earliest inventions were used to fashion other implements, including other tools, as well as to kill animals for food. We also use other kinds of machinery, such as plastic-molding machinery to make plastic parts, or sewing machines to put clothes together, or construction machinery to put buildings and infrastructure together. These all fall into the category of *structure-forming* production.

Aristotle asked what is the cause of the existence of a statue; a statue has two things, form and substance.[9] The substance is the marble of the statue, which had to be created in some way, and the sculptor creates the form with a chisel. In the same way, any material object has to be produced with structure-forming machinery (or tools), and has to be made from a substance, generally created with material-making equipment.

Third, we need some form of energy conversion to have the energy needed for production. During Aristotle's day, much of the industrial energy conversion came from people, that is, from slaves. Horses were also used, and a bit of wind and water. With the advent of steam engines humans captured a dependable source of machine-generated energy. Then came internal combustion engines, then the electricity-generating turbines, usually using a form of fossil fuel. Now we need to shift to fuel-less forms of energy, mostly electricity generation, for most of our *energy-converting* production.

Fourth, we need some way to transport materials from one part of the production system to another. The assembly line is an example of an important innovation in *goods-transporting* production, and there are other kinds of "materials handling" equipment that are used in factories. Trucks carrying goods between factories are another example. Of course, in the final goods and services stage of production, cars are the dominant transportation machinery right now.

Fifth, goods and services are created using some form of *information processing* production, even if it is as basic as one engineer explaining to another engineer how a piece of machinery works, face-to-face-to-machine. Writing and then printing were revolutionary innovations in information processing, while obviously computers of various forms fill that role now.

In other words, to make something we need to have a material, we need to shape the material, we need an energy source to make the object and perhaps to allow the object to use energy after it has been produced, we need to transport pieces around the production area or region, and we need information-processing equipment (or processes) to make the object and perhaps to enable the object to process information itself.

These categories of production—form-making, material-making, energy conversion, goods moving and information processing—are filled in the reproduction machinery stage by the most important technologies of their age. Currently, the machine tool fills that role for form-making, steel-making machinery for material-making, electricity-generating turbines for energy conversion, materials handling equipment for goods moving, and semiconductor-making equipment for information processing. These technologies, collectively, reproduce themselves.

THE PRODUCTION SYSTEM

When we transpose these five categories of production on top of the three stages of production, we have 15 production niches, in the same way that an ecosystem has a multiplicity of niches of production. So each stage of production has five categories of production. Conceptually, stages of production are more important than categories of production, because each stage of production uses all five categories of production, while a category of production needs more than just the other stages of production in its category. We can also model another stage of production for physical infrastructure, each infrastructure niche corresponding to a category of production. Ever since the early 1800s water infrastructure has probably been the most important system, because it enables large cities to function by bringing fresh water in and taking waste water out. Water is a kind of material, and so occupies part of the material infrastructure niche. Garbage landfills form part of this niche; hopefully, an omnipresent recycling system will eventually exist as well.

Buildings are themselves structures, and are created by structure-forming equipment, construction machinery. The way buildings are situated in relation to one another is also a kind of structure; the structure-forming part of the infrastructure can be called the urban structure. Currently, the United States is mostly composed of sprawl urban structure, although there are islands of walkable environments like Manhattan.

The energy infrastructure is a critical part of all energy niches. We need a robust transmission system and electrical grid to carry electricity from where it is created, mostly with electricity-generated turbines, but more and more with wind turbines.

The information processing part of the infrastructure is in the best shape of any other, having been overinvested in during the dot com boom, providing cable, phone, and data at rates which enable the Internet to be the force that it is. If we add these infrastructure niches to the previous 15 niches, the production system is composed of a total of 20 niches, which we can see in Figure 3.1.

I've now specified an ecosystem for the economy. This system is composed of units that each serves a specific function, each one being necessary for the efficient operation of the system as a whole. The economic ecosystem is greater than the sum of its parts. It has a structure emanating from two kinds of orderings of niches. First, there are stages of production, moving from the reproduction machinery stage, which makes and uses reproduction machinery to make reproduction machinery for the second stage, the production machinery stage. At the production machinery stage, reproduction machinery makes production machinery for the third stage. This stage uses production machinery to make the wealth of the society: consumer final goods and services, and the physical infrastructure:, that is, the urban, resources, energy, transportation, and information

Figure 3.1 The structure of a sustainable production system

infrastructure systems that envelope and enable the activity of the society. The second ordering of niches divides each stage into material-making, structure-forming, energy-converting, goods-transporting, and information-processing categories of production. Figure 3.1 shows many of the various technologies and infrastructure systems that might exist in a sustainable production system.

Now we need to understand how this system grows—and decays—both from its own internal processes and also when it damages the natural ecosystems that surround and nourish it.

CHAPTER 4

How to Create Sustainable Growth

What causes economic growth? Is economic growth possible without destroying life on the planet? Is it possible to create economic growth and maximize social justice?

Economic growth can be defined as the increase in the output of goods and services of an economy. As I will explain in Chapter 7, neoclassical economics does not have an adequate theory for explaining the technological change that underlies economic growth.

In an ecosystem, populations of organisms grow all the time. Organisms contain within themselves production systems, which take inputs from the outside, and then using various mechanical and chemical processes, convert those inputs into additions to themselves. In a stable ecosystem, the inputs come from within the ecosystem, and the use of those elements usually does not prevent their reuse in the ecosystem. Similarly, outputs (such as waste) generally do not affect the structure of the ecosystem. Sometimes, a new organism (say a predator) may enter an ecosystem and completely change the system; for instance, cats introduced into island ecosystems have led to the extinction of many species. Sometimes the "waste" product can change ecosystems, as when the ancient bacteria hundreds of millions of years ago produced oxygen as waste, leading to their demise as the central organism on the planet and enabling the rise of oxygen-breathing organisms.

The core mechanism of growth in an ecosystem is the process of reproduction. Most species are capable of incredible increases in population, given enough time. Whether they divide, as in the case of bacteria; spread seeds or spores, in the case of plants or fungi; or lay eggs or give birth to live offspring, as animals do; populations grow exponentially—that is, given the right set of circumstances, the larger the population, the more the population can grow. This process is *exponential* because if you take any number and multiply it by itself, say 2 times 2, and keep doing this, for example you multiply the result of 2 times 2, 4, by 2 again, and multiply the result by 2 again, you get to some pretty big numbers pretty fast (and even bigger numbers if your multiplier increases with your numbers). A few pairs of rabbits can lead to a huge horde of rabbits in very short order.

Thus, virtually any population of organism can "explode." Not only do populations increase in size if they can, each member of the population is different from all others. In Darwin's terminology, each "organic being" is a different "variation," that is, a different version, which means that life has an incredible ability to exploit any ecosystem, given enough time, no matter how much the organisms and physical components of the ecosystem also change.

Because of all of this variation (which we now know happens because of DNA), an ecosystem is structured to allow for an enormous amount of change. The organisms are changing, which means that their technological characteristics are changing. For instance, the organism may change from moving at a slower speed to a faster one, or from having a duller set of teeth to a sharper set.

Most ecosystems, however, are already "filled up," that is, every part of their structure is filled with exquisitely adapted organisms, so that an increase in one population generally comes at the expense of another, for example, if predators have a particularly successful year capturing prey. This couldn't continue forever, or else all of the prey would die out, and with them, the predators. Occasionally, however, a part of an ecosystem, or a whole ecosystem, or even the entire biosphere, is wiped almost clean, as when an object hit the Earth 65 million years ago, wiping out the dinosaurs and allowing for the ecological "space" for mammals to "radiate," that is, to try out variations and explode in population over the entire planet.

Another way that ecosystem destruction can happen is when an intelligent species, in our case human beings, evolves on a planet, and proceeds to "explode," taking over the management of most ecosystems from the self-reproducing unconscious control of the group of organisms that inhabit an ecosystem. We are in the middle of the *sixth extinction*, the sixth time that the planet has been convulsed by a massive loss of species. The previous mass extinction was the aforementioned die-off of the dinosaurs. In the current case, the cause has emanated from within the Earth's community of organisms, namely human beings, as opposed to an extraterrestrial cause, such as an asteroid or meteor. The question for our species is whether we can consciously manage the biosphere or collapse along with our mismanagement of it.

Normally, when a population explodes, the consequences are the result of a simple increase in the numbers of the organism. Algae might take over a lake, for instance, because of a surplus of a nutrient, as when people use too much fertilizer in agriculture, which runs off and feeds algae blooms. Certainly the human population has been exploding, and this has caused quite a bit of destruction of ecosystems.

The greater impact has probably come from an increase in the resource intensity of use by human beings. In other words, economic growth has not just occurred as the population increases; the main driver of economic growth has been the increase in resource use per person. This can be called an increase in gross domestic product (GDP) per capita, or per person.

The authors of the *Limits to Growth* books have modeled the results of the overuse of resources and the output of pollution over the years, and they have been warning since the 1970s that at some point in the 21st century, human population and economies will crash as a result of the depletion of resources and the destruction of ecosystems.[1] William Catton also explored the situation where a species, in particular humans, sets up a process which is not sustainable, that is, at some point in the future, humanity will overshoot its ecosystems and fall off a cliff, figuratively.[2]

This process of overshooting the sustainable carrying capacity of the planet has been a very quick one by usual ecological standards, because human beings don't need to go through the long, random process of evolution-by-random-mutation. People can invent new technologies, and do it rather quickly. In fact, since the invention of the various group of technologies in the period known as the Industrial Revolution, this technological process of innovation has accelerated. What was it about the Industrial Revolution that allowed this to happen?

HOW ECONOMIES GROW

As I alluded in the previous chapter, there are a group of technologies that may be referred to collectively as reproduction machinery, which allow for the increasing, or exponential, growth of economies. For instance, all metal is cut or shaped by a group of technologies called machine tools. These metal pieces are used to make all pieces of machinery, including more machine tools. If we have a set of machine tools, we can use them to make more of the same kinds of machine tools (there are several major categories of machine tools). If we didn't use the machine tools to make anything else but more machine tools, we would soon have the parts for a double, triple, or a many-fold increase in the number of machine tools. With the help of skilled production workers, the machine tools will have reproduced themselves, just as surely as rabbits and algae.

Now, it turns out that machine tools were around before the Industrial Revolution, but they were generally made of wood, so they weren't very sharp (or precise), and they had to be rotated (the most common way to make a cut) by the person using the machine tool (sometimes waterwheels were used as an inanimate form of energy). The Industrial Revolution changed all of this because two changes took place—wood was replaced by iron, and coal was used to run steam engines that turned the machine tools.

In other words, machine tools became much more productive because they were made out of metal, and they were powered by a plentiful, reliable source of energy. In addition, many inventors made ingenious changes to the design of the machine tools. In the terminology of the previous chapter, the reproductive machinery niches of the structure-forming, material-making, and energy-converting categories of production formed a positive feedback loop of innovation among themselves.

Productivity measures how much of something comes out of a machine depending on how much of something else goes in. Productivity is most often measured in terms of the time it takes a person to do something. With a stronger cutting tool and more energy, the machine tool operator can cut more pieces than before.

The machinist not only can cut a greater quantity of pieces, but he also can cut better quality and different kinds of pieces. In other words, the quality and nature of the output changed as well. Thus we see, in the creation of the industrial machine tool, the two main causes of economic growth: an increase in the *quantity* of the output, in this case pieces, and a change in the *quality* of the output, that is, different and better kinds of output, in this case metal pieces made with high precision, often of a shape that was not possible before.

Before the machine tool, the only way to shape metal was by using the tools of the blacksmith, that is, heating up the metal and beating it into submission with a hammer. This process of heating up the metal used up so much wood that the English started to run out of forests to chop down, and thus many English businesses turned to coal. By 1776, James Watt had invented a steam engine that used coal to run a piston that moved machinery such as machine tools, which were then used to bore out the middle of the tubes that were used to make the pistons of the steam engine. In other words, the steam engine and the machine tool operated as a technological positive feedback loop. Advances in steam engines led to advances in machine tools, which led back to advances in steam engines, and back again.[3]

But this was not all; the increasing use of coal and the ability to cut and shape metal more precisely gave rise to advances in the machinery used to produce iron, and eventually steel, which led to stronger and less brittle machine tools and steam engines, which led to better iron and steel-making equipment. Eventually, whole new sets of machinery became possible, such as agricultural machinery and steam engine-based railroad locomotives, which in turn led to a complete transformation of the agricultural and transportation systems of the United States (and the world). Farmers in the middle of the country could now reliably move their agricultural products to the cities. Later, sewing machines changed the clothing industries, and then bicycles and cars changed the transportation systems again.

Machine tools stood at the center of these changes, as changes needed for one industry could then be transmitted to other industries. Reproduction machinery industries such as the machine tool industry serve as conveyor belts of innovation throughout the entire manufacturing system. As Nathan Rosenberg, the historian of these 19th-century changes, summarizes the process:

> Inventions hardly ever function in isolation. Time and again in the history of American technology, it has happened that the productivity of a given invention has turned on the question of the availability of complementary technologies. . . . Technologies depend upon one another and interact with one another in ways

that are not apparent to the casual observer, and often not to the specialist. . . . The growing productivity of industrial economies is the complex outcome of large numbers of interlocking, mutually reinforcing technologies, the individual components of which are of very limited economic consequence by themselves. The smallest relevant unit of observation, therefore, is seldom a single innovation but more typically, an interrelated clustering of innovations. . . . The importance of these complementarities suggests that it may be fruitful to think of each of these major clusterings of innovations from a system perspective.[4]

Using railroads, logging equipment, agricultural equipment, mining equipment, bulldozers, and myriad other technologies, the ability to extract and use the natural capital of the planet exploded exponentially. Steel replaced iron in machinery, making it much easier to shape precise pieces, making the machinery lighter and stronger, while oil and electricity led to the use of the internal combustion engine and electric motor and the abandonment of the large, heavy, fussy steam engines. The exploitation of the environment, the potential to create more machinery, and the volume of goods and services increased even faster in the 20th century—voila, a seemingly self-sustaining process of economic growth.

As the authors of the *Limits to Growth* point out,

Machines and factories collectively can make other machines and factories. A steel mill can make the steel for another steel mill. . . . Like population, capital has the inherent system structure (a positive feedback loop) to produce the behavior of exponential growth. Economies don't always grow, of course, any more than populations do. But they are structured to grow, and when they do, they grow exponentially.[5]

This process is neither economically self-sustaining nor ecologically sustainable. It is not self-sustaining because the processes of the domestic political economic system tend to work to destroy it; it is not sustainable because an awareness of the limits of growth set by the ecosystems does not accompany the growth of technological innovations and output.

Time and again, the elites of societies have looked at the bounty unleashed by the positive feedback loops inherent in production systems, and instead of seeking to preserve the engine of growth, they have starved the production system to increase their short-term power and wealth. The financial system is a system of control and expropriates much of the surplus of the production system; elites of many kinds may also decide to raid the production system for their own personal profit.

The government can also deplete the production system, mostly to increase the elites' power by creating a powerful military system, as the Soviets did. Soviet economics, developed during the relatively liberated 1920s, was based on Marx's insights about the economy. Marx labeled the consumer goods industries as "Department 3," the factories that made the goods as "Department 2," and the sector that makes the means of production, "Department 1." G.A. Feldman was the main Soviet economist who translated this scheme into a theory that Stalin[6] and the Soviets used to create a self-sustaining production system that made the Union of Soviet Socialist Republics (USSR) a Great Power. But what the state makes, the state can take away, and the Soviet state destroyed its creation in the service of a huge military industrial complex.

As tempting as it would be to blame the unsustainable nature of human economies on elites—and they certainly make things worse— the truth seems to be that most of humanity would like to live like an upper-middle-class person in the developed countries and accrue constantly increasing wealth. I'd even like to blame the market, or capitalism, or corporations, except that the central planners of the former Soviet Union were probably the worst offenders of all in terms of environmental destruction, and today's Communist Chinese leadership is not much better. If everybody thinks that the goal of a modern economy is to have a constantly larger house and car and to fill that house with lots of electricity-sucking products, then we're probably doomed. But it's also possible that most people would choose a more sustainable future, if they were able to choose among a number of attractive alternative futures. In other words, people must be made aware of the alternative civilizations that are possible.

Would people accept higher quality over higher quantity? Currently, the desire for both seems to be running rampant. To understand how the difference between quality and quantity might make a difference, we have to resume an exploration of the processes of technological innovation and economic growth.

Human beings now dominate the planet for one simple reason: we can make tools. We are not very good at much else. Lions are perfectly good at communicating with each other in order to hunt, as are other groups of animals that carry out social activities. We're rather weak physically, and not very fast, and our teeth are pathetic compared to most other animals. Walking upright is so undesirable that we are about the only animals that do it, except for birds that need their upper limbs for flying (according to recent research, we're very good at running for long periods of time, which helps us exhaust hunted prey). As for having a big brain, the reason most other animals don't have one is because the brain takes up so much energy that most animals would starve before they gathered enough food to feed it. That is, unless they had tools.

"Oh yeah," the biologically correct might object, "plenty of other animals use tools." Yes, but no other animal uses tools to make tools. I argued that reproduction machinery was the key to economic growth because it enables the creation of a positive feedback loop of machinery creating more machinery. In the same way, human beings first fashioned "mother stone" tools that they then used to make the tool that was used for everyday life. Thus, a hammer stone was used to create cutting surfaces out of pieces of flint, for instance, a technique used by our predecessors, Homo erectus.

We evolved with a tool in our hands; there is no mythical time before tools in which human beings simply ate with their hands. The 18th-century philosopher John Locke, for instance, claimed that all value comes from labor because the first human beings must have eaten with only their hands, as in eating fruit (Friedrich Von Hayek and Karl Marx made the same claim). Apes are designed to eat fruit without tools, and to survive thereby. Humans need tools, or we will die. Homo erectus and Homo sapiens both co-evolved with tools, that is, with capital; take a look at your hands, they make no sense without tools. The brain was largely expanded to make tools, and because of tools, the brain obtained enough nutrition to survive. Tools made hands and brains, and hands and brains make tools.

Tools break evolution, because they allow the organism to change its technology to suit the environment, and as is the wont of most organic beings, human beings try to reproduce and prosper without limit. Natural evolution is not only not necessary for the tool-maker, evolution cannot fight back by creating other niches or organisms in the ecosystem that would lead to a balance of power against the tool-maker. As we see, the tool-maker has available to it a positive feedback loop that allows it to conquer the entire planet.

In fact, the only living part of the ecosystem that can stop ourselves is ourselves, either by consciously managing the planet in a rational way, or by destroying the biosphere to such an extent that the species goes extinct.

It may be that when an intelligent species emerges on a planet, evolution of intelligence will occur because of success or failure at managing the planet. Intelligent species could conceivably keep appearing if humans fail, and if they can't manage the planet properly, they will eventually go extinct as well, until such a time as a species emerges that can handle the job. It is not clear yet whether human beings will be that species.

As the increasingly famous Pogo line has it, "We have met the enemy and he is us," to which I might amend, "and we have met the ally and he is us," if we use our intelligence, well, intelligently.

HOW TO MAKE A MIDDLE CLASS

We have the tools to live peacefully with the world, to live in "blessed unrest," the title of a book by Paul Hawken about the attempt on the part of millions of people around the world to fight for the planet's biosphere.[7] The history of technology has been the history of improving quality, as well as increasing quantity. If we can concentrate on quality instead of quantity, we might have a shot at creating a sustainable civilization. But we need to understand how machinery technologies evolve; there is a certain amount of "industrial literacy" that is necessary to discern a way forward. That means understanding how technologies interact with each other and change.

The reproduction and production machinery technologies help to make more of themselves, collectively, and technological improvements in one category of production reverberate around the entire group of technologies, and beyond to the entire economy. If we look from the perspective of machine tools, for instance, we can see that an improvement in the kinds of steel available can lead to a big improvement in cutting and precision; electricity is used to power the machine tools; and the development of semiconductors and computer control led to a revolution in the capability of machine tools. In turn, better machine tools means more precise parts to be used in steel factories; better turbines for making electricity; and better grinders for the optical equipment at the core of the production of semiconductors. And, of course, better machine tools mean better parts for more technologically complex machine tools.

Better steel means higher quality steel for steel-making equipment for better turbines and better materials for semiconductors. Continuously cheaper electricity from better turbines throughout the 20th century led to the penetration of electricity-using devices throughout society; and of course, the most spectacular example of technological progress in most of our lifetimes has been the ever-increasing power of semiconductors, which is made possible by advances in semiconductor-making equipment.

Improvements in machine tools, steel-making machinery, turbines, and semiconductor-making machinery also lead to improvements in all classes of production machinery such as agricultural machinery, computers, phones, construction machinery, trains, and other consumer machinery. Semiconductor technology, along with wind turbine technology, may lead to the replacement of most electricity-generating steam turbines as the key energy-converting technology.

The constant and steady advances in machinery have led to constant increases in the ability of people to increase production. From 1947 to 2000, manufacturing production increased by 6-and-two-thirds times (from an index of 15 to 100, value added). This growth was accompanied by an increase of production workers in manufacturing from 15 million full-time equivalent employees in 1947 to 18 million in 2000,[8] that is, by only one-fifth. That's an increase in labor productivity of about 5-and-one-half times, or an annual growth in productivity of 3.2 percent. That means that through all the ups and downs of the post-World War II period, manufacturing technology kept improving, on average, enough to double output every 22 years.

To keep up this pace of growth, engineers are constantly tweaking, fixing, learning about, or even stumbling on new innovations day after day. Industrial engineers discover different ways of organizing work. Scientists discover new behaviors and principles that can be applied to industrial processes. Skilled production workers, working at the actual point of production, can be an important part of the innovation process, if their ideas are listened to.

Another important reason that the United States used to be the technological leader in industry is that American wages were higher than anyone else's. How could this possibly be an advantage? Seymour Melman discovered that when wages rise faster than the price of production machinery, competent managers—that is, managers that want to minimize costs and know how to do it—turn to the use of more and more machinery. If machines are always becoming less inexpensive in comparison to wages, then when faced with the choice in a factory of hiring more workers or buying more machinery, managers tend to buy more machinery[9] (assuming that the managers can't ship production to a lower-wage area).

This theory of "alternate cost-productivity" almost got Melman fired from Columbia University, but an eminent economist came to his rescue. What raised the ire of other economists was the idea that high wages were actually a good idea. Of course, we now constantly hear the drumbeat of the need for lower-cost labor, but what really drives prices down, and gives wealth to a society, is better machinery and better organization of work. As Joel Mokyr pointed out,[10] Milton Friedman's admonition that "there is no free lunch" is contradicted by the history of technology—the discovery that just by adding a piece of machinery here, changing the recipe for steel there, moving a piece of metal some other place—one can get more from the same inputs. Without these technological improvements, there might be no lunch for most people, much less free ones.

In addition to the counterintuitive argument that higher wages lead to greater growth, it has also been evident that higher wages and more machinery lead to more and better jobs. Because the machinery is more productive, managements have often built more factories to accommodate the demand for the lower-priced and/or better goods that are the result of the greater use of machinery by a cost-minimizing management. They therefore hire back the workers they might not have needed anymore and even add more. In addition, the machinery makers hire more workers to make the machines that the factory owners covet.

There is a positive feedback process at work here: higher wages lead to more machinery, which leads to lower relative prices for the machinery, which leads to the use of yet more machinery and higher wages for the workers who must be highly skilled so that they can get the most out of the machinery. It is more important to keep the machinery running than it is to cut workers' wages.

The result, ideally, is a higher standard of living because people have more, better, and cheaper goods to choose from, while at the same time they have higher wages. And what is the term for a society in which this golden cycle is occurring? *A middle-class society.*

HOW TO MAKE A SUSTAINABLE ECONOMY

The various classes of human capital—engineers, scientists, skilled production workers—can more easily learn about and contribute to this stream of innovations, the closer physically that they are to each other. This is one of the reasons that cities have been so important in world history—the close proximity of many kinds of production system innovators has accelerated the pace of innovation within cities. There is a reason that certain districts such as Silicon Valley and Wall Street are centers of innovation and power, and it has to do with the importance of being close to other people and the processes of production (or distribution). People need to "kick the tires," as it were, within the factory, see for themselves how operations work, build up face-to-face, long-term discussions with similar groups of professionals, even speak the same language to expedite communication.[11]

Throughout history, and even to this day, we continue to think of economies in a regional sense, as an American economy, a Chinese economy, the European economy, more than we think of one globalized world economy. This is because economies work best at a world regional level, generally at the level of a subcontinent, as in India or China, or a continental level, such as North America or Europe, or ideally, Africa and South America. These large economic units have the potential to encompass a full suite of production niches, in other words, a complete production system, including positive feedback loops. Large regions also provide the space for the technological reverberations that take place because the human capital in these regions build dense, fast, fruitful webs of interactions. All of this leads to a steady stream of innovations.

This constant stream of innovations can be characterized as a natural rate of innovation. It is the foundation for all economic growth. Even if there was no growth in the use of resources, this background natural rate of innovation would continue.

The move from fossil-fuel power plants to solar and wind energy is an example of how improvements in machine technology can proceed without the need for using up more resources and destroying the environment. Transforming electricity generation so that it relies on renewable sources would complete the Industrial Revolution by replacing a resource with a machine—instead of using a fuel such as oil, natural gas, or coal, the machine would use the wind or the sun to power itself.

In other words, it is an inherent part of the industrialization process that it contains within itself the seeds for overcoming its most destructive tendencies; instead of using resources for economic activities, we can use machines. This is sometimes referred to as *dematerialization*.[12] Machines can replace resources.

Information-processing machinery is affecting this transformation with the computerization of information. Writing was the first important information technology; the pre-modern Industrial Revolution was made possible by the printing press; vacuum tubes led to an acceleration of information processing, and now semiconductors are threatening to put printing presses out of business (and maybe, finally, leading to a lesser need for paper). Information processing and energy conversion are now at the point where they can be dematerialized, if not completely, at least enough to allow for recycling of the materials they need to fulfill their functions.

Machine tools and other structure-forming machinery never used a significant amount of resources; there isn't enough industrial machinery to seriously tax ecosystems, and most of the weight of a machine is steel, which is recyclable. That leaves material-making as the last unsustainable holdout within the reproduction machinery sector, making recycling the obvious solution. Most steel is now recycled. Plastics will have to match steel in recycling capability to be sustainable, assuming that there is enough oil to make plastics, unless biological alternatives can be used sustainably. Even cement is increasingly recycled. The agricultural system needs to be restructured so that soil is built up, not chemically sterilized and washed away. Chemicals may be the most difficult to recycle and to produce without pollution; the question is, what chemicals can we afford to give up, and which can be produced sustainably?

For the most part, the innermost parts of the industrial system need not be environmentally unsustainable. If the production of machinery involved recycled materials, were recyclable, and used wind and/or solar energy, the machinery sectors could be among the greenest sectors of the economy.

The problem is not that these sectors are themselves unsustainable; the problem is that machinery can pump out such a huge wave of goods from factories that the ecosystems of the planet can be depleted and trashed. We've made a big mess, and only about one-fourth of the world's population enjoys the fruits of the destruction of the planet. How do we lift the other three-fourths up in a sustainable way?

The answer is that society will have to become much more efficient (the specification of an efficient civilization will be the task of Part 3 of this book). We should be aware that there is an enormous amount of waste and inefficiency in the current civilization, which means that there are plenty of resources available for the task of reconstruction.

THE INEFFICIENT SOCIETY

The troika of energy, transportation, and urban systems has seemingly been designed to be as wasteful as possible, particularly in the United States. It makes centrally planned Russia look far-seeing by comparison.[13]

First, the coal plants, which are used to generate half of our electricity, waste globally about 69 percent of their energy through heat loss.[14] Another 10 percent or so is lost in transmission. Oil plants aren't much better, and neither are natural gas-fired plants or nuclear-powered plants.

Second, the car-, truck-, and plane-centered transportation system could not have been more badly designed. About 1 percent of the energy generated by a car is actually used to transport the person or people inside, and most of the rest (about 80 percent) is used by that wonder of old and outdated technology, the internal combustion engine; the remainder is used to carry around the metal needed in a vain attempt to make the killing fields known as our roads and highways safer.

Having a spread-out system clogged with cars and trucks means trillions of vehicle-miles that could have been saved if the buildings had been built closer together. On top of this, cars are only being used 4 percent of the time[15]—96 percent of the time they're wasting space in parking spots.

The upshot of all of this is that if a rail-system replaced cars, and buildings were placed closer together, many fewer car factories would be needed. The global market very efficiently makes too much of a very inefficient product.

Meanwhile, buildings are built and allowed to operate with minimal attempts to insulate or otherwise design them to minimize energy use, particularly for heating and cooling. The return on investment for energy retrofitting is risk-free and pays itself back in less than 10 years, yet is almost never done. In addition, apartment buildings are much more energy efficient than single-family homes, because they have much less roof and wall space per person. While a single-family house has four sides (or more) and a roof, an apartment may have only one side facing the outside. In 2007, of 128 million housing units, 80 million were single-family detached houses.[16]

Agricultural products are very labor efficient while being very inefficient about everything else. Huge amounts of pesticides, fertilizer, and water are applied, and food is transported long distances. According to the journalist Fred Pearce,[17] it can take 24,000 liters of water to make one kilogram of beef, and 10 calories of energy to produce one calorie of food.[18] Worst of all, the soil is destroyed.

Resources, instead of being recycled, are transported to overflowing waste dumps that destroy ecosystems and that generate about 3 percent of all greenhouse gases. Massive mining efforts are needed to replace the nonrecycled materials, also destroying ecosystems.

In addition to this waste, the financial, insurance, and real estate (FIRE) systems now take up 20 percent of the GDP, the health system over 6 percent (value-added), and oil imports another 5 percent. Thirty-one percent of the economy is being used for systems that should probably add up to 10 percent.

The military, which is a government function, is also incredibly wasteful. The military in the United States constitutes about 42 percent of world military spending,[19] a figure that excludes much national security funding. The U.S. military has little useful function other than keeping a subset of the industrial economy afloat and allowing American political elites to play at building an empire. In addition, the worst aspects of what used to be Soviet central planning are present in the U.S. military industrial complex: unreliable systems that are much more expensive than they should be; systems designed by engineers who have a hard time moving back into civilian production where cost-consciousness is a part of an engineer's daily work life; and a level of complexity designed to make it difficult to control spending.[20]

The governance structure of the corporation is also grossly inefficient. Corporations are hierarchical in structure—that is, they are effectively a dictatorship, with a chief executive officer at the pinnacle, a generally supplicant board of directors under him, and a powerless mass of shareholders under them.

As in a political system, within the corporation the consequences of a centralized distribution of power is that the top of the structure, the upper management, has it within their power to divert a large percentage of the firm's resources for their own personal gain. Thus we see the explosion of chief executive officers' compensation, for instance. Louis XIV would understand this behavior, which is a consequence of the centralization of power.

Perhaps even more malignant is the effect hierarchy has on efficiency within the organization. Those at the bottom or even the middle are the ones who are doing the actual work of the organization. But they are not the ones with the decision-making power—the managers at the top have that power. Not only is the managerial level farther away from the information about the actual conditions of production and the possibilities for innovation, they generally monopolize decisions relating to either how innovation takes place or what to do with innovations that occur.

Because power that emanates from the top of the organization is unconstrained, top managers tend to hire more people than they need to extend their power throughout the organization. Melman found that the ratio of administrative personnel to production workers within manufacturing firms soared from 22 per 100 to 53 per 100 from 1947 to 1996, and that the total for salaries increased from 31 per 100 to 99 per 100. In other words, by 1996 manufacturing firms were spending as much on administrative personnel as on production workers. For the economy as a whole, the ratio of decision-making personnel to consumer-goods production moved from 42 per 100 in 1940 to 140 per 100 in 1990.[21]

According to David Gordon, by the early 1990s, Japan and Germany were using about one-third the number of administrative employees per production worker as the United States. Gordon argued that the burden of corporate bureaucracy costs four times as much as the military for the country as a whole.[22]

If corporations were owned and operated by all of their employees, in other words, if the corporation became democratic, the resources going into the managerial levels would drastically decline, and the innovation and efficiency going on within production would greatly increase.[23]

The financial industry not only controls more resources than it needs to as a result of its power of control, it also redirects resources into the wrong sectors of the economy. The financial system should be used as part of an effort to transform the economy into something more sustainable, and the best way to do that is to turn them into public institutions, on a federal, state, or local level.

Add all of these inefficiencies together, and it is a wonder that advanced economies, and particularly the United States, are able to function at all. The economy would be *more* efficient, not less, if certain sectors of the economy, such as health and finance, became a part of citizen-controlled government, and if the government designed and financed a transformation of various infrastructures. Society as a whole must decide how to direct the construction of technologically sophisticated systems, not the large concentrations of centralized economic power that control the market.

Intelligent design and democracy can take us far in constructing a society that can grow in quality, at the natural rate of innovation from improvements in machinery, without growing from the use and abuse of the biosphere.

Human beings have stopped evolution, but our market-driven economies and stupid design threaten a de-evolution instead. We can no longer assume that human society will develop as if it were an automatically self-adjusting system, as proposed by the neoclassical economic paradigm. The planet needs intelligent design, and the neoclassical model is of little help in this task.

Instead of relying on disengaged models of reality to guide us in the future, we should look at the historical record. History is civilization's laboratory; it can provide the empirical evidence in support of or in contradiction to the hypotheses of any economic paradigm.

PART TWO

THE RISE AND POSSIBLE DECLINE OF MODERN SOCIETY

Ideas are very powerful, but they should be tested against the historical record, current conditions, and the future as best we can discern it. In Part 2 of this book, the alternative paradigm constructed in the first part will be used to try to explain how history has been unfolding, and what lies in the future if we carry on with business-as usual. Manufacturing and production have always had a critical effect on the course of history, and particularly on the influence and capabilities of the group of nations often referred to as "Great Powers," that is, those nations that can shape how humanity manages the whole planet. Fights between Great Powers can lead to world wars, but cooperation could lead to the improvement of life for people and the other organisms on this planet. Chapter 5 explores the processes of rise and decline up to the time of the Industrial Revolution.

The British were in the forefront of the Industrial Revolution that began in 1776 when the steam engine was invented, but in 1776 the United States also came into existence. Much of the time since its first centennial, the United States has been in a starring role, owing to its rise as a manufacturing nation. Chapter 6 traces this rise, as well as the changes in other parts of the international system, particularly with respect to Germany and the former Soviet Union.

No country has ever been so powerful, relative to other countries, as the United States was just after World War II. Some sort of decline was inevitable, but the focus of American dynamism shifted from manufacturing to matters military and financial during the six decades after the last world war. The military obsession also brought down the Soviet Union during this time. Although the United States is still powerful, its middle class may not be for very much longer. Chapter 7 shows how we can use a production-centered approach to economics to explain both rise *and* decline.

Although the economic prognosis for a United States with a declining manufacturing sector might be grim, the entire global civilization will be in trouble if global warming, peak oil, and ecosystem destruction are not dealt with in a serious way. Except for some indigenous cultures, human beings have almost always been hard on the environment, and many past civilizations have fallen because of ecological mismanagement. Chapter 8 looks at the sources of the greenhouse gas emissions that threaten the stability of the climate; the effects that the end of the era of cheap oil will have on a civilization addicted to cars, trucks, and airplanes; and the dire results of destroying ecosystems, particularly for the provision of food.

CHAPTER 5

The Rise and Decline of Great Powers

The rise and decline of nations have profound effects on the state of the planet. Depending on who is ascendant and why, life can be miserable or comfortable, for both people and other living things. Depending on who is rising or declining, the international situation may be peaceful or war-like, open to constructive improvement or whole-scale destruction.

We now exist in a time when nations must collectively do the right thing, that is, they must act to prevent climate change, ecosystem destruction, and an economic collapse that will attend the end of cheap oil. In addition, if there is any hope of ameliorating global poverty and preventing nations, such as the United States, from becoming poor, thriving manufacturing sectors will have to be established within all world regions, and these sectors will have to output no or little pollution and use recycled materials. It is imperative to learn the lessons of the past to understand how best to create an economically and ecologically sustainable society.

In the short term, superior force will determine the outcome of conflict, but in the long run superior productive power will determine the level of force. This applies on many time levels. As Paul Kennedy argued,[1] the side in a global war that has superior industrial power will eventually, in the course of that war, translate that industrial might into military power and usually victory. For example, the United States started World War II with the greatest industrial system in human history and a tiny military. Because of its industrial base, by the end of World War II it was able to create the world's greatest military. Now, the United States risks losing much of its power because it is maximizing its short-term international power by directing resources into the military, resources that should be used to recreate its economy and infrastructure.

THE CONTRADICTION OF MILITARY POWER

The processes of the rise and decline of nations occur again and again. Somehow a nation, or more generally a society, figures out how to unify an area and at the same time increase its productive capacity. It then expands, economically and territorially. However, this expansion also disproportionately enriches sectors of society that do not feed back resources into the productive system. On the contrary, these forces—the military, the very wealthy, the financial system—act like parasites, sucking the resources out of the system and into their own sectors. Their sectors become more and more powerful, even as the production system, which is the basis for their power, starts to buckle under the strain.

We can use my specification of a domestic political economic system to see how this takes place. The economic system is composed of two subsystems, the distribution system and the production system. The financial sector is the main player in the distribution system. It starts out small, with less power than the production system. The political system is the sister system to the economy within a nation, and it too has several subsystems. One such subsystem is the military, which uses the reproduction machinery sector of the economy's production system to make its destruction machinery. It, too, is generally small when the society is starting to rise.

At first, the production system enjoys the full effects of various economic positive feedback loops. Eventually, however, the financial and military systems start to pick up speed, siphoning more and more resources from the production system. Eventually, the production system cannot even replace its own capital, and it starts to decline. The financial and military system by this time are probably gaining capital from their own investments or conquests from other countries, so it may take some time for them to experience decline, a decline which is masked by their international resources; in the meantime, they have less reason to worry about the decline of the domestic production system, and they have more time to squeeze the remaining

capital out of it. But eventually some other country, or set of countries, passes the declining Great Power, and the Great Power eventually drops out of Great Power status altogether—and its citizens
become considerably poorer in the process.

It can be very difficult not to become caught up in an international race to acquire a large military. It may be the case that there
are several belligerent nations that are close enough to cause real
trouble if you don't keep up. It might also become difficult to stay
out of local conflicts; if you're big enough, there are quite a lot of
things going on at your borders, and so you feel you have to keep
the neighborhood safe, as it were. It is also difficult for people with
power to resist the temptation of easy influence or conquest.

So you may have good reasons, besides lust for power, to expand
your military; but if building up a large military depletes your productive system, the other nations are not going to give you a pass. If
you decline because you had to carry the expenses of a huge military,
nobody is going to save you. If you don't indulge in the build-up of
a large-scale military and there are other nations that can then conquer you, unless you are very good at getting other countries to do
your defending for you, nobody will help you defend yourself either.
So most societies, at some point or another, have had to contend
with the problem of creating a big enough military to fend off conquest, but still keep the military under control to give their productive system the capacity to renew itself and grow.

Ideally you would have as small a military as possible to be able to
have as big a military as possible should you need it. The more your
military controls resources, the less your productive sector will, and
vice-versa. In the long run, the smaller your military, the larger it
can be in an emergency.

There are other problems with a big military besides depleting
the economy. A big military generally leads to a large role for financial institutions, which has to raise the financial capital necessary for
military construction, and this establishes the financial sector in a
powerful role. Even more fundamentally, the militarization of society stifles the creativity and linkages that a society needs to innovate;
because innovation is the key to the growth that underlies both
wealth and military power, militarization of a society eventually leads
to a collapsing society, and with it, a collapsing military.

The safer the international environment is, the easier it is to keep
the military under control, although a peaceful situation can give an

unscrupulous country an opening for conquest. On the other hand, if a nation's people are passionate about the defense of their country, conquest of that country becomes more difficult. But that means that the government has to gain widespread legitimacy, that is, most people have to believe that the government is working on their behalf. The easiest way to gain this legitimacy is through democracy that allows people clearly to have some control; however, dictatorships also try to maintain their own legitimacy in various ways. This is one reason democracy keeps advancing; it is easier to defend a democratic country than a dictatorial one.

The contradictions of military power affect the most powerful nation most of all. For countries that are not on top, elites may feel that they must suppress some of their own worst tendencies because they need to catch up to the leading power, lest the leading power take advantage of their relative backwardness. In other words, fear of those more powerful than you acts as a constraint. No such constraint exists for the top power. A short-term decision by elites of the top country to profit by very slightly decreasing the capital base of the country might seem harmless, say by moving production overseas. After all, the country will continue to be the top power, whether the change is made or not. Pretty soon, other elites will notice that this bit of capital destruction is yielding big profits, and more and more will create a self-reinforcing "tipping point" of offshoring production, lest the firms be left behind by the pioneers of the capital destruction movement. Much like nations, companies feel that they have to emulate the successful or risk annihilation. Soon capital destruction is all the rage, and the country is on its way to poverty—like the United States.

Production is the most critical factor in understanding how nations rise and fall, including the disposition of the basis of production, ecosystems. The military and financial sectors play a big role in decline, but the nonmilitary part of the government can play a big part in creating the conditions for the rise of a nation, as well as keeping a country wealthy and wise.

THE CONTRADICTION OF CONTROLLING NATURE

Throughout history, it has seemed as if the more a society destroys its ecosystems, the greater advantage it has over other societies, at least in the short term. This occurs when liquidating or drawing down capital, to use William Catton's term.[2] Capital is turned into income, which is used to provision armies and conquer other societies. This process first took place with the invention of agriculture, which involved a radical shift in the management of ecosystems.

Most ecosystems progress through time in a cycle of stability and fast change. For instance, forests are generally able to withstand even bad fires, because they have evolved to function on the assumption that there will be fires; thus some trees, such as redwoods, only germinate in a fire. Destruction is part of this natural progression. Early ecologists thought that many ecosystems, after a period of disturbance, work their way up to a "climax" stage, that is, a fully mature stage that is stable. More recently, however, some ecologists have pointed out that a "mature" stage is only one of many, and that ecosystems regularly reform themselves, such as a forest after a fire. An ecosystem that has the capacity to withstand, or even welcome, large-scale, long-rhythm changes is referred to as *resilient*.[3]

After a fire or other form of environmental devastation such as a flood, the land has been wiped fairly clean—there are no large plants around, for instance, that suppress the growth of smaller plants. This is where grasses and what we know as grains jump in and thrive. They grow very quickly, and reproduce prodigiously in an effort to get a foothold while they still have a chance. In most ecosystems, the larger plants, such as trees, eventually take over, and the grasses might even disappear after a while.

It is these fast-growing and reproducing grasses, or grains, which human beings domesticated for the purposes of agriculture.[4] By choosing the fastest-growing species, humans enjoyed a huge increase in food productivity. By doing so, we also started to depend on an intense and unnatural management of the ecosystems in which farming takes place, because ecosystems are always trying to reassert themselves and move onto the next stage of an ecosystem. So we eliminate weeds, which are often simply the next stage's plants. Because we maximize productivity by concentrating on one plant, we defeat the natural feedback mechanisms of the ecosystem and pests become a problem, threatening to eat up most of the crop. Probably worst of all, though, we destroy the natural capital of soil by constantly planting these very nutrient-hungry grasses, which are often also very thirsty, necessitating vast irrigation systems or even

flooding, as in the case of rice, which can destroy the soil by encouraging salt to rise from deep in the ground.

Thus it was that the first agricultural-based society, the Sumer-
ians, probably disappeared because they over-irrigated and ran into
salt problems. Indeed, the entire Middle East was known originally
as the "Fertile Crescent," which is fertile no more, probably thanks
to the wholesale destruction of forests and grassland ecosystems. Egypt
remained the breadbasket of the Mediterranean world through Roman
times because the Nile River always deposited a nice new layer of
nutrients on the fields during the annual floods.

The agricultural productivity of grains gave the societies that
domesticated them a short-term jump (sometimes lasting centuries)
on other peoples of the area by providing the food for nonfarmers
such as artisans and soldiers to pursue their professions, mainly in
the cities. While agriculture provided the extra food to feed an army,
which is always a hugely expensive operation, it also fed the artisans
who made the weapons and provisions for the army and for the political elites. Artisans need cities to pass along skills and to interact
with other knowledge workers, as they are now affectionately known.

How formerly relatively independent hunters and gatherers were
convinced or coerced into becoming overworked farmers in the
fields seems to be lost in the mists of time, but these grain-based
societies became very hierarchical, that is, power emanated from the
top of the society down; there was virtually no democracy, as far as
we can tell. It is quite possible that these militarized societies conquered other peoples who were in much greater harmony with their
local ecosystems, and who seem to have worshiped the Earth god-
desses, as opposed to the male war gods of the conquerors.[5] However, lacking the productive power of the militaristic societies, the
indigenous peoples were essentially wiped out, as in Europe.

THE CREATION OF THE MODERN WORLD

As the historian William McNeil explained, until industrial technology came into its own, the resultant large, grain-based empires
and societies had one other group that occasionally bested them
in combat: the steppe peoples, coming from the huge plains of central Eurasia (what is now Russia).[6] These people were nomadic
herders and had one huge technological advantage over centers of

civilization: they had superior skills in handling horses, which were the premiere transportation vehicle and power source before industrial society. In addition to making the best bows and arrows, these peoples, culminating in the Mongols, used advanced military techniques and were able to defeat what looked like more "advanced" civilizations.

Speed can be very important in warfare because simply confronting an enemy head-on and annihilating them is a fairly rare occurrence. The ideal is to surround one's enemy, and therefore starve them out, or what generally precedes starvation, make the enemy panic and disperse as a fighting force. Horses give an army the speed to achieve this end, which is why the cavalry was always the most important part of an army, until cannons and artillery started to chip away at this advantage. So the Mongols and other steppe peoples were not simply blood-thirsty barbarians who overran their adversaries by being insanely aggressive, they used cutting-edge technology as well.

Janet Abu-Lughod's *Before European Hegemony*[7] discusses the era before the 1400s, when China, India, the Middle East, and Europe, in approximately that order, were the leading technological centers of the world. As she explains, the Mongol hegemony over much of central Eurasia allowed these civilizations to interact with each other, because the Mongols made commerce on their vast territory relatively safe; this is the era when Marco Polo crossed into China and enabled Europe to "discover" this more advanced civilization.

However, that doesn't mean that the steppe peoples were nice. The development of the pre-modern power centers was being continuously interrupted by major invasions of the steppe peoples. The Mongol conquest of China led to a period of looking inward that followed Mongol rule, even though during this time the Chinese had constructed ships that were much bigger than the Europeans' and that explored South Asia and East Africa. The Mongols also unified India under the Moghuls, and the Ottoman Turks, another steppe people, unified the Middle East, although they probably overtaxed the fledgling manufacturing centers.[8] Baghdad was grievously harmed by the Mongols, an insult from which it never fully recovered.

The Mongols also encouraged one of their Russian principalities, Moscow, to be the administrative center of their conquests there, and by so doing initiated a centuries-long positive feedback loop of conquest enabling further conquest, until Moscow took over most of

Russia under Ivan the Terrible and eventually controlled most of the former Mongol lands of central Eurasia. Central Eurasia is a good example of a geographically logical place to have a complete production system, of a subcontinental type.

One area the Mongols did not influence, however, was Europe. The Romans had developed superior technologies, mostly in the area of civil engineering for roads and infrastructure. Although it allowed them to initiate their own positive feedback process of empire creation, the steppe peoples (such as the Huns) broke this up. The Romans had allowed their military to sap the resources out of the empire, an example of the process of decline which I have outlined above. The Romans had also overtaxed their empire ecologically.[9] The lack of a strong state that followed the Roman collapse gave an opening to outside powers. The Mongols, who had been on the verge of adding Europe to their imperial collection in the 1200s when their leader (great khan) died, had to retreat to pick a new leader, never to return.

The Europeans had a few advantages, besides the leftover technologies of the Romans. They were close enough to more advanced civilizations, such as the Arabs, to learn a great deal, but far enough away that it was difficult for these civilizations (and steppe peoples) to take them over. This geographic "sweet spot," of being not too far away and not too close, has repeated itself quite often in history. England and Japan definitely benefited from their geographic status as islands, as did the United States in a similar way much later. The Europeans seem to have also benefited from not being unified into one central empire,[10] making it possible for different kinds of systems to develop. A central authority did not suck the capital out of the rest of Europe. At the same time, Europe defined a single trading region, and so technologies and people were able to intermingle and produce economic growth.

The world of 1500 became much more interconnected. The Turkish, Indian, and Chinese empires were fairly content to administer their rather large realms, while the Europeans started to use their technological advantages in guns, germs, and steel, as Jared Diamond put it in the book of the same name,[11] to take over the indigenous peoples of Africa and the northern and southern continents of the Americas.

The sub-Saharan Africans had managed not to destroy their particularly delicate and difficult ecosystems. Because of those ecosystems, the Africans had a hard time establishing large agricultural systems. They also did not have recourse to the horse; their species of horse, the zebra, is too smart to be lassoed and domesticated.

However, the Africans had an advantage that the native Americans didn't have; being connected to the Asian supercontinent as they were, they had become immune to many of the diseases that were constantly sweeping across most of that part of the planet. As William McNeil explains,[12] the relative ease of transit across Eurasia by all organisms enabled the production of an enormous number of variations, such as the horse, and also various germs that the peoples of Eurasia and Africa became immune to.

In the Americas, on the other hand, the north-south routes are much more difficult to traverse than the Eurasian east-west routes, and in any case, there is not as much variation in the Americas because the Americas are smaller than Eurasia. When the Eurasians invaded the Americas, the native peoples were not prepared, for either the technological onslaught of guns and horses, or for the biological invasion of Eurasian germs; the flora and fauna of the Americas were also no match for the invaders.[13]

The indigenous peoples of the Americas had also kept their respective ecosystems intact, while the Europeans did not after they took over. In North America, European farmers continually moved west from the east coast because they overused and eroded the soil. Although the North American "Indians" learned to use horses and guns, they could not manufacture guns, and despite the efforts of some leaders such as Tecumseh, they did not unify and thwart the Europeans.

As the Europeans learned to manipulate iron and steel and to compete against each other militarily by using their metals to develop better guns and cannon, they also slowly pushed the Mongols out of central Eurasia. The British then started to push the Moghuls out of India, as they engaged in another example of a positive feedback process of conquest, first gaining a toehold in India, then gaining more and more of the subcontinent.

INDUSTRY DOMINATES RESOURCES

Meanwhile, most of the Americas became resource-extraction economies. This is the worst kind of economy, and compares quite unfavorably to an industrially based economy. In a resource-based economy, the main idea is to extract natural capital as quickly as possible, either by mining from underneath the ground or by exploiting the soil in huge plantations above ground. Either way, the work force is usually brutalized in one way or another; Christopher Columbus killed off the Taino of Hispaniola by working them to death in mines, while the English enslaved a large part of Africa to provide the labor for plantations in the Caribbean and northern America.

A resource-based economy is easily militarized, because economic wealth is measured by the quantity of land and the natural capital that is on, or under, that land. Military force is needed to take over and control that land, and to force the workers to accept miserable and low-paid conditions. Even today, for instance, the possession of oil leads to narrow dictatorships and wars for oil, not economic development. Latin America still feels the legacy of being mainly a plantation economy for hundreds of years; it is only now emerging into deep-rooted democracy.

A political system can be defined as a territory over which an organization, the state (or government), controls a monopoly over the legitimate means of coercion.[14] Therefore, a resource-based economy becomes a politicized economy by definition; control over the means of coercion is the main route to economic wealth, not industry. The wealth of the resources becomes concentrated in a small political and economic elite.

On the other hand, if an economy is industrial, its power is based on its skill and knowledge, not on its territory. Contrary to recent conventional wisdom, our economy did not recently become mainly a "knowledge" economy—the most advanced economies have always been knowledge-based. Eventually, even resource-based economies fall under the influence of industrial economies, because industrial economies can *create* an advanced military, while resource-based economies can only *buy* a military. As Immanuel Wallerstein extensively documented,[15] in the early modern world, the industrializing "core" of northwestern Europe regularly exploited the resource-rich "periphery" of Africa and the Americas.

By the 1700s, the global distribution of power was tilting toward the Europeans, partly by default. Most critically, the Chinese became very insular, and the Moghul empire started to disintegrate, allowing the British to digest more and more of it, so that there was no balance of power in Asia against the Europeans. The Spanish, having decided that gold was more important than industry, promptly headed toward second-rate power status, and the British, French, and Dutch fought it out for leadership. The Germans and Italians, although technologically sophisticated, were much too divided to challenge for leadership, and the Dutch dropped out because they were too small. The Americas were being exploited for sugar, tobacco, and gold, but these were not as important as industrial know-how, which the French and, in particular, the British, were making great strides in developing.

WHY ENGLAND?

The scientific advances that helped lead to the first Industrial Revolution were international and open in nature, and no European country had a great advantage since the knowledge was easy to obtain. But the British certainly took the lead in the industrial revolution, even though the French seemed to be running a very close second. For instance, the famous pin factory that Adam Smith used to explain the division of labor came from the French Diderot's exhaustive *Encyclopedie*,[16] which showed a huge assortment of very advanced industrial techniques that seemed to have been common in France in the mid-1700s. During the American Revolution, Thomas Jefferson was very impressed while Ambassador to France by a French demonstration of a critical part of the mass production of manufactured goods, the ability to put together an artifact (in the French case, a gun) using standardized parts, which can only be done if a manufacturing process is advanced enough to be able to output precisely formed parts.

There were other factors at work. The English, like much of Europe, faced a shortage of trees, since they had been logging them for centuries for use in making houses, ships, and most other implements. They also used lumber to create the charcoal used by blacksmiths and by iron makers to create the heat needed to make and shape metal. Without wood, how could they even make military weapons? The answer was to turn to the use of coal,[17] a momentous decision, both technologically and, a couple of centuries later, climatologically.

The English had lots of coal, and they needed to pump water out of deep coal mines, so they started to exploit scientific advances concerning vacuums. Eventually they invented crude steam engines that used coal to pump water out. To create the steam engines, they needed better tools to shape the metal, called machine tools. Eventually, James Watt would be able to use the containers bored out using the machine tools of John Wilkinson, who used steel to create more precise sizes of containers. As a result of several synergistic technological innovations including his own, Watt invented a steam engine in 1776 that could be used for all kinds of industrial machinery. In particular, textile mills, which had recently also been the scene of machinery advancements, could be hooked up to an energy source without having to be close to a river, hydropower being the previous best-case energy source.[18]

Eventually, the steam engine was used to increase the output of iron furnaces and to improve the quality of the iron; the steam engines were hooked up to iron works and then steel factories. A self-reinforcing set of synergistic technologies, machine tools, steam engines, and iron-making, was established, which led to the production of all kinds of machinery that could then be used to produce various consumer, industrial, and military goods.

Perhaps the British established this explosive set of innovations by historical accident, or perhaps they were helped indirectly by the French government. Colbert, the great minister of Louis XIV in the 17th century, had had thousands of entrepreneurs put to death simply for buying English wool.[19] In that kind of environment, it must have been difficult to set out on one's own in France, as evidently one could in England, and invent and use new machinery. The French government commissioned quite a bit of productive infrastructural investment and industrial development, but they still maintained internal tariffs until the French Revolution. The English, on the other hand, had a Parliament, which served as a constraint on the arbitrary actions of government. Parliament, in fact, represented the interests of businessmen, quite often in direct opposition to the interests of most Englishmen. They forced farmers off of their land so that the businessmen could raise sheep for the wool that the French businessmen were executed for buying. So democracy, however shallow, was probably an important determinant in the lead that Britain forged as the "workshop of the world" in the first part of the 18th century.

Besides the steam engine, the United States was also born in 1776, as was Adam Smith's book *The Wealth of Nations*.[20] Smith pointed out that the division of labor led to great gains in productivity—and a critical component of Smith's definition of the division of labor was the use of machinery. Smith also argued that it was not gold, as some mercantilists held, that defined national wealth, but the production of goods and services that the people of a nation created. In the new United States, Alexander Hamilton argued that manufacturing was the key to national wealth and power, and that the nation should impose tariffs to allow "infant industries" to grow to full maturity. It was the southern plantation and slave owners who wanted no tariffs so that they could import luxury goods from Europe for less money, and they fought the tariff for much of the 19th century, while the industrial North kept a strong tariff barrier up to encourage the "industrial arts" that they had inherited from England.

RICARDO TAKES A WRONG TURN

Ironically, just as England launched the Industrial Revolution, the field of economics took a turn toward pre-industrial logic, where it has remained to this day. Its chief architect was the British economist David Ricardo, who invented the ideas of "diminishing returns" to try to explain production, and "comparative advantage" to try to understand trade. Both ideas underlie much of mainstream economics, and both ideas lead to exactly the wrong conclusions about the economy and economic policy.

Adam Smith was very concerned about capital, unlike Ricardo. In Smith's schema, there are two types of capital: *circulating capital* are those goods that move from producer to producer—that is, they are ordinarily intermediate goods that are in the process of being turned into final products; and *fixed capital*, which is comprised of "all useful machines and instruments of trade that facilitate and abridge labour," commercial buildings, improvements of land, and the "acquired and useful abilities" of labor:

> To maintain and augment the stock which may be reserved for immediate consumption, is the sole end and purpose both of the fixed and circulating capitals. It is this stock that feeds, clothes, and lodges the people. Their riches or poverty depends upon the abundant or sparing supplies which those two capitals can afford to the stock for immediate consumption.[21]

Ricardo,[22] on the other hand, tried to invent an economics that could use analytic mathematics. Capital is difficult to model mathematically, because it can feed back into itself. That is, capital can create capital; therefore, capital affects capital, and it is difficult to write equations for a system in which something loops back to affect itself at some later time. Ricardo tried to deal with this problem by assuming, for the sake of his model, that all products in the economy were corn, which can reproduce itself. But corn is not like machinery; you can't use corn to make other things, there is no concept of technological change, which in any case Ricardo, like mainstream economics ever since, assumed does not exist!

At least Ricardo wrestled with the self-reproducing nature of capital, which his successors did not even do. However, he also introduced the idea of diminishing returns, which as Erik Reinert[23] has argued is only useful for explaining why poor countries are poor. Let's say we have a certain amount of land. The best land for farming would be used first; after that, each added parcel of land would yield less and less of a return in terms of food (assume each parcel is the same size). You would get diminishing returns as you added land. Or, if you had the same amount of land, but you kept adding more and more labor, at some point you would get diminishing returns from each added person.

As Reinert points out, however, the whole idea behind making manufacturing the center of an economy is that manufacturing often leads to increasing, not decreasing, returns. That is, as you add more and more machinery, and more and more people, your output actually goes up per person or per piece of machinery. You achieve what are called economies of scale, which is why most factories are big. Actually, at some point bigger doesn't mean better; there is usually some optimal point in size, so in a sense there are diminishing returns at some point, but the main focus of factory design is not on the diminishing returns, the focus is on how to increase output with the same equipment and labor, or how to increase output with better machinery and labor, or how to organize the machinery and labor better, all of which leads to greater productivity. In an agricultural situation like the one Ricardo models, it may be hard to find those increases in productivity, which is why Reinert can accuse Ricardo of simply describing poverty. Only in poor countries are people reduced to using less and less productive land, instead of more and more productive machinery in industry.

Sometimes mainstream, or neoclassical, economics is also called "marginalist" economics, the "marginal" referring to this phenomenon of diminishing returns. When something decreases in time, it makes it much easier to model with analytic mathematical techniques. Since analytical math is the core of mainstream economics' toolkit, diminishing returns fit in beautifully, even if they don't have much to do with reality. The idea of diminishing returns, combined with the inability to explain or discuss the phenomenon of capital, means that mainstream economics, ironically, is pre-industrial.

But it gets worse, because Ricardo's theory of trade, which to this day is the key concept used to justify globalization and free trade, also ignores technological change. The theory of comparative advantage states that each country should specialize in something different, and should choose that specialty that it is relatively best at, even if it is absolutely worse than another country. So, for instance, if the United States uses fewer person hours to produce clothing than Europe, and also uses fewer person hours to produce food, but Europe is relatively better at food than at clothing, the United States should stop making food and concentrate on clothing, while Europe should stop making clothing and concentrate on making food.

At the end of his explanation of his theory, Ricardo, writing in the early 19th century, said that his theory "determines that wine shall be made in France and Portugal, that corn shall be grown in America and Poland, and that hardware and other goods shall be manufactured in England."[24] A worse prediction of world economics would be hard to find, but it is consistent with his theory. His theory, in other words, seeks to justify the status quo, and the dominant position that a manufacturing power happens to have at one moment in time (in Ricardo's time, that power was England). Since world history is to a great extent the history of the rise and decline of nations, and more recently of the industrialization of much of the planet, claiming that all nations should not work toward industrialization is absurd.

But there is an even deeper problem. Ricardo assumes that there are no synergies among the different parts of the economic system. Maybe if you are good at raising food, some of the technological innovations would leak over to clothing, or vice versa. I am claiming that an economy is like an ecosystem, a holistic, interdependent system, and that splitting an economy apart will negatively impact all of the elements of the system. That perspective is completely counter to the argument that Ricardo, and current economic theory, asserts is true. They claim that the United States can even outsource manufacturing, much less subsets such as industrial machinery.

Alexis de Tocqueville, the French observer of the early United States and author of *Democracy in America*, had better insight than Ricardo. He observed the democratic nature of American society, and the widespread use of "industrial arts" by its citizenry, and could see that the United States would extend to the Pacific Ocean; he famously predicted that by the 20th century, both the United States and Russia would become the most powerful nations, because of size and industry.[25]

How did de Tocqueville, never considered an economist, get it so right, and David Ricardo, the founding father of economics, get it so wrong? De Tocqueville observed an actually existing society; he based his conclusions on empirical data, like a scientist. Ricardo created an ideal, formal world, with no foundation in the real world. But because Ricardo's methodology was amenable to mathematics—and because it also happened to justify the status quo—while de Tocqueville's analysis was descriptive, Ricardo is canon, while de Tocqueville is not.

We have arrived at the launching of the Industrial Revolution, when machinery would become the basis of international and national power. For the rest of the 19th century, nations that wanted to be wealthy and powerful would pursue policies supportive of manufacturing, while the rest of the world would become the pawns of those who successfully industrialized. At the end of this process, the United States was, indeed, not only just one of the Great Powers, but the greatest one of all.

CHAPTER 6

The Rise of the United States

The United States started life with the only industrial economy in the Americas. Even in the United States, however, the southern half had been based on slavery and plantations, like much of Latin America. As a result of the Civil War, the industrial North was able to extend the foundations of a manufacturing system within much of North America, and thus set the stage for the rise of the greatest manufacturing power in world history.

THE CIVIL WAR BETWEEN INDUSTRY AND RESOURCES

Part of the reason for the revolt of the United States in 1775 was the English attempt to suppress industrial activity. Iron making was declared illegal, as were other forms of manufacture. The colonies had also been printing their own money, and thus they didn't need to borrow money from banks. In fact, the colonies started their own banks, and the interest from the loans meant that they didn't even need to impose taxes on their citizens. The English closed these all down as well.[1]

The English idea, formalized by Ricardo in his theory of comparative advantage, was to exploit its colonies by monopolizing manufacturing in the home country, while making everyone in the colonies pay for the English manufactured goods by trading raw materials in return. Since manufactured goods lead to greater wealth than resources, the English would stay wealthy, while the rest of the Empire stayed poor. Manufactured goods embody the knowledge it takes to make them and the sophisticated machinery that is used to produce them, while resources mostly involved, in the 19th century at least, the use of backbreaking, very low-skill labor. When you can barely eke out a profit using large amounts of slaves in a sugar plantation, then the slaves will be oppressed and poor. When you can use very few workers to put together machinery, then the workers in those establishments will probably share a very large pie.

Even if the owners make a lot of money in a resource-based enterprise, they won't put the profits back into better machinery, because the use of slaves or very-low-wage workers make using better and better machinery a losing proposition. On the other hand, in the United States, there was a shortage of skilled production workers in the North, and the ones that were found had to be paid high wages, or else they would work for someone else.[2] The northern industrialists therefore had incentives to continually upgrade their machinery; it was an early example of Melman's alternative cost-productivity process discussed in Chapter 4.

On the other hand, the invention of the cotton gin made the growing of cotton much more profitable, particularly since the English and Northern economies were creating new kinds of textile machinery, leading to the production of low-cost clothing. The intensive cultivation of cotton in the South also led to the despoliation of the soils, so cotton farms had to be continually moved west. Would the American West become the site for slave-based plantations like the South, or be amenable to industrial uses like the North? The ecological crisis of soil loss drove the country toward a war to determine which type of production would dominate. The South, while increasing its wealth, was not increasing as fast as the industrial North. Much as the ancient Greek historian Thucydides claimed that Sparta attacked Athens because Athens was gaining relative power,[3] so the South had to attack the North before its own domination of the entire United States faded.

When the Civil War came, the South's superior officer corps and soldiers were no match for the industrial power of the North. The South couldn't make their own locomotives, and though they managed to steal a few, this lack of transportational capacity was one of the reasons they lost. The torrent of guns, clothing, and supplies from the North was no match for the South. What was the South going to do, drown the Northern soldiers in cotton?

During the Civil War, Congress was not shackled by the presence of conservative Southerners, and so some of the most progressive legislation in U.S. history was passed: the establishment of land grant colleges, the Homestead Act that gave millions of acres of farmland to families, and the building of the transcontinental railroad. Lincoln had the freedom to use the government to print money, called greenbacks, instead of giving in to the demands of bankers for 30 percent interest rates on war loans.[4] When the conservative forces of the South came fully back into Congress after Reconstruction, they continued to act as a drag on legislation, as they do right up to the present day.

The Radical Republicans in Congress at the end of the Civil War wanted to enact a land reform on the South, proposing to give the freed slaves 40 acres and a mule, which would have had the effect of breaking the power of the Southern elite. Such land reforms were essential, a century later, to the rise of East Asian countries such as Japan, Korea, Taiwan, and China, but the United States missed this golden opportunity to fully integrate the African American population and to break up a very regressive bloc of power among the plantation owners.

As the sociologist Barrington Moore argued in reviewing the 19th century, "no bourgeoisie, no democracy."[5] That is, when land-based elites prospered and wielded a great deal of influence over national policy, the result by the 20th century was usually dictatorship. Either a revolt among the peasantry would bring on a Communist dictatorship, or the land-based elites would join up with the industrial elites to repress the workers and enable the establishment of fascism. The United States has had extreme right-wing politics throughout its history; had the South remained dominant, the United States probably would have gone in a fascist direction.

INDUSTRIALIZE OR BE LEFT BEHIND

By 1870, with the South in ruins, the United States was poised for explosive industrial growth. The second Industrial Revolution spurred the expansion of steel making, the critical material that replaced iron in machinery, used for railroads and buildings. All around the globe, nations were reconfiguring themselves to keep up with the world leaders, in particular, the United Kingdom, to avoid elimination as a serious player in global affairs.

In France, a revolution in 1870 brought down Louis Napoleon, and ushered in what has become a continuously democratic republic ever since. In Russia, the Czar abolished serfdom in 1861 in an effort to make industrialization possible; serfdom was in many respects a system that was similar to slavery.[6] Italy was finally unified in 1870 and freed from foreign domination. Japan was threatened and forced by the United States to open its borders after a couple of hundred years of closure, which led Japan to embark on its Meiji restoration in 1868, laying the groundwork for an independent and industrial country.

Perhaps most spectacularly, Germany was finally united in 1870. Before 1618, Germany had been an odd assortment of over 300 principalities, cities, and even Church-owned districts. The 30 Years War that started in 1618 devastated Germany, which then began a long, slow rise out of the ashes. A hyper-militaristic state emerged from the area of Brandenburg, which encompassed the city of Berlin, and was controlled by the royal family called the Hohenzollerns. Set on its path by a series of King Fredericks, it came to have a single-minded goal of grabbing as much territory as possible, by building up the biggest and best trained army possible. Eventually it formed the country of Prussia, taking a piece of Poland in the process. This had the unfortunate side effect of incorporating the Junkers, a very regressive group of landowners with large plantations in or near Poland who believed that their serfs should live in slave-like conditions and continue to work the land. The Junkers provided the bulk of the Prussian officer corps, and much later helped hand Germany over to the Nazi regime.[7]

The Germans led in the development of the field of chemistry, and in the development of many different kinds of machinery, including the automobile, owing to a long tradition of skill and education. They also excelled in the production of industrial machinery.

Thus, by 1870 all of the Great Powers of the next century had set themselves on an industrial trajectory. In the second half of the 19th century, the generation of electricity from steam turbines became well established, setting up the industrial and technological advances of the first part of the 20th century. Steam engines still dominated factories, which were filled with machine tools, a focus of technological innovation.[8]

Various categories of machine tools were invented and produced during the late 19th century. Because of machine tool innovations, several other classes of machinery became possible, including, in rough order, agricultural machinery, sewing machines, bicycles, and culminating in the creation of automobiles.[9] Locomotives and passenger and freight cars were the main transportation machinery being created in the late 19th century, as a rail boom extended all around the world. As Alfred Chandler documents, the rail industry pioneered many of the necessary innovations needed to create the modern corporation: the coordination of processes over an entire continent, a large administrative bureaucracy, modern accounting, distribution chains and distributed production. These all entailed administrative control, not market control, and also involved increasing returns to scale.[10] In fact, the returns increased so much that the rail system should have been a monopoly; in most countries outside the United States, it was therefore controlled by the government, which is the normal structure of the industry to this day.

Besides the United States, Germany was the country that most quickly caught up to the world leader, Britain. Britain had pretty much had industrial technology to itself on the world stage during the first two-thirds of the 19th century; it had used its enormous lead to build a globe-spanning empire, centered on the positive feedback process of the conquest of India. Perhaps other nations were attempting to catch up to Britain as quickly as possible because they saw, in the case of India, what happens when you fall behind. India had had a superior textile industry to Britain as the 19th century dawned, but Britain, through both the export of cheap textiles to India and the suppression of Indian manufacturing, had crushed that country's textile industry, dooming India to exploitation for over 100 years.

Britain had taken its world leadership in industry and converted it into world military leadership. France had been its main adversary in the 18th century and Napoleon had almost consolidated French rule over the European continent, until like Hitler over 100 years later, Napoleon overextended his forces and came to ruin by invading Russia. In any case, Britain would have gained over France in the long term because of its lead in manufacturing technology. But by the middle of the 19th century, British elites were becoming more interested in imperial and financial control than in manufacturing innovation.

THE DECLINE OF BRITAIN

In the middle of the 19th century, Britain's leading machine tool engineer, Joseph Whitworth, led a team to the United States to figure out how it could produce such a large amount of rifles and other products. The American System of Manufactures, as it was known, enabled the United States to output large numbers of the same item because the parts of those items could be made with such precision that they were interchangeable, that is, a workman could quickly grab any of the same kind of part and fit it to the new item. As we saw in the previous chapter, Jefferson had witnessed something like this in France; by the middle of the 19th century, the Americans had vastly improved on the system, which became the envy of British engineers. Whitworth concluded that

> the labouring classes [there] are comparatively few in number, but this is counterbalanced by, and indeed may be regarded as one of the chief causes of, the eagerness with which they call in the aid of machinery . . . wherever it is introduced, it is universally and willingly resorted to.[11]

The British workers, on the other hand, were numerous and badly paid.

By the end of the 19th century, British journalists were wringing their hands over the decline of British industry, particularly compared to the Americans and Germans. By about 1900, in fact, a wave of American manufactured goods hit Europe, which was just coming out of a deep economic depression. Machinery makers always get hit hardest in depressions, because their orders completely dry up—consumer goods producers might need to make at least some goods for the public at the beginning of a depression, but they certainly don't need to buy more machinery. The American market was so dynamic that the American machine tool makers were able to catch the British machinery makers flat-footed,[12] and they permanently took much of the European market away from the British as a result.

The British government also supported two policies that were good for short-term power but bad for their manufacturing sectors in the long term: free trade and a strong currency. Ever since the early 1800s, when it was clear that Britain was the leading industrial power, the British conveniently decided that free trade was best for all economies, even though it was clearly best mainly for the British economy because British goods could overwhelm any challenges. Alexander Hamilton in the United States and Freidrich List in

Germany inveighed against this obvious self-interested ideology, and most nations adopted high tariffs, that is, imports were slapped with a tax, or fee. These tariffs allowed the countries that used them to protect their "infant industries," as Alexander Hamilton called them, and to develop industrial systems, so that when tariffs came down to some extent toward the end of the 19th century, there was much more trade than there would have been had everyone but Britain not built manufacturing systems.

The period before World War I is often characterized as a high point in the globalization of the international economy, a peak not repeated until well after World War II. But that level of trade would not have been possible without multiple centers of industrial expertise, and that multiplication would not have occurred had they not been protected in one way or another. As Erik Reinert has pointed out, protection actually leads to more trade in the long term than free trade, because countries that protect their developing industries can at least develop industries, and with industries, a country can create the goods needed for trade.[13] As we saw in Chapter 2, even the United States needs to be competent enough in manufacturing to be able to trade goods for other goods.

Another policy that doomed the competitiveness of British industry was the support of an expensive British pound. The more expensive the pound, the more expensive were British exports. The British colonies had no choice but to take British manufactured goods, since they were not allowed to take anyone else's. So a high pound still offered an outlet for British manufacturers, but British manufacturers didn't have to produce at a globally competitive level because there was no competition in the colonies. The high pound meant that the people of Britain could afford to import all kinds of things into Britain, and to enjoy the fruits of domination, but in the process, they lost the basis for that domination by eliminating any incentives for technological advance.

A century later, the United States was to repeat much of the same process of decline as the British, involving a focus on the military and finance, and a desire to enjoy high purchasing power at the expense of long-term economic wealth. While the United States faces an emerging China, which doesn't seem to be expansionary, the British faced two rising challengers, the United States and Germany. The United States was not expansionary, at least, not toward the British; Germany was.

THE GERMAN PROBLEM

To some extent, the difference between the American and German responses to increased power can be explained by geography. The German historian Ludwig Dehio introduced the idea that a nation can be "satisfied" if it is big enough. If a nation encompasses a large enough territory, the demands of simply keeping that territory together and well-functioning prevents, or at least, minimizes the tendency for the satisfied nation to choose conquest as a policy.[14] A territory is big enough, following my framework, when it encompasses an entire production system, as the United States did throughout much of its history.

But if a country does not encompass an entire economic region, and would naturally complete its production system by integrating it with its neighbors, then there is a tendency for the country to want to "satisfy" itself by absorbing, that is, conquering, its neighbors. Such was the problem in Europe, at least the continental part (that is, outside Britain). The Europeans had been fighting with each other for supremacy for centuries, and no one could get the upper hand, at least not for very long. By 1870 a united Germany had become more powerful than France, which had been the leading country in continental Europe for a few hundred years. Germany was controlled by a dynasty that had always encouraged warfare as a way to increase its domains; that was how Germany was finally unified, by fighting the French in the Franco-Prussian War of 1870.

Germany and Britain, being the two leading industrial economies in Europe, were also very good trading partners. There had been a hope, going back to the philosopher Immanuel Kant in the early 19th century, that trade would lead to peace, because war would destroy trade between two warring countries, which presumably trading partners would want to avoid.[15] Unfortunately, despite their rising trade, tension between Germany and Britain increased even more rapidly in the early 20th century. The Germans, who were controlled by Prussia, which was controlled by a militaristic royal family, a class of landowners that were belligerent, and a rapidly expanding military, were in no mood to allow a geographic problem like being stuck in the middle of a continent to stop them from global expansion. Instead of trade, the result was one of the greatest follies of all time, World War I.[16]

To understand World War I and much of the 20th century, it may be helpful to look at Table 6.1, which shows the share of the global production of industrial machinery among major nations during much of the 20th century. We can see from this table that there were usually only about four countries that controlled about 80 percent of global machinery production during this period. This group we can call the "Great Powers," those countries that have the most influence on the functioning of global events, particularly in global wars. The reason machinery is so important is that by using machinery, not only can a country create more machinery and wealth, it can create military machinery, and thus gain an independent capability to fight major wars. Great Powers can also influence other countries that must depend on those Great Powers for their supply of machinery and thus for their own military capability. With machinery, a country has long-term influence; without machinery, a country is influenced.

By 1913, the United States accounted for a whopping 50 percent of global machinery production, Germany for a rising 21 percent, and the United Kingdom for a sinking 12 percent. Together, these three Great Powers accounted for over 80 percent of world machinery production.

WORLD WAR I

The other alleged Great Powers (depending on the author)— France, Russia, Austria-Hungary, and Italy—only controlled about 10 percent of machinery production between them all. Russia was no match for Germany in World War I, and France survived thanks to the help of Britain, and belatedly, the United States, while Austria-Hungary and Italy gummed each other to death, militarily speaking. In human terms, however, World War I was a disaster; even worse, populations were so immiserated afterward that the world's worst pandemic, the flu of 1919, wiped out more people than the fighting of World War I. But the carnage that underlay that flu and that led a large percentage of the adult male population to its death was the result of the culmination of a militaristic ideology that had been developing since the first agricultural societies burst forth from the Middle East.

Table 6.1 Global Nonelectrical (Industrial) Machinery (in percent), 1913–2007

Percentage Global Output	1913	1925	1938	1948	1953	1958	1963	1970	1975	1980	1985	1990	1995	2000	2007
United States	50	57.6	41.7	55.2	54.1	36.5	43.9	37.8	27.3	26.6	29.2	25.6	26.4	20.3	15
Germany	20.6	13.1	14.4	3.8	4.7	6.5	11.1	9.8	9.6	8.9	8.6	16.5	15.3	12.8	12
USSR/Russia	3.5	1.8	14	10.1	12.4	17.8	13.2	15.8	21.7	22	20.5	3.9	0.5	1.1	1.5
United Kingdom	11.8	13.6	10.2	8.4	8.3	7.8	6.1	6	5.2	5.4	3.8	5.3	4.3	4	3.4
Japan	0.3	1	3.5				4.9	10	9.6	10.1	13.6	22.4	25.5	22.4	19.5
China										3.4	2.7	1.8	2.5	6.5	15.9
"Big 4" economies of Europe (Germany, Italy, France, UK)										20.8	17.6	29.8	25.9	24.9	22.6

Sources: For the years 1913–1995: Jon Rynn, "The Power to Create Wealth: A Systems-Based Theory of the Rise and Decline of Great Powers in the 20th Century," PhD Diss., City University of New York, 2001, Statistical Annex, pp. 120–145, available at http://www.manufacturinggreenprosperity.com; for the years 2000 and 2007, United Nations International Development Organization, *International Yearbook of Industrial Statistics, 2009,* Vienna, 2009, Table 1.7, "Leading Producers in Selected Divisions, 2000 and 2007, Machinery and Equipment N.E.C." (ISIC 29). Note: All data for 1913–1995, except 1938, from League of Nations and UN publications.

Before World War I, offense in wars had been the domain of the theretofore most important transportation technology, the horse. Cavalries had been the elite of the elite for thousands of years. Militaries around the world, however, should have anticipated what mechanized firepower, particularly the forerunners to machine guns could do: destroy the horse's speed and intimidation advantages, and turn wars into gruesome battles of attrition, that is, the side with the most industrial power wears down its lesser foe. Such had been the lesson of the American Civil War, which the Europeans should have paid attention to.

The Franco-Prussian War of 1870, which enabled Prussia to incorporate the remaining parts of Germany, gave military elites a false sense of hope about offense, because the French did not effectively use their superior machine guns and the Germans literally ran circles around them. Much of military strategy involves encircling the enemy, so that the enemy collapses from panic and from an inability to obtain food and supplies.

The machine gun negates the power of the horse; but the tank negates the power of the machine gun. Technological development, by 1914, had allowed for the mass production of machine guns, but had not yet led to the internal combustion engine's ubiquitous position in the economy, and then to the tank. The macho, imperialistic, racist, egotistical, social Darwinist attitudes of the world's elites were at their height by 1914, as was a cult of offense within the various officer corps. The result was perhaps the dumbest military decisions made in human history, if the number of clearly avoidable deaths of one's own soldiers is any measure. British, French, German, and other military officers sent their own men to their certain deaths by the millions because they believed that soldiers could somehow overwhelm dug-in machine gun nests.[17]

Not only did the European countries lose much of their adult male talent, resources, and economic capital, they also wiped out most of their monarchies in the process. To recruit the huge armies that were necessary for such a large war, the political structure had to change to incorporate the vast majority of the people. This trend began in the wars started during the French Revolution and consummated by the Napoleonic wars a century before, when, desperate to stave off conquest, the French revolutionary government enforced a levee-en-masse, that is, for the first time since the ancient Greeks and Romans, all free men were inducted into the army.[18]

For hundreds and even thousands of years previously, armies had been filled by mercenaries, that is, most soldiers had been paid to fight—and they might decide to quit at just the wrong time. Even worse, armies had been filled by the dregs of society, picked up off the street and beaten until they followed orders like automatons.[19] A highly motivated, if not particularly skilled, huge mass of soldiers could fairly easily sweep away these kinds of armies, and Napoleon did just that.

Napoleon was a dictator, but he invented the role of the *popular* dictator, one that tries to rally the people—or enough of the people—to his cause by the use of charisma and worship, in addition to brutality. The totalitarians of the 20th century would use the same techniques, but the royalty of the 19th century had no interest in the little people. As World War I empowered the little people because of the need for large, motivated armies, the people no longer had any use for the royalty, and so monarchy, except as window-dressing, disappeared.

Democracy was propelled forward, in part, because the country that could use the capacity of most of its citizens by building a huge army and enormous military economy would defeat a regime or regimes that were built on narrower foundations. A couple of other variations on this theme were also created, namely fascism and communism, which used various techniques to inspire or scare people enough to provide mass support. Those variations have hopefully burned themselves out, although a total collapse of civilization might bring them back if people become desperate enough.

A wave of democratization swept the world after World War I, particularly in Germany, and even for a while in Russia and China. Women got the vote in the United States and other countries. Technologically, the electrification of society gathered force, and created an economic boom in the 1920s. But there were still significant imbalances that were laying the groundwork for the even greater conflagration of World War II, and for a Cold War between superpowers beyond that.

SINGING THE SOCIETY ELECTRIC

Even though the United States was clearly the leading industrial power, Britain was the top military power after World War I, and controlled by far the largest empire. With its industrial power lagging, it attempted to stay on top by making things more difficult for its man-ufacturing sector with, again, a strong pound, a huge military, and a pliable colonial system. Meanwhile, the victorious powers had decided to try to weigh Germany down with large reparations. Since Germany was such an important part of the European economy and had been Britain's best trading partner, reparations hurt both Germany and Europe, and encouraged the rise of the Nazis by stoking frustration in the German population. In 1923, when the Germans refused to give their coal to France, France invaded the Ruhr region of Germany, and the German currency went into hyperinflation, wiping out the savings of the German middle class and embittering them.

To make matters worse, the Communist takeover in what became the Soviet Union created a backlash in many countries; in the United States many intellectuals were literally put on boats and kicked out of the country, and in Germany many economic elites started to flirt with right-wing groups like the Nazis. The Communist regime did not really know how to create a communist society, but waged a bit-ter civil war and tried various policies in the 1920s.

Despite these problems, there was a great deal of technological innovation in the 1920s, which particularly the United States capital-ized on, led by the electrification of the cities. With electricity wired to homes, many appliances could be sold, from radios to washing machines to toasters. Trolley systems and subway systems were in-stalled, although mostly before the 1920s, because by the 1920s the production of automobiles was booming. This created a modern oil industry. Vacuum tubes, which were used in radios, were also start-ing to be used to more precisely control machinery, and would even-tually lead to the development of the computer.

Perhaps most importantly, electricity increased productivity in the factories. Prior to this time, factories had usually used one big steam engine to power all of the machinery. To transfer energy from the steam engine to the machines, a huge, long, rotating rod emanated from the steam engine, and for each machine on the factory floor, a long rotating leather belt had to extend from the rod on the roof to the floor. Not only was this system not very precise and wasteful of energy, not only did machinery have to have different width wheels to hook onto the leather belts to control the speed, but the noise and dirt being thrown around were very unhealthy. By plugging a machine into the wall for electricity, all of this apparatus could be eliminated, and very precise speeds could be incorporated into factory machinery, and thus, higher quality products could be produced at faster rates.[20]

Like the expansion of the railroads and other technologies in the 19th century, all of this activity led to a speculative frenzy. There was very little regulation of the financial industry, and so a full cycle of speculation developed.[21] A speculative environment develops when people are investing in something, not because that something inherently yields a certain profit from its operations, but because people think that other people will buy it for more than it is currently being bought for. In that case, if the price should start to go down, investors will panic and then all try to get out at once, since they thought that the investment would always go up.

The U.S. stock market became gripped by speculation. A panic set in, simultaneously with bank collapses in Europe, whose economy was brittle in any case because Germany was being held down. When economies crashed all around the world, no one knew what to do, because economic theory taught that the government cannot help, and that the market is self-correcting.

Except that the market was not self-correcting. As John Maynard Keynes pointed out, economies can produce a vicious kind of positive feedback loop that he called a "liquidity trap."[22] Positive feedback loops can lead to indefinite growth, subject to environmental constraints, as when rabbits multiply. But positive feedback loops can also lead to a "lock-in," often to a "floor," that is, the system keeps wanting to go "down," and since zero is the lowest one can go, it stays locked at zero. This is essentially what happened in the Great Depression and what happened, or may still be happening, in the Great Recession that started in 2008: investors and banks panic. Then they won't lend to anyone. Because no one can get any money to keep their operations going, the economy worsens; the bankers panic even more, and they convince themselves even more not to lend anything. Keynes claimed that the economy can stay stuck like this, essentially forever. The only way out of this, he argued, is for the government to start lending or spending, and give the economy a kick to get it out of its locked position.

A *Business Week* editorial of the time declared:

The business situation in the United States or any other country is not made or destroyed by conditions in the security market. Prosperity does not depend on the price of stocks . . . Security trading is a . . . relatively small part of the vast aggregate American economic activity. There are many others much larger, much more important, and quite as exciting—such as mining the world's coal, making its iron and steel, manufacturing its clothing, raising its food, transporting and distributing the goods it needs. These are the basis of business here and everywhere. Without them, the stock market is merely a game of tiddlywinks, and security prices are simply statistical sawdust.[23]

The Nazi regime, ironically, was the first to figure this out in the 1930s. The Germans, like the Americans, had plenty of spare manufacturing capacity since the factories were shut down for lack of orders. So the Germans got the factories going again, and employed millions of people, by building up the infrastructure with a program of construction of highways, cars, and most ominously, a military.

The United States eventually figured out that it was acceptable for the government to run a deficit, that is, to spend more than it takes in with taxes. In fact, it may be to everyone's benefit if the government spends more than it takes in. By doing so, the government creates new money, and if it creates new money by creating productive systems such as infrastructures and factories, then the new money simply reflects the addition to the wealth of the nation. Having the government create new money can often be better than the "normal" method, having private banks do it, because private banks can get caught in speculative fevers and, as happened in the 2000s, lose most of the surplus money. After a speculative bubble bursts there isn't enough money to go around, people cut back on spending, prices decline (there's a deflation), and you get stuck in a liquidity trap again.

In fact, one could even nationalize the entire financial system to prevent liquidity traps from occurring; the main impediment to this line of action being that the financial industry is generally very powerful owing to their control over so much financial capital. Instead of nationalizing, the New Deal in the United States heavily regulated the financial industry, including prohibiting banks from financially speculating, at least to some extent, by not allowing them to invest for their own profit, like investment banks. Then the Congress and the executive branch in the 1990s eliminated that provision, called the Glass-Steagall Act, contributing to the meltdown of 2008.

THE RISE OF THE UNION OF SOVIET SOCIALIST REPUBLICS

The economic collapse of the early 1930s led to the following dangerous situation: a resurgent and militaristic Germany, no longer constrained by reparations that the Nazis unilaterally stopped paying; a weak Union of Soviet Socialist Republics (USSR); a weakening Britain; a potentially very strong but temporarily very weak United States, whose public was not interested in stopping an expansionary power; and a similar vacuum in East Asia, where China was being picked apart by opportunistic imperial countries, including an industrializing Japan, which was challenging a declining Britain for hegemony over East Asia. The structure of the international system enabled Germany and Japan to start a campaign of conquest.

If we look at this numerically in Table 6.1, the United States produced about 42 percent of machinery in 1938, more than the USSR and Germany combined, each of whom constituted about 14 percent of global machinery production. The United Kingdom still generated 11 percent. France and Japan each had about 4 percent of world capacity, with Italy at about 3 percent.

The USSR, by 1938, had caught up with Germany, because of one of the fastest programs of industrial expansion in world history. In the 1920s, as Soviet economists thrashed around for an economic theory that would help them develop in a short spurt, they used part of Marx's economic theory plus some of their own, as I explained in Chapter 3, and came to the conclusion that they needed to develop the resources for creating the means of production. In other words, they needed to create a reproduction machinery sector that would reproduce itself and build production machinery, which could then be used to create the goods and services for the general society.

However, instead of producing for the final stage of goods and services, the Soviet system was always focused on producing for the military. Even at the beginning of the Communist takeover of Russia, Leon Trotsky, who ran the operations of the ensuing Civil War, developed the idea of "War Communism," that is, planning all production to provide for the war effort. The Soviets then dropped the word "war" from "war communism," but communism for the Soviet regime was always, first and foremost, about building a military paradise, not a workers' one.[24]

This militaristic attitude was, if not preordained, then partly caused simply by the geographic position that Russia occupies in the huge land mass known as Eurasia. Russia had been militarized since it rose under Ivan the Terrible in the 1400s because it is vulnerable to attack from so many sides. Stalin, in a speech that set off the rapid industrialization of the 1930s, laid out this problem by pointing out that the Russians had been invaded by Mongols, Swedes, Poles, Germans, Germans again, and would be invaded by, yes, Germans yet again, unless the Soviets jumped ahead economically 100 years within 10 years' time. That "jump" meant industrialization, by any means necessary, and the Soviets used any means, including taking the entire harvests of the Ukraine and letting millions of peasants starve so that the sale of the food could obtain the best American and German engineering help that money could buy.[25]

The Soviets constructed vast electrical networks, huge factories for producing machine tools, cement, and steel; schools filled with engineers who could design and build these factories; and myriad other factories filled with workers straight off of the farms.

For instance, in 1929 *Business Week* breathlessly relayed the news that "Russia determined a year ago to lift herself into thorough industrialization by 1933. In the twelve months since, order after order in large globular figures has been coming out of there. Foreign goods, mostly tools to make tools, will be needed to the amount of $3,500,000." The article, entitled "Russia Asks Cleveland to Build a Tiny Detroit" about how the Soviet government contracted with a company to build an entire industrial city, describes how a small industrial ecosystem was going to be constructed from scratch, with a huge car factory, fabrication shops, homes for workers, and buildings for all services, including even sports.[26]

Another article tells of how Americans would build clock factories so that the factory workers and railroad passengers would know what time it was; between 1924 and 1929, the Soviets bought $430 million dollars worth of tools and machinery.[27] An article called "Brains—Our Biggest Export to Russia" relates how Americans were setting up factories for cars, tractors, steel, sewing machines, chemicals, ammonia, and drug manufacture, building hydroelectric projects, modernizing coal mining, road building, establishing foundries (where large steel objects are formed), irrigation systems, and oil drilling installations and meat-packing plants, buying electrical machinery and patents, even a large mechanical bakery in Moscow. Yet in 1930, the United States represented only 35 percent of Soviet foreign purchases, much of the rest coming from England and Germany.[28]

The Soviet farms were turned into rigidly controlled pseudo-factories, which had terrible effects on agricultural productivity, particularly after the most skilled and prosperous peasants (kulaks) were either killed or driven off, but such regimentation allowed the regime to provide food for the cities and factory workers. It was a very short-term way to solve a long-term problem. Although it allowed the Soviet Union to rise to superpower status, ruthlessly empowering the central government and military laid the ground for the depletion of the hastily erected production system, and eventually to the fall of the Soviet Union.

In 1942, the Germans made a huge mistake and assumed that the Soviets were still weak. After signing a nonaggression pact with the Soviets, the Germans had swept France and other Western European countries away in 1940, but couldn't quite solve the age-old problem of attacking Britain across the English Channel. Hitler adopted an important military innovation that originated in Great Britain, the modernization of the old idea of encircling an enemy, developed by the British strategist Liddell-Hart.[29] By using the new technology of tanks to quickly fight and defeat an enemy, mostly by encircling it, the Germans could fight a "blitzkrieg," or "lightning war." Hitler wouldn't stress his manufacturing economy to the breaking point by producing a huge military apparatus, as Germany had done in World War I. He could just make do with tanks and some supporting aircraft, instead of a horribly expensive army.

When he took over France and other countries, instead of needing a huge German bureaucracy, Hitler simply co-opted the existing bureaucracy. To succeed, the strategy of blitzkrieg required an intact, conquered government, a lesson lost on the George W. Bush administration when, like Hitler, they used a tank-led blitzkrieg to quickly conquer Iraq, and then, incredibly, destroyed Iraq's governmental bureaucracy, leading to a long civil war.

Hitler's strategy worked perfectly while he was taking over continental Europe, which constitutes a natural economic area. Like Napoleon, he could have stopped there and consolidated his holdings—as horrible as that would have been—but fortunately for Europe, like Napoleon, his lust for power got the best of him[30] and he miscalculated, attacking the Soviet Union in 1942, which threw him back, until in 1944, the United States and Britain delivered the crushing blow from the west and the German Reich collapsed in 1945.

WINNING BY LOSING

At the end of the war, German society caught some lucky breaks. First, in July 1944, the German nobility, the group that had come from the land-owning, serf-owning Junker class, which had been leading German expansion for hundreds of years, turned on Hitler and tried to kill him. They failed, and Hitler wiped most of them out; then the second lucky break occurred, because the Soviets occupied what had been Prussia, and expropriated the survivors of the Junker class. The Junker class had been eliminated, and the militaristic, regressive power elites in German society were gone forever.[31]

A similar process of expropriation of elites occurred in Japan, where the remnants of the samurai class, in alliance with the land-based elites, had constructed a fascistic, racist, xenophobic imperial system that had terrorized much of East Asia, only to be flattened in World War II by the overwhelming superiority of American industrial output. Here the Japanese were also lucky, because the American occupiers were from the progressive, New Deal-inspired part of government, and they instituted land and other reforms that broke the power of the old elites, including the industrial conglomerates that had supported war. The newly empowered Japanese unions also played a large role, basically negotiating for labor peace with the new, vulnerable economic elites for what came to be known as the lifetime employment system, in which Japanese workers—at least, with the big companies—are assured that they won't be fired. This gave the Japanese middle class a good deal of economic power.[32]

In France and Italy, too, the old elites were swept away; in France because they collaborated with Hitler's blitzkrieg-and-let-the-bureaucrats-stay strategy, and in Italy because Mussolini and the fascists had joined up with Hitler for most of the war. The French and Italian governments then created national economic policies that have created some of the wealthiest regions on the planet.[33]

In Germany, an extraordinary shift of economic power occurred, as the principle of "codetermination," or institutionalized power for all employees of a company, became more and more widespread through national legislation. Workplace democracy had been a very active topic in pre-war Germany; after the war in the largest companies supervisory boards were set up that were elected by all of the employees of the company. These supervisory boards are separate from the board of directors, and have a say over the most important decisions of each company. The laws have been expanded so that now only the smallest companies do not have to have them.[34]

Germany, Japan, Italy, and depending on how you look at it, France won by losing World War II. The United States, United Kingdom, and USSR lost by winning, because their elites remained intact, in a position to slowly strangle their respective economies. Stalin rewarded the travails of his people by engaging in a murderous new campaign of oppression, and the United Kingdom tried to hang on to its former glory; at least it fairly graciously finally gave up India. The United States, the only major economy to not be devastated by war, encompassed within its borders fully one-half of the world's entire GDP at the end of the war and embarked on a policy of trying to replicate Britain's long-term decline.

CHAPTER 7

The Decline of the United States

LESSONS OF HISTORY

The experiences of the Great Depression and World War II set the United States on a trajectory that it is still on, toward a large military, free trade, suburbanization and the use of oil, and little structural governmental intervention. These trends did not have to happen as they did; in fact, the lessons of the Depression and war could moved the country in a completely different direction.

Policy discussions have often revolved around the alleged "lessons of history." For example, during the 1990s Vice President Al Gore and presidential candidate Ross Perot conducted a debate about the North America Free Trade Agreement, or NAFTA, and Gore used the example of the raising of tariffs during the Depression (the Smoot–Hawley Act) to argue that a lack of free trade can lead to global depression. Although the passage of Smoot-Hawley sparked tariff hikes in other countries, there is disagreement over its importance as a cause of the Depression. The United States only imported and exported about 5 percent of its gross domestic product (GDP) in 1930, so the effect could not have been that substantial. The European countries mostly traded with each other. Still, it became conventional wisdom that free trade is necessary to avoid a global depression, even though out-of-control financial speculation was a much more important cause.

The economic historian Charles Kindleberger argued that the most important factor that could have prevented the severity of the

Great Depression would have been the existence of what he called a global "lender of last resort," that is, had the United States government been ready and willing to lend in the United States and around the world, the financial system could have regrouped much more quickly and avoided much of what Keynes called a liquidity trap.[1] When the financial system failed in 2008, that is exactly what Ben Bernanke, chairman of the Federal Reserve and a scholar very familiar with the history of the Great Depression, proceeded to do.

A lesson allegedly learned from World War II is that military spending can be good for the economy. In the years 1943 through 1945, the U.S. government spent over 40 percent of the GDP, and of that, up to 60 percent was for military spending.[2] A different accounting shows that as much as 50 percent of the resources of the United States went into the war effort.[3] By 1940, even after many years of the New Deal, unemployment had been stuck at 15 percent; unemployment went down to 1 percent during the war. After the war, the economy stayed strong for over 60 years, taking into account several ups and downs.

The same effect as military spending, however, would have been achieved in the 1940s had that level of spending been applied to upgrading the country's infrastructure, for instance, or its cities. During the Depression, the cities steadily deteriorated for lack of maintenance. Capital always requires maintenance, whether it is a road, a building, a piece of factory machinery, or an engineer's capabilities. During World War II, infrastructure and the cities were not attended to; by the end of World War II, some parts of the economy had not been upgraded for 16 years, since 1929.

The attack on Pearl Harbor in 1941 provided the political will to spend vast sums of money to pull the economy out of its liquidity trap. A military attack was required to move conventional wisdom to the point that the government could intervene enough to do what was required. It wasn't dilapidated infrastructure that caused this change; even today, despite a crumbling infrastructure, billions can be poured into the quagmire of the war in Afghanistan while water mains break and bridges collapse.

As explained in the last chapter, Stalin also justified governmental intervention by arguing in military terms; Japan began to industrialize only after America's Commodore Perry showed up and bombarded its capital. Over thousands of years, the state—government plus its territory and people—have learned to bond over warfare like nothing else. Soldiers are trained to overcome their most basic instinct, preservation of life, to further the glory or defend the sacred territory of the "motherland," "fatherland," "country," "way of life," or what have you. Even though the United States was born possessing a heavy dose of skepticism about the military, and had a smaller army than Bulgaria's as late as 1939, war and the fear of conquest in 1941 was able to overcome another deep-seated bias of American history, the disapproval of governmental intervention into the economy.

The exigencies of the Depression laid the foundation for what are called *macroeconomic policies*—running deficits in times of recession in an effort to prevent a liquidity trap, or the need for a certain amount of regulation to prevent damage to the economy. But when it comes to directly participating in the economy, partly as a result of World War II, it is only the military that has a blank check to do what it wants.

When the war ended, it was feared that the military would not be able to give a big enough assist to the economy to prevent a return of depression, and so the third lesson of the war and depression years was that there needed to be an upgrade in living conditions—not by rebuilding the cities, but by building an entirely new arrangement, the suburbs. Part of the so-called "G.I. Bill," which gave returning soldiers a free education, among other things, was to also provide guaranteed mortgages, and the federal government encouraged the use of those mortgages in the suburbs, not the cities.[4]

This rush to suburbanize was partly the result of efforts by the automobile industry, and also the American oil industry, which was by far the world's most important source of oil. Another lesson of the war seems to have been that oil is very important. Oil is certainly critical for military forces, which need to easily store and move an energy source that can reliably provide large amounts of energy. Much of Hitler's setbacks late in the war were due to his need to find more oil, which doesn't exist anywhere near Germany. So oil had a very good image as the war came to a close.

Yet another lesson of World War II was the idea that countries should not appease an aggressor, and this lesson was used to argue that the United States had to be ever ready to battle the Soviet Union. Before World War II, Hitler had been appeased, that is, his demands had been met to avoid the consequences of its threats. In particular, in 1938 Hitler demanded that Germany should own the part of Czechoslovakia that was predominantly German, and the European powers agreed, on the condition that Hitler would stop demanding more territory. He didn't. After the war, the Soviet Union gobbled up much of Eastern Europe; therefore, the argument went, a large military is required to avoid a repeat of World War II; the Cold War was born.

The English had argued in favor of free trade in the 19th century, because they were in a position to overwhelm every country with their goods. They had built the world's largest military, without too much justification except for a rather feeble attempt at taking up the mantle of the "white man's burden." By contrast, the United States had an entire bookshelf of explanations and lessons of history to choose from to justify its economic and military adventures: constraints on trade caused the Depression, the war pulled the country out of the Depression, oil is a critical resource, suburbs is the next stop on the highway of progress, and appeasement is a bad idea. A world based on free trade, a strong American military, oil, and suburbia seemed to be the answer to the questions of the Depression and World War II.

A CONSTRAINED SUPERPOWER

The United States did have one constraint that the British did not have: the existence of another military superpower, the Soviet Union. We will never know what the United States would have done without this threat, but with it, they became very determined to encourage the development of Europe and Japan and East Asia to balance the power of the Soviet Union. As part of its quest, the United States ignored the gross violations of free trade that those countries engaged in. Except for an occasional effort to open up a weak country's trade, for example, in Latin America, free trade policies were mostly applied to the United States itself. The United States became a huge market for Europe, Japan, and eventually much of East Asia, which considerably helped those nations to support their industrialization agendas.

We also don't know what the U.S. elites would have done internationally had they not been constrained internally, that is, had there not been democracy in the United States. Judging from the many interventions and violent changes of regimes that the United States encouraged in the 1950s and 1960s, one may presume that, armed with a huge military and half of the world's GDP, a dictatorial

United States would have been constantly waging wars of conquest. When it did intervene, as in Vietnam, public opinion was able to eventually stop the spread of war.

When China was "lost," that is, in 1949 when the Chinese Communists took over and reunified the country, defeating the U.S.-backed Kuomintang regime, a sharp, right-wing reaction took place in the United States, which led to the rise of Senator Joseph McCarthy and a witch-hunt against supposed "communists" and sympathizers within government. This was a dangerous moment for American democracy. My grandfather, a Jewish immigrant from Europe, had left Germany for the United States in 1923 when Hitler staged his "beer hall putsch" and tried to force a coup there. When McCarthy was at the height of his power in the early 1950s, my grandfather packed the family's bags in anticipation of having to move again. But McCarthy was defeated; democracy held in America.

Fortunately, the United States helped Europe maintain democracy and power with what came to be known as the Marshall Plan, which involved giving $13 billion to the Western Europeans to rebuild themselves back up after the war. This was in marked contrast, for western Germany at least, to what the United States had been doing there before 1948. The so-called Morgenthau Plan proposed stripping Germany of any industry at all, turning it into a "pastoral" state. This was similar to the punitive measures that the Europeans had taken against Germany after World War I, which eventually helped lead to the rise of the Nazis; apparently this lesson of history had not been learned.

Besides the mass starvation that this plan would have led to, the threat of Communist takeover did much to convince the United States to abandon the Morgenthau Plan and opt for aid in the form of the Marshall Plan instead. The most important part of the aid was the requirement that the money be spent by the Europeans as a coordinated whole. This was the first step to creating a Europe unified by cooperation and democracy, not unified by conquest, as had been tried for the previous 1,000 years.[5] Toward the end of the Marshall Plan, in 1951, the European Coal and Steel Community (ECSC) was formed with six members, the most crucial being France and Germany.

Except for a brief period 1,000 years earlier during the time of Charlemagne, the French and German parts of Europe had constantly vied for power. France went through a period of positive feedback conquest after Charlemagne, starting in Paris, leading to the establishment of a very strong country by the 1400s. Germany, as we saw in the last chapter, finally unified in 1870, by fighting France. Napoleon had actually helped the western part of Germany unify when he took them over in the early 19th century.

France and Germany, along with the three small countries of Netherlands, Belgium, and Luxembourg (Benelux), make a natural economic unit and need each other's industries to thrive. In particular, the French steel industries needed the coal in the German Ruhr region, and in 1923 when France invaded the Ruhr to get the coal, the German economy collapsed. To avoid that fate, and as a sign that the times had changed, the ECSC guaranteed that France would get its coal peacefully.

The ECSC eventually turned into the European Common Market, which turned into the European Community, which turned into the European Union. Even before the fall of the Communist regimes of eastern Europe in 1991, the European Community included, most importantly, Italy, and then Great Britain, so that the four most powerful countries in Europe—Germany, France, Great Britain, and Italy—finally started working together, instead of against each other. Europe had economically unified, and now constitutes an economic region that can encompass all of the different niches of a complete production system.

While Europe concentrated on unification and manufacturing, the United States in the 1950s concentrated on building a "military-industrial complex," as President Eisenhower called it in his farewell address. The Department of Defense became the largest political machine in U.S. history. Previously, a political machine in a big city was defined as an arrangement in which the party leaders would hand out jobs to people who voted for and worked for the party. The Progressive movement in the early part of the 20th century inveighed against the corruption that this brought, and sought to make city employment more professional. The U.S. military updated the old city techniques, spreading military factories and bases all across the country, into almost every Congressperson and Senator's district or state. The military budget means more than national defense, it means jobs. The military has become a critical part of most local economies.

The 1950s also saw the rise of the highway lobby, so-called because the automobile, oil, highway construction, tire, cement, and

suburban real estate interests all banded together to push for suburbs and the roads the suburbs needed to survive. The Interstate
Highway System was the crowning glory of this effort. General
Motors and several other companies were actually convicted in the
late 1940s of conspiring to buy up and destroy the nation's trolley
companies in an effort to force people to either use less convenient
buses or, more importantly, to not have any alternative but to use
cars and roads. The conspirators had to pay only a few thousand
dollars in fines, but by that time the damage had been done.[6] In the
1920s, one could take local trolleys from New York City to Madison,
Wisconsin, with only a few gaps in between. One of the only trolleys
left is a single, vintage car in Kenosha in southern Wisconsin; one of
its stops is at the Joseph McCarthy Transportation Center.

Meanwhile, in the Soviet Union, Stalin had died (or been pois-
oned) in 1953, and the new party boss, Sergei Kruschev, led an
industrial revival. In 1959 Seymour Melman took a trip to the Soviet
Union in which he reported on the front page of *The New York Times*
that the Soviet machine tool industry was advanced enough that they
were mass-producing sophisticated machine tools (his recommenda-
tion to the British to do the same fell on deaf ears).[7]

However, somehow news of the efficient production of machine
tools in the Soviet Union did not stir the blood of the American
public. What really got their attention was the fact that the Soviets
launched a satellite, called Sputnik, into outer space. Maybe it was
the effect of science fiction movies or just fear of being zapped from
outer space, but a "space race" ensued that had the benefit, in the
United States, that for perhaps the only time in American history,
science education in the public schools was given top priority. In the
Soviet Union, however, the focus moved from machine tools to
rockets, with disastrous consequences for the Soviet production system. When Kruschev ventured to voice the opinion that maybe the
military should stop getting the lion's share of the country's scientists, engineers, and resources, he was promptly replaced with the
military's man in the Politburo (the Soviet equivalent of the board of
directors). That man, Leonid Brezhnev, did not spare any expense in
the pursuit of a completely extravagant military system.

Germany and Japan had not only been shorn of their militaristic
nobilities after the war, they had been prohibited from building a
large military. In Japan, the American-designed Constitution prevents the government from spending more than 1 percent of GDP

on the military. Instead of the best and brightest pursuing careers in the military-industrial complex, as often happened in the United States and almost always happened in the Soviet Union, in Japan the Ministry of International Trade and Industry (MITI) and the top industrial firms like Toyota and Mitsubishi attracted Japan's top graduates. MITI practices "administrative guidance," that is, it brings together the top firms in a particular industry, or firms that MITI thinks can create an industry, and cajoles and lobbies them to move in a particular direction. MITI will then often close the Japanese market to, say, certain American products, then encourage the American companies to sell their technology to the Japanese companies. MITI also used to control any flows of money out of Japan, ensuring that all available financial capital would be used inside the country.[8] To go back to our table of machinery in Chapter 6 (Table 6.1), by 1970 Japan was tied with Germany with 10 percent of global machinery production, while Britain had sunk to a 6 percent share.

In the 1970s, MITI successfully brought together companies such as Nikon and Canon to create what is now the world's top semiconductor-making equipment industry, which supplies the machinery that makes the semiconductors that are the brains in electronic products.[9]

Observers sometimes use the image of flying geese to convey the process of development in East Asia; Japan acted like the leading goose in a V-formation, while the other East Asian nations, particularly South Korea, Taiwan, Hong Kong, and Singapore, copied the Japanese policies.[10]

Taiwan and South Korea enacted land reforms early in their postwar history. Taiwan was invaded by the remnants of the Kuomintang who were expelled from China when the Communists took over that country. Instead of making the mistakes they had made in China of allying themselves with large landholding families, the Kuomintang expropriated the indigenous Taiwanese large landowners, and gave them industrial bonds as compensation. The former landholders were forced to build factories to redeem their bonds, and the government encouraged other firms to industrialize as well.[11]

South Korea imposed a land reform after the brutal war with North Korea in the early 1950s. The North Koreans had taken over much of South Korea at one point, and had given all lands held by big landowners to the peasants. To avoid a repeat of a communist takeover, the returning South Korean regime let the peasants keep their land.

Starting in 1960, with a change in the dictator, a very deliberate policy of industrialization took place. Several industrial conglomerates, or chaebol, were formed. If they exported enough goods—much of it to the free-trading United States—then they were rewarded by the government. If they didn't perform up to expectations, the government could actually take them over and distribute their various parts to the other chaebol. Alice Amsden calls this "performance-based" industrial policy. In return for help, partly in the form of trade barriers, the government holds companies accountable. According to Amsden,

> the growth rate of output increases as the growth rate of productivity increases, and in closed-loop fashion, depending on institutional constraints, the growth rate of productivity increases as the growth rate of output increases—through investments that embody foreign designs, economies of scale, and learning-by-doing.[12]

Korea moved from being one of the poorest countries in the world to one of the richest. Korea is now much more digitally wired than the United States.

THE MILITARY AND SUBURBIA TEAM UP

By the 1960s, U.S. manufacturing dominance was carrying it to an extraordinary period of growth. But there were already clouds on the horizon; in 1963 Seymour Melman's *Our Depleted Society* warned that the manufacturing system was being ignored in favor of military industries.[13] In the Department of Defense, things were getting worse, as the new Secretary of Defense, Robert McNamara, former president of Ford Motor Company, was turning a military-industrial complex into a permanent war economy, centralized in the Pentagon. Outside of the Soviet Union, the U.S. military system was the largest manifestation of central planning anywhere in the world. In addition, Melman was documenting the immense "overkill," as he popularized the term, of the nuclear arsenal. It was, he claimed, the biggest waste of money in world history. Between 1940 and 1996, national defense cost $16.23 trillion (in constant 1996 dollars), with $5.82 trillion of that just for nuclear weapons and infrastructure, fully 50 percent of federal outlays in that period.

James Howard Kunstler called the construction of suburbia in America the biggest waste of money in American history.[14] The military and suburbia have starved manufacturing and cities of resources for the past 50 years. Cities are the natural centers of manufacturing innovation, because cities offer people the opportunity to work together and take advantage of the synergies of various fields of endeavor. By emptying the cities, the government cut off a source of manufacturing leadership; by encouraging free trade, at least into the United States, the government encouraged the loss of manufacturing production.

Part of the suburbanization of the United States was driven by racism and fear of other ethnic groups. The U.S. housing bureaucracies encouraged banks to refuse loans to African Americans. They color-coded different parts of the city, and the riskiest zones were colored red, which invariably were where African Americans lived; thus the term *red-lining* came to mean that African Americans could not get home loans. By 1960, Levittown, the pioneering suburb in Long Island, had 88,000 people and not a single African-American.[15] With the middle-class tax base moving to the suburbs, which were supplied by roads and other infrastructure built with government money, the cities deteriorated even further.[16]

The outcome was different if the city was in the South, in which case the city was showered with military contract monies. For instance, Martin Marietta, the huge defense contractor, was headquartered in Marietta, Georgia, which came to be the district of one of the 20th century's most important conservative legislators, Newt Gingrich. The most fervent defenders of the market were, and are, completely committed to what is now the largest example of central planning-type socialism, the American military system. Contrary to conventional wisdom, the Republican Party loves government—for the military, for expansion of suburbs, and for subsidies for the industries that support the Republicans.

In the 1960s, the United States and USSR engaged in an arms race that benefited both of their militaries, but both military leaderships had one big problem: they weren't engaged in an expansionary war that took advantage of their military dominance. To some extent, this was because they constrained each other. Their governments were also, objectively speaking, rather "satisfied," that is, they had their hands full just keeping their continental-sized systems running. The United States ran Latin America without having to administer those countries as colonies, and the Soviets did the same with eastern Europe (Stalin had wondered why the United States was upset about his takeover of eastern Europe, because Stalin felt that the United States had done the same with Latin America). China was finally out of service as a target of colonization, as was India, and in any event, Africa, the Middle East, and the rest of Asia had just thrown off its own colonizers, sometimes rather messily, which didn't make them attractive targets for conquest either.

According to Franz Schurmann,[17] there were still forces within the United States that wanted to expand into China, since the Pacific had been the U.S. Navy's lake for quite some time. Schurmann argues that to avoid that minefield, Vietnam became an attractive way for Lyndon Johnson to deflect the U.S. military into something less dangerous. In Vietnam, the U.S. military found a way to flex their considerable muscle, even if the spoils were rather thin. Better to fight somewhere than not to fight at all, seemed to be the decision-making process within the "national security" apparatus, a train of thought that was repeated in the Iraq invasion of 2003.

This military diversion into Vietnam had another consequence, whether deliberate or not we may never know—the movement toward a social democratic society in the United States was short-circuited. Lyndon Johnson had succeeded in passing Medicare and civil rights legislation. Some form of universal health care, solid environmental protections, and even help for the cities and education were possible. Tragically, he became obsessed with Vietnam, and the cities went into even further decline.

With that decline came a decline in manufacturing. According to Table 6.1, whereas the United States produced almost 38 percent of global industrial machinery in 1970, between the mid-1970s and the 1990s, the percentage bounced around in the mid-20s, until by 2000 the United States hit 20 percent—all the while increasing its imports. In 2007, the United States was surpassed by China, which had 16 percent of total output compared to the United States' 15 percent. In 2000, the Japanese passed the United States in industrial machinery output at 22 percent of global output, as did the combination of the four top economies of the European Union, Germany, Italy, France, and the United Kingdom, at 25 percent. At the beginning of the 2010's, the United States is declining, the European Union and Japan are holding their own, and China is rising.

THE ACHILLES HEAL OF NEOCLASSICAL ECONOMICS

Unlike Europe and East Asia's long experience with targeted economic intervention in encouraging manufacturing, the U.S. government is still not supposed to interfere—even ensuring health care for all is considered to be overstepping the government's proper role. The ideology of preventing government intervention in the economy is a significant impediment to solving the ecological and economic crises of the 21st century.

The theoretical core of this ideology is embodied in every economics department in the country, in the form of neoclassical economics. But neoclassical economics is singularly unable to explain and guide policy in the modern world, much to the detriment of the U.S. economy. It is worthwhile understanding why this is so, in order to build the case for an alternative to neoclassical economics for national economic policy.

As I explained in the previous chapter, David Ricardo had introduced the idea of *diminishing returns* into economic thought, that is, the idea that the more one uses of a factor of production, assuming other factors of production stay constant, at a certain point, one will receive in return less than the cost of that factor of production. It is at the point when we cross over from *making* a profit from employing a factor of production (such as a worker) to *not* making a profit that one should stop hiring, and further, that one should pay all of the factors of production (such as all workers) the wage one pays the last one. This idea had a very convenient ideological benefit—it meant that everybody was theoretically receiving in income that which they were contributing to the economy.

At least, that's what John Bates Clark of Columbia University claimed when he came up with the idea around 1900.[18] Karl Marx and other radicals had been arguing that workers should receive what they deserved, not what the owners could force them to take. Clark argued that this socialist paradise was already in existence. Because every worker got what the worker who was at the point of not yielding a profit was getting, they all received as income that which they contributed to the enterprise. The market was just, and automatically and fairly distributed the gains from the economy.

However, this idea of *marginal productivity* gave rise to another problem when it came time to try to figure out what causes economic growth. While economists had been focusing on understanding why goods have the price that they have, they had been ignoring the question of what causes economic growth. Understanding how supply and demand affect a price is not the same thing as understanding why the economy grows.

One would think that understanding economic growth would be the most important question in economics. Ultimately, that is what populations expect their governments to do; at the very least, a government is not supposed to let an economy decline. A government will, at a minimum, want to keep up with the growth rate of other countries, lest it lose relative power and be at the mercy of those who grow faster.

Besides, the most important economic phenomenon of the past 200 years is not that goods have prices, it is that economies have grown by orders of magnitude. The economic historian Paul Bairoch calculated that global per capita (that is, for each person) manufacturing production increased by seven-and-one-half times from 1900 to 1980.[19] According to Angus Maddison, between 1913 and 1989 the per-person income for most developed countries went up almost five times.[20] And yet, Jonathan Temple has gone so far as to call growth theory a "backwater"[21]; for Nicholas Stern, growth theory "has, however, been a popular topic for those involved in formal economic theory only for short periods, notably from the mid-1950s to the late 1960s."[22] How can this be? Aren't economists attacked for only being interested in economic growth?

One problem with neoclassical theory is the aforementioned marginal productivity problem. When you actually look at the data, labor, that is, working people, take in about two-thirds of the country's income, and profits, or by implication capital, takes in about one-third. According to theory, that must mean that labor is responsible for two-thirds of growth per person and capital for one-third. So the quantity of labor must have increased by quite a bit, according to this line of logic. The problem is that labor has *not* increased by much; the number of annual hours worked per person has stayed about the same over much of the past 70 years or so. On the other hand, capital has increased by a large multiplier. In fact, both capital and GDP increase at about the same rate—so capital must be responsible for economic growth, right?

Not if the theory of marginal productivity is correct. In fact, since the amount of labor has pretty much stayed the same, then the factor of production that is increasing, capital, should be experiencing those diminishing returns that Ricardo was so interested in. That means that when capital goes up, output should still go up, but at a decreasing rate. But that's not what happened—the *capital-output ratio*, as it is called, did not go down as a result of *capital deepening*, that is, more capital being used in the economy.

This is how the dean of post-war American economists, Paul Samuelson, put it in his famous textbook on economics:

> Instead of observing a steady rise in the capital-output ratio as the deepening of capital invokes the law of diminishing returns, we find that the capital-output ratio has been approximately constant in this century . . . A steady profit rate [that is, share of capital in national income] and a steady capital-output ratio are incompatible with the more basic law of diminishing returns under deepening of capital. We are forced, therefore, to introduce *technical innovations* into our [static] neoclassical analysis to explain these dynamic facts.[23]

In other words, neoclassical economists can't explain an anomaly in economic theory; the theory is not supported by the facts. Rather than overthrow the theory, one inserts an "X" factor, some unknown force, which can explain the anomaly. Before Copernicus (and others) suggested that the sun is at the center of the solar system, Ptolemaic astronomers explained problems in their observations of the planets by introducing "circles within circles" within the solar system, desperate attempts to save the paradigm. The introduced measure of "technological innovation" does not solve the problem, it is simply a way to fit a hole in the theory.

In the 1950s, Robert Solow at the Massachusetts Institute of Technology (MIT) tried to explain how economic growth occurs, and calculated that this "X" factor, which he attributed to technological change, contributed as much as seven-eighths to economic growth.[24] In other words, neoclassical theory can't explain economic growth, even using its own techniques. Moses Abramowitz, who took the first look at these data in the 1950s, simply called this unknown force a "measure of our ignorance."[25] Solow presented an elegant model, and so he received a Nobel Prize, but Abramowitz was closer to the truth.

The fatal flaw in the neoclassical paradigm is that the concept of fixed capital is basically absent from its paradigm. Ricardo tried to

model capital as corn; John Bates Clark tried the metaphors of wine
and a forest, more in an attempt to understand how capital changes
in time than to understand how it affects the rest of the economy;
Frank Knight at the University of Chicago used the image of a cac-
tus, something that grows and can be used in pieces. The subject after the 1950s was pretty much dropped, except for an occasional
dispute among different schools of thought, the last one occurring
in the 1960s when U.K. economists at the University of Cambridge
argued that there was a contradiction in the use of the ideas of capital
and profit in the economics as developed in Cambridge, Massachusetts,
meaning mostly Samuelson and Solow.[26]

These discussions petered out by the 1970s. There was a short-
lived burst of interest in the 1980s in an idea called *new growth
theory*, in which research and development, or information, was said
to be a factor of production and not subject to diminishing returns,
but that idea faded as well. Neoclassical economics depends on
branches of mathematics that cannot handle positive feedback loops,
whose outcomes are horribly difficult to predict with precision; a
branch of science called chaos theory has emerged, in part, to try to
deal with positive feedback loops. The best way to model positive
feedback loops, as ecologists have done, is with computer models
that use *iteration*, that is, they show how forces work from one time
period to another, including the operation of cycles

Neoclassical economics is constructed in such a way as to describe
how short-term phenomena work within a single competitive industry, like short-term prices. It is not designed to explain how industries interact, or how technological change and economic growth
occur in the long run.

So what kinds of advice are economists dispensing, if they are not,
technically speaking, trying to increase economic growth? They are
extrapolating from the way that competitive markets work in the
short term, where the interference of government, say by imposing
taxes or price controls, yields a less than optimal outcome. Or, they
are using the ideas of John Maynard Keynes to try to move the economy out of a liquidity trap. Or they are explaining how trade could
help all countries if technological change does not exist.

In other words, except for the problem of stopping a liquidity trap
in the short term, we should be paying attention to the historical record to understand how countries have industrialized and encouraged
their manufacturing sectors, instead of listening to what neoclassical

economists have to say about what their models tell us about how the economy should be run, or not run.

GETTING THE MILITARY ON OUR BACKS

And yet, all post-war administrations in the United States have been listening to neoclassical economists, and most governments in the rest of the developed world have not. This puts the United States at a disadvantage, and means that other industrialized countries, particularly in Europe and Asia, can be expected to rise relative to the United States and for the United States to decline, relatively.

The United States could also decline absolutely if the manufacturing sector is allowed to deteriorate too far. But the United States has another major economic problem: of all the developed countries, it is by far the most dependent on cheap oil. The suburbanization process has gone much further in the United States than in Europe or Asia.

The trends of militarization of the economy, a hands-off approach to economic policy, and suburbanization and a growing dependence on oil all came together in the early 1970s. Like the British, the United States had fixed the currency at a very high level since the end of the war, tied at a fixed rate to the price of gold. Because the United States had been declining relative to Europe and East Asia throughout the 1960s, the fixed exchange rates mandating that the dollar should be worth so many German deutsche marks, Japanese yen, or French francs, did not reflect the reality of the relative strengths of these economies. At the same time, the U.S. dominance in oil was declining because the output of oil was declining—starting in 1971, just as Hubbert had predicted in 1956. The United States started to import large quantities of oil. Richard Nixon decided to let the dollar float, that is, let the global market decide what the relative worth of the various currencies would be. A couple of years later, during the Yom Kippur War in the Middle East, the Saudi and other oil producers decided to flex their economic muscles against a less powerful United States, and drastically raised the price of oil, laying the groundwork for the economic slowdown of the 1970s.

The late 1970s were a turning point. The United States could have moved to an economy less dependent on oil, but that would have required rebuilding the cities and the electric train-based transportation systems within them, which would have meant a reversal of the subsidization of suburbia and spread-out southwestern cities. It would also have required a reversal of the expansion of the military budget, to provide resources to the cities and manufacturing.

Decreasing the military budget would have had a salutary effect on manufacturing, if managed properly. A smaller military budget would have decreased that part of the economy that was, and continues to be, fundamentally shaped by central governmental planning. That is, the military industries don't need to satisfy the needs of consumers, they need to satisfy the needs of generals and admirals, who want something different than a product that is as cheap as possible and that is as reliable as possible. The military doesn't need to worry about price, because they have a massive political machine devoted to bringing them all the resources they need. They don't even have to worry too much about reliability, because with that never-ending flow of money, they can always buy more if something breaks. Instead, they construct equipment that can do certain things, like fly in a certain way, or move in a certain way, or deliver a certain kind of weapon in a certain way. Performance is important, not price or reliability.

Robert McNamara, Secretary of Defense in the 1960s, not only centralized this whole system, he also instituted the policy of *cost plus*, that is, no matter what it costs to produce something, the manufacturer gets a certain percentage of profit. If something costs more to produce than originally specified, the firm receives *more* money and the percentage of the profit stays the same, and so the absolute amount of profit grows larger. There is actually an incentive in the military production system to make equipment more and more costly to produce, which is part of the reason why, famously, toilet seats and coffee makers can cost thousands of dollars when made by military contractors.

A manufacturer would therefore prefer to produce for a military firm, not a civilian one. Why not make more money and be assured of a steady, long-term income? Once a firm gets on this money train, it's very difficult to get off. The engineers become used to making overly complex machinery that is hard to maintain and that costs more than consumers would want to pay. The military firms can offer the best engineers more money than civilian firms, so slowly but surely the entire manufacturing system is depleted of engineers, scientists, and the competence to produce for most markets.[27]

IMPERIAL REQUIEM

By the late 1970s, high oil prices plus a sagging manufacturing sector meant that wages and salaries could not buy what they could buy before, which manifested itself as inflation and high unemployment. Instead of seeing this slowdown as the result of not enough intervention by the government, much of the public saw it as the result of too much intervention. Ronald Reagan was elected, ushering in an institutionalization of the world view of neoclassical economics, that is, "getting the government off our backs." In addition, instead of reining in the military economy, Reagan gave it a big boost.

During this move to a more conservative government, the Federal Reserve under Paul Volker, the Chairman appointed by Jimmy Carter, decided to kill inflation by killing much of the economy, raising interest rates to 18 percent. This would have led to a full-scale depression had it continued, so the rates were brought back down; however, the long-term effect was to seriously damage what was left of the exporting capacity of the American manufacturing system. The high interest rates led to a highly valued dollar, because those interest rates brought in money from abroad, looking for easy profits. Just as an economic downturn around 1900 had allowed the United States to overtake Britain as the major machinery maker, so the "strong" dollar of the early 1980s gave German and in particular Japanese machinery makers the opening to break into the American market in a serious way. American machinery makers have never recovered.

Meanwhile, the economy of the other superpower, the Soviet Union, had probably started to decline absolutely from about 1980 on, according to Russian economists.[28] The neglect of machinery industries, particularly in reproduction industries such as machine tools, had become so great that output could not even be maintained. Instead of trying to fix this situation, the Soviet elites decided to finally use their oversized, idle military to conquer a country— Afghanistan, one of the most difficult military environments in the world, a country that even outlasted Alexander the Great, much less the British, Soviets, or the Americans. Evidently, the Soviet political economy was so ossified and inflexible, and the military-industrial complex was so powerful, that nothing could reverse its claim on the country's resources except a collapse of the entire Soviet system. And so it did.[29]

John Kenneth Galbraith was moved to observe in 1982 that "No one can look at the history of the last twenty years and conclude that there has been anything but a race to see which of the great powers can lose influence most rapidly."[30]

The American elite followed the path of the British and Soviets in giving priority to the military, and followed the British in also allowing more and more power to accrue to the financial elites. A "strong" dollar, like a strong pound, was bad for manufacturing but good for banks and other financial services firms. Once financial considerations become paramount, decline accelerates because financial processes move at a faster speed than in other services or manufacturing. If one can get a very short-term advantage in finance, one can leverage that small advantage into a bigger and bigger one, in a process of positive feedback. In a manufacturing setting, growth occurs from innovation and the development of products that incorporate those innovations. That process is at the root of economic growth, but it takes some time, perhaps years or even decades. Financial firms, on the other hand, can grow in seconds, or within one quarter of a year, which is how often firms usually report their financial figures.

With manufacturing faltering and finance flourishing, even manufacturing firms moved to make themselves more "financial" by appealing to Wall Street and the stock market, and by improving their short-term performance. Normally, changes in short-term performance might reflect a temporary condition that doesn't have much to do with long-term performance, such as a large expense for research. But if one needs to show short-term performance every quarter, then expenditures that depress that performance must go, such as research and development. The fastest way to show short-term performance is to eat one's capital, that is, to sell off one's capital, which gives you a short-term increase in wealth, but dooms you in the long-term because you don't have the capacity to create wealth at some point in the future.

The favorite way for Wall Street to encourage the short-term performance of firms has been to urge the firm to close up shop in the high-wage United States and reopen in low-wage countries such as Mexico in the 1980s, or later on, China. The firms that do this lose the human capital of the workers that they lay off, and their engineers lose the ability to walk into the factory to see how a new design is working; eventually the engineers often lose their jobs as well. By destroying human capital, the firms decrease their ability to innovate, and therefore they lose the ability to grow in the long term. Eventually, the economy follows the firms in a downward positive feedback loop of job loss and failure to innovate.

The remaining firms in the United States also lose, because they can no longer take advantage of close interactions with the closed factory. Perhaps the closed factory used to provide another factory with machinery. The relationship may have been long-term, and so human capital for the dependent factory disappears when relationships with the closed supplier disappears. Perhaps a closed factory used to supply material for another factory. It is also human nature for the suppliers in other countries to try out their most recent, best innovations on their neighbors instead of someone across the ocean.

Eventually, an entire industrial ecosystem may collapse, as happened with the U.S. automobile industry. There are certainly many reasons for this collapse, starting with an arrogant management, but no industry is safe if large sectors of the manufacturing sector decline and disappear. No corporation is an island; the production system involves cooperation as much as competition, and if there are no other firms to cooperate with, the remaining firms will fail just as surely as if they were unable to compete.

By the early 1990s, a key element in the creation of American wealth was disappearing: the ability to increase the wages of production workers faster than the prices of machinery. As I explained in Chapter 4, a competent, cost-minimizing management can take advantage of rising wages to install new, relatively cheaper machinery. Between 1971 and 1991, Germany and Japan continued to do so, while in the United States the rise in the prices of machine tools eventually outpaced the rise in the production wages by up to 13 percent.[31]

BLOWING BUBBLES

It is quite possible that, just as the Soviet Union collapsed because of its inability to maintain its machinery sectors, the United States was about to move to a lower overall standard of living during the recession of 1991, except that the speculative dot-com bubble emerged. This was based on a real burst of productivity and innovation, as the diffusion of the microprocessor finally reached a tipping point. It took a good 20 years for the development of electricity-generating steam turbines to lead to the electrification of much of society in the 1920s, and it took almost as long for the development of the microprocessor in the late 1970s to hit the rest of the economy with full force, in the 1990s.

By the time the dot-com bubble burst, the Federal Reserve initiated the opposite of its policy in the late 1970s and early 1980s, and drove interest rates down to almost zero, setting off the real estate bubble of the 2000s.

As *Business Week* stated,

> Corporate financial resources have been withheld in enormous amount from use in business expansion, and the profits of corporations have reflected in considerable part earnings from banking and investment activities irrelevant to their real business. Great as our progress has been under these conditions, how much greater might it not have been if the energies and resources of business had been devoted during these years to the essential task of producing and distributing the goods and services that create real national prosperity.[32]

However, it stated this opinion in 1929, not 2009. After 1929, the federal government moved to regulate finance so that banking became "boring," to use Paul Krugman's phrase,[33] until deregulation hit with full force in the 1980s and particularly the 1990s.

Now, after at least a decade of bubbles, the economy has sunk to what may be a new "normal": persistent unemployment, lower income levels for those who are employed, a sense that the economy has nowhere to go but down, and the big dark cloud of rising oil prices over the horizon.

OIL AND MONEY

Oil had a large part to play in the real estate bubble of the 2000s and in the course of the American economy for the last several decades. Henry Kissinger, when he was secretary of state, pulled off his most important diplomatic move when he arranged for all of the oil-producing nations to agree to sell their oil only for dollars. By doing so, the United States could run a persistent trade deficit, that is, they could buy more goods than they sold, because foreigners could always use their dollars to buy oil; in fact, they would *have* to use their dollars to buy the oil to power the cars, trucks, airplanes, and ships that they all seemed to want to have.

When the oil producers raised their prices a second time in the late 1970s, they overreached. Prices rose so high that people started to think seriously about, if not eliminating the use of oil, at least reworking society so that much less oil would be needed. The Saudis and others wanted to stop the movement to a more efficient society, and instituted an era of very cheap gas that lasted until about 2005. The sport utility vehicle (SUV) was a consequence of cheap gas, as was much of the real estate boom of the 2000s, because cheap gas meant that housing developments could be built that were very far from a city, and that housing would be fairly cheap to buy—but very expensive if gas went up in price.

Which it eventually did; just as Hubbert predicted, the global supply of petroleum started to peak soon after the millennium changed. The bubble that was created by cheap oil was burst by peak oil. The sharp drop in demand in the world economy led to a sharp drop in demand for oil, but as the world economy picks up, so will the price of oil, producing an up-and-down cycle in the world economy. This will turn into a mostly down cycle until the global economy shifts from an oil-based transportation system.

The other financial prop for the U.S. economy has been the huge amount of dollars that have flowed outward as a result of the trade deficit and have acted like an international currency for the rest of the world. Many central banks like to hold onto dollars as a kind of insurance policy to keep their own currencies stable, and this also adds to the demand for the dollar. Apparently most countries do not print enough money to cover their expanding economies and when they need more currency, they can always turn to the money-printer of last resort, the United States.

However, by relying on the demand for the dollar to keep the American economy afloat, the financial sector is empowered even more, leading to a worse situation for what remains of the manufacturing sector. From a steady 25 percent of the workforce, manufacturing employment in the United States has declined to 11 percent. Americans are consuming a larger and larger percentage of goods from abroad, as we saw in Chapter 2.

SLIPPING AWAY

Meanwhile, much of America is getting stuck in what Elizabeth Warren calls the *two-income trap*. That is, in an effort to maintain one's standard of living in the face of stagnating wages and salaries for most of the country, more and more families have wives working as well as the husbands. One of the consequences of this increase in income has been that housing prices have been going up, as we saw in the 2000s, because families had more to spend on residences, and this intersected with a deteriorating quality of schools. The result was a scramble for houses, not just that are big or nice enough, but that are in the right area so that a family can send their children to a good school. Warren found that families, on average, are actually spending less for necessities like food and clothing than decades ago, but the cost of housing, health insurance, and education have eaten up all of the income increases and more, so that many families became caught in a cycle of debt, both with credit cards and home equity loans.

This problem is compounded with the loss of good manufacturing jobs. By 2008, the employment in production occupations had dipped below 10 million.[34] In 2000, there were 12.6 million production workers.[35] The numbers for all manufacturing employees fell from 17.3 million in 2000 to 13.4 million in 2008.[36]

This massive layoff of manufacturing employees took place while the current infrastructure needs $2.2 trillion dollars of investment to be brought up to an adequate level, according to the American Society of Civil Engineers.[37] Their report looks at the state of infrastructure for various categories, and I have included what they see as the needed spending over a five-year plan, in billions of dollars, for each one: aviation (87), dams (12.5), drinking water and waste water (255), energy (75), hazardous waste and solid waste (77), inland waterways (50), levees (50), public parks and recreation (85), rail (63), roads and bridges (930), schools (160), and transit (265). Although they estimate that about $930 billion is being spent per year for all of these systems, it still leaves a shortfall of $1.3 trillion per year. That total doesn't even include what is needed to make the infrastructure ecologically sustainable and petroleum-free.

Europe is in much better shape than the United States in terms of manufacturing. Its manufacturing work force makes up about

25 percent of its work force, and 32 percent of its nonfinancial sector is in manufacturing,[38] as opposed to 13 percent for the United States. Their cumulative trade deficit is one-quarter of the United States (mostly with China). Europeans use about half the oil that Americans use, per person, which is a result of very high gasoline taxes instituted after the war. Unlike the United States, Europe has little oil. There is a very extensive electrified rail system, including truly high-speed rail, often running close to 200 miles per hour.

The Japanese use trains more than any other country, about 27 percent of all travel, including an extensive high-speed rail system. Their manufacturing firms continue to be among the best, if not the best, in the world. Their machinery firms are prospering; in the United States, by contrast, not a single major U.S.-owned machine tool firm survives, and there are no manufacturers of electrified trains, either high-speed or subway.

Overshadowing all of these regions is the phenomenal rise of China, caused by the rise of its manufacturing. In 1990, China's manufacturing, construction, and electrical industries output $145 billion worth of goods and constituted 36 percent of its GDP. In 1997, this figure had grown to $373 billion (using constant 1990 dollars to account for inflation), while the same industrial sectors constituted 43 percent of GDP. In 2008, these sectors accounted for $1,118 billion and 47 percent of GDP. That is just below Japan's industrial output of $1,123 billion, and still behind the $2,057 billion of the United States (all figures in 1990 dollars).[39]

While the Chinese are over-investing in roads and automobiles, apparently from an uncritical view that somehow the existence of automobiles leads to wealth, they are also constructing extensive rail and subway systems, and have become the world leader in solar panel and wind turbine production.[40] They also overtook the United States in greenhouse emissions, mainly because of an expanding system of coal-based electricity generating plants.

Like the other East Asian industrial countries, the Chinese started by specializing in simpler manufacturing technologies, and have moved to more and more sophisticated ones, including machinery technologies; as Table 6.1 shows, they now produce more industrial machinery than the United States (15.9 percent to 15 percent of global production). They train a massive amount of engineers, and send others abroad to learn the best technologies. Just as one would expect, U.S. firms that first moved factories to China are now moving engineering design departments over there as well, because engineers benefit from proximity to factories. The Chinese government has no compunction about manipulating its currency down, as opposed to the U.S. movement up, and the leadership requires that many goods be manufactured in China when it provides government assistance. The United States, by contrast, recently saw many of its stimulus dollars leak away, often to China, when buying equipment such as wind turbines. The Chinese require that factories be set up as joint ventures between foreign and domestic firms, and often require that their engineers be trained by the foreign firms, just like the Koreans.

These are not evil actions, belligerent policies, or unfair trading practices. They are policies that every country, including the United States, has been practicing, at one time or another, for hundreds of years. For any country to be rich, it needs to have an innovative, complete suite of manufacturing industries. The United States was once accused of merely copying the technologies invented in Britain, and of unfairly giving domestic firms too many advantages. The result then was a very wealthy country that came to the defense of Britain and the other democracies in two world wars. It would be to the benefit of the United States, and the rest of the world, if the United States decided to rebuild its manufacturing sector and again become a full trading partner.

But even that won't be enough to propel the United States, or the rest of the world, very far into the 21st century. For on top of the imperative to rebuild the manufacturing system, we now need a green transformation of the economy. The ecosystems of the planet have been under assault for some time, and so we now turn to consider their future.

CHAPTER 8

Driving Civilization off a Cliff

The central problem of our time is production, both because production is the key to wealth and because we have to figure out how to produce without destroying the planet. As we have seen in the last three chapters, countries that take care of their wealth-producing potential—that is, their capital—thrive, while countries that destroy their capital, don't. Manufacturing and skilled people are the most important kinds of capital, along with natural capital. Natural capital—ecosystems, climate, and resources—are under global assault right now.

There are three main ecological calamities facing civilization in general: global warming, peak oil (and other commodities), and ecosystem destruction.

Both global warming and ecosystem destruction could put most of civilization out of action, but the worst effects of these processes will not be felt for a decade or more. Unfortunately, people are best at dealing with problems when it is the most difficult to stop them. Peak oil is very close at hand, but cuts to the core of the current version of modern global civilization, and so will be very difficult to deal with until it is also too late.

We have been looking at the history and present of the global system; now is the time to look at possible futures.

THE END OF THE ERA OF CHEAP OIL

Peak oil—that is, the concept that we are near or at the peak of the global production of oil, and that fairly soon we will see a decline in global production—is really an ecological problem, although it is usually seen as purely an economic problem. All ecosystems involve material flows. In fact, ecosystems, like human production systems, involve material making, energy conversion, structure forming, goods movement, and information processing. For instance, plants use solar energy via chloroplasts, use and move nutrients as material from the soil (including nitrogen bound by bacteria at their roots) and water, and create the cells and structure of the plant using information in the nucleus of the cells. If something critical disappears or changes in quantity—water, for instance—then the entire ecosystem may have to adapt, or may change rather quickly and fundamentally.

In just the same way, if a human economy runs out of a critical resource, such as oil, it will have to adapt or collapse. We have a problem, though, that we don't have in the study of global warming—we don't really know, or know to the accuracy we would like, how much oil is out there. Part of the problem is that it is very difficult to know what is under the crust of the Earth, but worse, the countries under whose soil the oil exists are not being wholly truthful about how much they have. They will not allow outside experts to independently verify the countries' claims about how much oil they have.

The best known example of oil data duplicity occurred in the mid-1980s, when the reported oil reserves of many Middle Eastern oil-producing countries doubled almost overnight, because the Organization of Petroleum Exporting Countries (OPEC) decided to allow rates of production of oil depending on how large the reserves were. Those estimates have never been revised downward, and they were never independently confirmed.

However, a general rule that petroleum engineers have about oil-well production is that they follow the famous bell curve; on average, that is, they ramp up production, peak, and ramp back down in approximately the same way they ramped up. It was on this basis that one of the most famous petroleum engineers in history, a Shell engineer, M. King Hubbert, predicted in 1956 that the United States would peak in oil production (at the top of that bell curve) by 1971. Nobody believed him, and oil production in the United States peaked in 1971. He then applied the same techniques to global production, forecasting that world production would peak in 2000.[1]

Oil production probably peaked around 2007—the oil crises of 1973 and 1979 may have delayed it a few years—although we will only know for sure after the peak has come. In 2008, of course, we saw the spike in prices that probably burst the mortgage/financial bubble. Many people seem to think that this must have been some sort of evil plot on the part of the oil companies, or speculators, or oil-producing countries. Speculators probably put two and two together, and figured that with oil peaking, the price would eventually go up—which it will. But neither oil companies nor oil-producing countries want people to think that oil won't, like diamonds, be forever.

Private oil companies, as manipulative as they may be, only control about 10 percent of the world's oil anyway. If the United States and United Kingdom followed the lead of virtually every other oil-producing nation and nationalized their oil companies—that is, they controlled the drilling, extraction, and selling of the oil—then the "majors," as the remaining private firms are called, would remain as experts in the technologies of drilling, pumping, and moving oil, not owning it. Currently, the majors generally pump what the United States owns anyway, at a low royalty. If the U.S. treasury took in the revenues from constantly increasing oil prices, it would make the coming oil crunch much easier to deal with.

As it is, even in a country that owns its oil company, Hugo Chavez of Venezuela is just as conservative as the oil royalty of the House of Saud when it comes to proposing post-oil solutions—in other words, he doesn't want anyone to think about it. And like most of his oil-producing brethren, Chavez wastes huge sums of money keeping gas prices low for his population, which brings the world ever closer to the brink. The real problem for most of the world is not that global *production* of oil in general is peaking, the real problem is that the oil that is being *exported* is peaking.

As Jeff Rubin[2] explains, more and more oil is being used by the countries that everyone is counting on to boost oil exports to feed their growing appetite for oil. The Gulf States have another resource problem, the decline of freshwater reserves, and therefore, they are using their oil to desalinate the salt water of the Indian Ocean. They're also using oil to power the greater and greater number of cars that their expanding economies and populations are demanding as well as using the oil to provide air conditioning. Meanwhile, their oil fields are declining in output, and their capacity to export is declining even faster.

Because many countries are jumping on the manufacturing band-wagon that I am trying to intellectually justify in this book, they have the resources to drive more cars further and faster and live in bigger houses further away from transit, driving up demand, particularly in China. It doesn't have to be this way—China is a dictatorship, and could, if it so chose, decide that cars have no long-term future and delink itself from the entire oil system.

But China, because it is a dictatorship, has a legitimacy problem, particularly since the crackdown on the democracy movement of Tianamen Square in 1989; apparently it's easier for them to go down the dead end of highways, cars, and dwindling oil supplies than to supply democracy to their country. This is a good example of preferring business-as-usual to planning for the future, even for a country that has a 2,000-year tradition of planning.

Of course, the Chinese government can use car driving as a support for their regime because so many people want to drive. China in 2009 overtook the United States in car sales, at 13.5 million, and experts think the sales will go even higher, as people use their new found wealth to tie themselves to a way of life that has no long-term future.[3]

When countries such as Iran attempt to reverse their economically suicidal gas subsidies, there are riots in the streets and the increases are canceled. I wonder what would happen if, before decreasing subsidies, these regimes installed world-class transit and train systems so that people would have an attractive alternative to cars; but again, that would take not only far-sighted planning, but also the willingness to try something new—moving a society dependent on cars, trucks, and planes toward one centered on electric trains.

Manufacturing would be hit hard by a rise in oil prices, too, but not because oil is used in the process of manufacturing. About 10 percent to 20 percent of oil is used as "feedstock" for the chemical industry, the output of which is used in just about every product, which then leads to predictions of doom when authors list all of the things that use oil. A bigger problem is that manufacturing has dispersed from befouling the center of cities to being spread out all over the country, and indeed, the world, enabling the rise of globalization. Moving factories closer to cities would not lead to the downfall of civilization. The Soviets moved all of their factories over the Ural Mountains to escape the Germans in World War II, so our advanced companies could surely move the machinery and even buildings to more central locations if they had to—after all, they have quite a bit of experience moving factories overseas.

More problematic is the case of agriculture, which has become very dependent on oil for the production of pesticides, and for running the huge machines used to prepare and harvest fields. Then there are the trucks now needed to transport our salad greens thousands of miles, for example. Oil has enabled the construction of a vast trading system called "globalization," but a globalization death watch might be in order. Eventually all of China's, and most everybody else's, trade advantages will be eaten away by the increased cost of running cargo container ships across large oceans. Jeff Rubin and Benjamin Tal wrote at the height of the oil price spike in 2008:

> Including inland costs, shipping a standard 40-foot container from Shanghai to the U.S. eastern seaboard now costs $8,000. In 2000, when oil prices were $20 per barrel, it cost only $3,000 to ship the same container. But at $200 per barrel, it will soon cost $15,000 in transport costs to ship from China to the U.S. eastern seaboard.[4]

Container cargo ships are what makes globalization possible, because they can transport such large quantities of output very inexpensively, due to the fact that each container is a standard size, and so the ports that load and unload the containers can use huge cranes that make the movement of goods much faster than before container ships and ports became dominant in the 1980s. Because all of the business strategies developed by the Walmarts and Dells of the world assume cheap container cargo ships can carry their goods from China and elsewhere, they will have to manufacture within rail distance of distribution centers when oil becomes expensive.

Air travel will be a luxury that only the rich can afford. According to Christopher Steiner, at $8 per gallon, flights under 350 miles will no longer be profitable, and at $12 per gallon, flights under 500 miles won't be.[5] Only large cities will rate as destinations. Car trips between cities will be too expensive. Without an electric rail network, long-distance travel within the large expanse of the United States will not be economically feasible, for the first time since before the railroads became a cohesive system, since at least the 1880s. The end of cheap oil will lead to a devolution of the U.S. economy, unless plans are developed and implemented soon.

The rest of the world will not be as hard hit as the United States. Europe's high-speed and regular rail network run mostly on electricity, and most towns and cities are compact enough that they could return to a nonautomobile-based existence without the massive disruptions that will take place in the United States. After all, they are already paying about $8 to $10 per gallon for gasoline.

The election of 2008 had two pivotal moments: most importantly, the financial crisis hit, which was itself partly caused by the spike in oil prices, which caused housing prices far from cities to plummet; and second, when John McCain's response to the price spike was "Drill, baby, drill," the Democrats had no good response; however, the "drill" argument was diminished by the crash in oil prices toward the end of the year. The last thing a politician can talk about, all over the world, is how gasoline prices are going to escalate forever. When I asked a New York state assemblyman why, when he was arguing for high-speed rail, he didn't talk about how gas prices will steadily increase, he basically replied, "No politician wants to make their constituents mad at them."

Laying down rail systems, relocating and/or constructing buildings, transforming agriculture and manufacturing—these would all take a decade or two, and trillions of dollars (see Chapters 9 through 11). Depending on how quickly oil production descends the other side of the bell curve, the people of the world, and particularly the United States, will have trouble feeding themselves; buying affordable goods; getting to work, the store, or anywhere else; and moving outside of one's immediate urban area.

Oil is not the only resource that can peak. Perhaps the biggest problem after oil is water and soil. The other fossil fuels, natural gas and coal, are just as depletable as oil, and just as critical at this point. In the United States, only about 10 percent of electricity is generated by oil, but about 50 percent comes from coal, with about one-third from natural gas. Natural gas is very difficult to transport if it's not moving inside a pipe, and the supply of natural gas in the United States has become problematic, although much gas has allegedly been found that can be reclaimed by exacerbating another resource problem, water. Coal has been hailed as being virtually inexhaustible, but it turns out that these pronouncements were based on inaccurate and old data. It is quite possible that coal production will peak within a few decades, not the centuries often portrayed,[6] in which case manufacturing would come to a screeching halt (assuming that not much progress has been made in renewable electricity by that point), buildings would mostly shut down, and civilization would regress back to before the Industrial Revolution, at best.

The reason for the real estate bubble, in addition to cheap oil, was the lack of places for investment because of the decline of manufacturing in the United States. The previous bubble, for the "new economy" Internet-based stocks, had been similar to many previous bubbles in that there was a certain amount of what Alan Greenspan, the former head of the Federal Reserve, called "irrational exuberance." Similar bubbles had been occurring in the United States since railroads first burst on the scene in the mid-19th century. But with these bubbles, at least there was a certain amount of production going on—the bubbles were part of the "froth" of real growth.

The mortgage bubble also resulted in building new homes, but most of what was built should not have been, and the price rise of all existing real estate did nothing to increase the real wealth of the country. A purely financial bubble, built on top of the creation of wealth that is worthless if oil is expensive, was popped by the upward spike of oil prices, caused by the first major consequence of peak oil, exacerbated by the lack of investment opportunities created by the decline of manufacturing in the United States.

GLOBAL WARMING

Unlike the situation with peak oil, no one is trying to hide the amount of carbon dioxide in the atmosphere or deny access to knowledge of how the oceans distribute heat. The problem is that the Earth's climate is extremely complex, probably as complex as anything people have ever attempted to model. Because the potential destruction of a breathable atmosphere would be a good thing to know about, one would think that billions and billions of dollars would be poured into modeling and measuring the atmosphere, but that is not the case.

Part of the problem is that some of the attitudes that have made science so successful, skepticism and the slow building of consensus, is getting in the way of sounding the alarms as loudly as they should be. Besides James Hansen, who is probably the single most important climate scientist and the one who first called Congress' attention to the problem, there are very few scientists who are telling the public things that it does not want to hear, such as that we must shut down all coal plants. But there may be an even deeper problem.

Scientists have a tendency to underestimate global warming. They are not used to dealing with positive feedback; the last scientific book that focused on the general phenomenon of positive feedback was published in 1986.[7] Positive feedback loops are very difficult to model because, when things are growing faster and faster, it's hard to predict what will happen next. When you have a system that calms down when things get messy, which is what happens in a negative feedback loop, it's much easier to model. Which, again, encourages scientists to look for things that aren't as messy as, say, climate change.

When the Intergovernmental Panel on Climate Change, or IPCC, submits their reports, they need the approval of every single government on the panel, which is almost every government in the world. The reports are therefore the least scary possible, because there are plenty of governments that are protecting their wealth generators like oil or coal, or simply not interested in dealing with inconvenient facts.

So it has been pretty common to see an article that begins with a statement like "Global warming indicators like [fill in the blank] are much worse than the most pessimistic predictions of the IPCC." Much of this underprediction has occurred because positive feedback loops have been underestimated. The most talked-about positive feedback loop is the "albedo effect," that is, the white snow and ice of the Arctic (and other cold places) bounces sunlight, and thus heat, back into space, but when the oceans warm up and melt the snow and ice, the oceans absorb more sunlight, and thus more heat, leading to yet more snow and ice melting, leading to more heat being absorbed, and before you know it, scientists are predicting that soon there will be no ice in the Arctic in summers.

But that is by far not the scariest positive feedback problem. Probably the scariest positive feedback loop—or second scariest, depending on what you think of the scenario after this one—is the thawing out of the frozen ground known as tundra, particularly in Siberia. There are massive amounts of methane trapped all around the world, and it will all come out, and is now starting to come out, as the temperature in the areas just below the Arctic warm up.[8] Methane is about 25 times more powerful as a greenhouse gas (GHG) than carbon dioxide, although it stays in the atmosphere a shorter period of time.

The really bad scenario is if the oceans warm up enough to release methane clathrates, another level entirely of methane release,[9] which could possibly lead to conditions as they were 55 million years ago, when there were an enormous amount of extinctions, almost as many as when the meteor hit that wiped out the dinosaurs. If this comes to pass, all of the ice in Antarctica will melt, and sea levels will be 300 feet above where they are now, meaning Chicago would have beachfront property—*ocean* beachfront property.

There are even more lurid possibilities, such as that something could tip the global biosphere into an event as bad as the Permian extinction, the worst extinction in Earth's history, which may have at least partially been caused by global warming. In the Permian Extinction, oceans became so warm that the oxygen disappeared, killing all life except anaerobic bacteria, which emitted clouds of sulfuric acid over the land-masses of the planet, killing most of the rest of life. We just don't know how bad it could get, and we're pouring carbon dioxide into the atmosphere at a very fast pace.

Even assuming we don't trigger this cataclysm, things could still get really bad. There are the heretofore mentioned rising of the seas; even if "just" Greenland or part of Antarctica melted, the seas would rise a good 20 to 30 feet, inundating much of our coasts and their associated cities. If the glaciers around the world melt, billions of people will lose water for much of the year. Glaciers are water storage units of the most massive kind. The ones in the Himalayas feed some of our largest rivers for much of the year, rivers such as the Yellow River in China, the Ganges in India, and the Mekong River in Southeast Asia.

Then there are the changes to weather patterns, which we can only dimly perceive, the most important being the droughts that could affect very important areas, such as the world's breadbasket, the American Great Plains. The American Southwest has always been prone to killer droughts that probably brought an end to at least one Native American civilization. The Colorado River provides water for much of the Southwest, and it would be in danger of drying up if weather patterns changed.

Nothing would be biblical in its proportions, though, if it didn't include some pestilence and disease, and when the temperature increases start marching toward the North and South poles—which they are doing—then so will pests and tropical diseases. It might be pretty difficult for the human race to come through in one piece.

Speaking of biblical, sometimes it seems like God (or Earth, depending on your spiritual proclivities), doesn't want to provide helpful warning signs of global warming; most evidence is showing up in some pretty remote areas. Only a handful of scientists have more than a passing knowledge of Arctic annual ice patterns, and it's not as if anything close to 1 percent of the Earth's population would notice if the Arctic never had ice. Tundra melting in Alaska has made for some pretty spectacular pictures of houses and forests leaning over, but unfortunately the plight of Eskimo peoples does not elicit enough outrage, and it takes the hardiest scientists to spend enough time in Siberia to figure out that methane is already starting to issue from the melting ice. Who would notice if methane was bubbling up from remote regions of the oceans? If the oceans rise and the droughts start, it will probably affect the poorest and most powerless first, as it probably has in the case of Darfur, and will in places like Bangladesh.

On top of all of this, several other factors are making support for climate mitigation policies more difficult to pass. Since there haven't been any obvious warning signs, such as Hurricane Katrina, hitting the United States recently, the public's proclivity to have a short attention span has led to a loss of interest in the subject. The advocacy of complex, obscure ideas such as cap-and-trade and carbon taxes, whatever their merits—and I will argue in Part 3 that a green transformation will do a better job—has only added to the complexity of the issue of global warming. Had the attention to scientific education not ended soon after the launch of the Sputnik satellite by the Soviets in 1959, the scientific complexity of the subject might not have been such a barrier to public support for constructive policies, but adding policy complexity to the mix has had, I think, unfortunate consequences.

So it will take some leaps of imagination and understanding and some soul-searching about people far away in time and/or space for people of the developed nations to really want to change their lifestyles, and perhaps worse, their configurations of power, to deal with bad climate change.

CONVENIENT FACTS ABOUT AN INCONVENIENT TRUTH

We can at least get a clear picture of the sources of global warming, the greenhouse gases, mostly carbon dioxide and methane. Greenhouse gases come from many sources.[10] As we shall see, they come from things that we don't want for a variety of reasons—coal and oil because of their deadly pollution and limited supply, deforestation because of the overall importance of forests, agriculture because we're going to need to save soil and water in the long run to grow food, and natural gas because it is becoming increasingly dirty and difficult to get at it.

Coal has probably been most in the public eye because of its emissions. All coal-fired power plants together are responsible for 18 percent of global greenhouse gases. Shutting down all coal-fired power plants would decrease greenhouse gas emissions by 18 percent—but that would still leave 82 percent, so even if we succeeded in shutting down all coal plants, we would still have a long way to go to a carbon-free society.

Surprisingly, the fossil fuels (coal, oil, and natural gas) used to provide heat for buildings and industry are responsible for 21 percent of greenhouse gas emissions—more than all the coal-fired power plants. So it is very important to concentrate on ways in which buildings can heat themselves.

Forests might be some of the cheapest of the "lowest hanging fruit" to save, since they account for almost 16 percent of emissions. But belching livestock are responsible for 4 percent of emissions. It might be easier to prevent the 5 percent of all emissions caused by the overuse of nitrogen-based fertilizers.

Before we get into details, however, let's take a stroll through the basics of greenhouse gas accounting. There are various ways to look at the sources of greenhouse gas emissions, depending on the problem in which you are interested. The variation comes from the fact that fossil fuels are used to generate electricity, which is used for buildings and industry, and fossil fuels are also used directly in buildings, industry, and transportation. So the amount of GHG emissions that fossil fuels emit are part of what the generation of electricity emits, and the emissions of fossil fuels are also what buildings or industry emit as a result of heating and other processes that don't have anything to do with electrical generation.

Let's start with my recalculation of a pie chart that the IPCC uses,[11] which separates electricity as a source of GHGs from each sector:

What Table 8.1 illustrates is that buildings emit 11 percent of GHGs *before considering the electricity they use*; industry, 22 percent. If we want to take the full account of GHG emissions for buildings and industry, integrating electricity into the buildings and industries, then we have to present a table that allocates electricity among

Table 8.1 Global Greenhouse Gas Emissions, with Electricity as a Separate
Category

Source	Carbon Dioxide Equivalent in Megatonnes	% of Total
Electricity	11,215	22.84
Buildings	5,515	11.23
Industry + Fossil Fuel Processing	10,851	22.09
Transportation	6,468	13.17
Agriculture	6,100	12.42
Deforestation	5,800	11.81
Other Forests	1,862	3.79
Waste Management	1,300	2.65
Total	49,000	100

buildings and industry, without showing the emissions for electricity
(see Table 8.2).

Notice that the last four entries didn't change at all when we integrated electricity into the calculations, because electricity doesn't
lead to emissions in those sectors. Those unelectric four I'll call *land
use* sources of emissions.

Now, let's say we want to know the responsibility of fossil fuels by
separating them out in the calculations (see Table 8.3). Notice how

Table 8.2 Global Greenhouse Gas Emissions with Electricity Integrated
into Buildings, Industry, and Transportation

Source	Carbon dioxide equivalent in Megatonnes	% of Total
Buildings	13,215	26.97
Industry	13,893	28.35
Transportation	6,829	13.94
Agriculture	6,100	12.42
Deforestation	5,800	11.81
Other forests	18.62	3.79
Waste Management	1,300	2.65

Abbreviation: CO_2, Carbon dioxide

buildings can be held responsible for 11 percent of total GHG emissions if electricity is separated out, up to 27 percent if electricity emissions are allotted to housing, and down to 4 percent if all fossil fuels are taken out (that last 4 percent is mostly gases from air conditioning). The decision about which to use depends on the question: What if we wanted to make all buildings zero emissions, that is, self-reliant for most energy needs and nonpolluting? Then we need to know that we would thereby eliminate 27 percent of GHGs. What would we be left with if all fossil fuels were replaced with carbon-free sources? We would still have the 4 percent left for buildings. And so on, for all sectors.

Greenhouse gases come in two basic flavors: carbon dioxide from fossil fuels, and emissions from land use—agriculture, forests, peat bogs, and waste management. Fossil fuels are primarily used for energy in three sectors: buildings, industry, and transportation. Transportation is almost entirely oil-based—according to the International Energy Association, about 0.1 percent of transportation energy currently comes from electricity.[12]

We use fossil fuels to make electricity to use in buildings and industry, *and* we use fossil fuels to make heat to use in buildings and industry.

Table 8.3 Global Greenhouse Gas Emissions, with Fossil Fuels Listed as Categories

Source	Carbon dioxide equivalent in Megatonnes	% of Total
Coal CO_2	10,600	21.63
Oil CO_2	10,200	20.82
Natural gas CO_2	5,300	10.82
Buildings	2,000	4.08
Industry	2,130	4.35
Agriculture	6,100	12.42
Deforestation	5,800	11.81
Other Forests	1,862	3.79
Waste Management	1,300	2.65
Methane from Fossil Fuel Processing	3,071	6.27
Transportation non-CO_2	636	1.30

Abbreviation: CO_2, Carbon dioxide

At 28 percent of all GHGs, industry is the single largest source of emissions. However, there is so much variation in manufacturing and construction—and the data are so hard to collect—that an exact allocation is difficult. The relevant part of the IPCC "Working Group III Industry Report" states:

> Iron and steel, non-ferrous metals, chemicals, petroleum refining, minerals (cement, lime, and glass), and pulp and paper . . . (ex-petroleum refining) . . . accounted for 72% of industrial final energy use in 2003. With petroleum refining, the total is about 85%.[13]

Concrete is the only industry that seems to produce a major amount of carbon dioxide that does not come from fossil fuels. Steel and aluminum constitute about 4 percent of emissions, but this gives some cause for hope: to produce recycled steel—from scrap—uses only about 40 percent of the energy that making steel from iron requires. And scrap is a bigger and bigger part of global steel production. Recycled aluminum uses only 5 percent of the energy of "virgin" aluminum. In other words, recycling can drastically decrease industrial emissions (see Table 8.4 for industry).

Table 8.4 Global Industrial Greenhouse Gas Emissions

Source	Carbon dioxide equivalent in Megatonnes	% of Total
Fertilizer (Ammonia)	500	1.02
Ethylene	180	0.37
Chlorine	78	0.16
Other Chemicals	4,455	9.09
Concrete	1,650	3.37
Petroleum Refining	1,508	3.08
Steel	1,550	3.16
Aluminum	526	1.07
Glass, Ceramics	445	0.91
Paper	400	0.82
Other	2,601	5.31
Total Industry CO_2	11,600	28.35

Abbreviation: CO_2, Carbon dioxide

We know the general categories of energy use in residential and commercial buildings, but the percentages of such usages vary considerably around the world, making it very difficult to determine exact breakdowns. In Table 8.5, electricity is used for appliances, some heating, refrigeration, and cooling; heat of all sorts is used for space heating, cooking, and water-heating.

To bring these emissions down, we'll not only need to use carbon-free electricity—and to do more heating from such electricity—but we will also have to decrease the *need* for electricity by making buildings better able to retain heat and cold. It will be necessary to try to use as much solar heating and ground-source heat pumps as possible.

As far as transportation goes, we'll have to find a way to convert transportation from virtually complete dependence on oil to almost complete dependence on electricity. The current figures are shown in Table 8.6.

However, just as decreasing industrial emissions should come from decreasing the *need* for energy, so too transportation emissions should diminish as a result of changing the structure of our living patterns. The denser we can make our residential, commercial, and industrial buildings, and the more we can mix those various functions in a smart way, the less energy will be required for transportation. Electrified trains will be the most efficient way to move people and freight.

Agricultural GHGs are most notable for what is missing in the data: carbon dioxide emissions. Virtually all of the emissions from agriculture come from methane and nitrous oxide because the IPCC assumes that the carbon lost from agriculture is balanced almost exactly by the carbon sequestered in agricultural lands. But what if agricultural regions weren't being degraded by modern agricultural

Table 8.5 Global Greenhouse Gas Emissions from Buildings

Source	Carbon dioxide equivalent in Megatonnes	% of Total
Electricity CO_2	7,145	14.58
Heat CO_2	4,071	8.31
Cooling Non-CO_2	1,500	3.06
Heating Non-CO_2	500	1.02
Total Buildings	11,600	28.35

Abbreviation: CO_2, Carbon dioxide

Table 8.6 Global Greenhouse Gas Emissions from Transportation

Source	Carbon dioxide equivalent in Megatonnes	% of Total
Cars, SUVs, Light Trucks	3,039	6.2
2 wheelers	109	0.22
Heavy and Medium Trucks	1,707	3.49
Air	792	1.62
Shipping	649	1.32
Buses	423	0.86
Rail	102	0.21
Total Transportation	6,829	13.94

Abbreviation: SUV, sport utility vehicle

techniques? According to the IPCC agricultural report,[14] by 2030, 6,000 megatons of carbon dioxide emissions are preventable provided the soils of the world are built up instead of worn down. That would take care of over 10% of the current 49 megatons total of carbon dioxide equivalents. But sticking to methane and nitrous oxide, Table 8.7 has the breakdown for agriculture.

Organic agriculture could easily remove excess nitrogen from fertilizer. But as far as I can tell, there's no good way to remove methane emissions from livestock belching (and some gas passing), although there is some evidence that factory farms increase belching. So does this mean that a lifestyle change would be necessary? Could we eat much less meat? Or, eat mostly fish? The latter would mean

Table 8.7 Global Greenhouse Gas Emissions from Agriculture

Source	Carbon dioxide equivalent in Megatonnes	% of Total
Excess Nitrogen from Fertilizers	2,318	4.37
Methane from Livestock Belching and Gas	1,952	3.98
Biomass Burning	732	1.49
Rice Production	671	1.37
Livestock Manure	427	0.87
Total Agriculture	6,100	12.45

that to solve the problem of too much livestock, we'll have to pro-tect the oceans. By saving the ocean's fisheries we could indirectly prevent the worst impacts of climate change.

The worst effects of livestock and agriculture may actually be their effects on the world's forests. According to the IPCC, the amount of emissions from forests is the most difficult to estimate. We also don't know how much can be attributed to livestock, agricultural clearing, or logging for timber. Table 8.8 presents the loss in forests, by area of the world.

Finally, it turns out that waste management contributes almost 3 percent of GHGs—mostly methane from garbage landfills. Again, recycling could eliminate the need for most landfills.

Even without global warming, our energy, transportation, agricul-ture, and forestry systems are unsustainable. Fossil fuels will eventually become too expensive to use, our agricultural systems destroy the soil, water, and other ecological systems on which they are dependent, and the planet cannot survive without its forests. With the threat of global warming, the need for a transformation of our civilization has never been more necessary.

MIXING PEAK OIL AND GLOBAL WARMING

The interaction between the problems of global warming and peak oil could yield benefits as well as worsening problems. There are two main interactions.

First, there is a set of shared solutions to both global warming and peak oil. If the transportation system was powered by electricity, and if that electricity was generated from wind and solar, then there

Table 8.8 Global Carbon Dioxide Loss from Forests

Source	CO_2 Carbon Stock, 2000–2005	% of Total Forests
South America	−12,833	51.47
Asia	−11,000	44.12
Africa	−5,134	20.59
Rest of World	4,035	−16.18
Global Total of Forest Loss	−24,392	100

Abbreviation: CO_2, Carbon dioxide

would be significantly less GHG emissions, and the need for oil, coal, and natural gas would plummet.

Secondly, however, there is also a set of solutions that could temporarily improve the fuel situation while exacerbating the global warming problem. This would involve, first, using coal to make gasoline, which releases even more carbon dioxide into the atmosphere than oil-derived gasoline; second, the use of tar sands, such as are found in Canada and Venezuela, which are horribly destructive environmentally and waste an enormous amount of water, while at the same time doubling carbon dioxide emissions; and third, biofuels, which, unless they are carefully controlled, can destroy or use much of our agricultural areas. For instance, the growth in the planting of oil palm in Indonesia has led to the burning of vast fields of peat, which releases so many GHGs that Indonesia is now the third biggest emitter, after China and the United States.

In other words, if the first path is not pursued, and both problems are solved at once, then the second path, which will not solve either problem, will be embarked on, in a more and more hysterical tone, leading quite conceivably to societal breakdown and wars for the little remaining oil that is left.

Ironically, the existence of most oil in the world is due to a period of global warming tens of millions of years ago that produced enormous algae blooms in the oceans, that were then pushed together by the movement of the continents. The resulting organic brew was then cooked by the pressure of the Earth's geothermal energy. One of the reasons that people become too enthusiastic about biofuels is because they think that the main energy source of oil is the organic material, the ancient algae, which stored the ancient sunlight. But that is not the main reason that oil is so useful; the main reason is that the organic material has been cooked and processed by the Earth, into a chemically perfect form. If we try to recreate the organic material, we will lose most of the energy we could gain because growing the bio-material, harvesting it over large areas, processing it, and then transporting it over long distances will use more energy than it creates.

ECOSYSTEM DESTRUCTION

Human beings have been busy destroying the foundations of their economic systems for millennia, and right now we are doing it for much the same reason as we have always done it: to grow food and build towns and cities.

There are two main foundations for life on the planet: the oceans and soil. We are in the process of destroying the life-generating properties of both. At the rate we're going, the oceans[15] and land will functionally turn into deserts. Global warming will exacerbate the problem, because the basic direction of temperatures will be to increase; the destruction of ecosystems exacerbates the problem of global warming, because deserts tend to warm up the atmosphere.

The basic problem in the oceans, and for life in freshwater ecosystems such as lakes and rivers, is overfishing, that is, overexploitation of living things that need a certain minimal population to reproduce. For the most part, fish and other seafood are not "grown," as agricultural products are, they are simply taken. Ideally, they would be taken in a sustainable way, as Marine Stewardship Council-certified fish and seafood are. At the very least, areas of the oceans designated as hatcheries, that is, areas where large numbers of fish spawn, would be protected. If they are not, whole species can disappear, as appears to be happening to tuna and other widely eaten fish.

Farming fish may not be an answer either, except for freshwater fish that are sustainably farmed in lakes, such as tilapia and catfish, which can also be fed plant products. Fish such as salmon that are farmed are often fed ground-up seafood, thus doing nothing to stop the overexploitation problem.

Using freshwater farmed fish and sustainably caught fish from oceans could actually indirectly help with the global warming problem if it enabled people to stop eating cows and pigs, which generate over 10 percent of GHGs because of belching, passing gas, and pooping, in addition to livestock-induced deforestation. But fish can't replace mammal products if there are no fish.

Rivers and lakes have long been threatened and killed by pollution, for instance, by the acid rain emitted, mainly by coal plants but also by factories. Overfertilization in agriculture leads to run-offs of nitrogen into rivers and even oceans, leading to huge blooms of algae that destroy life. Unfortunately for petroleum-users, it would take millions of years for those algae blooms to turn into oil deposits.

On land, agriculture, livestock grazing, and town and city building, along with industrial pollution, have destroyed ecosystems for millennia.[16] The rate of destruction has been increasing in the last century,[17] and business-as-usual will lead to collapse in the future.[18]

Forests, in particular, have been destroyed; some forest soils can easily disappear once the forests are gone, such as in the Amazon. Much of South America might become a desert without the Amazon. Grasslands can also turn into desert, particularly if they are close to an already existing one, because animals, particularly sheep, eat too much of the grasses. The soil is swept away, leading to desert conditions.

Agriculture, which generally takes place in former grassland or former forest, can also lead to soil being swept away by winds or rain, particularly if, as is often the case, people want to maximize the amount of land planted and farm on hillsides. Without the trees that have been logged to make way for the farmland, water and wind make the hillsides barren.[19]

Irrigation can spell the death-knell for soil. Too much water applied to land can bring salt to the surface, which ruins its ability to grow life; or else irrigation can use up underground reservoirs (called aquifers), and the farmland dependent on those aquifers then dries up and blows away. Cities, and particularly sparse suburbs, have been burying ecosystems and farmland at an accelerating rate.[20]

Global warming will interact with ecosystem destruction, mostly by taking rain away from areas that need it, but in some areas, too much rain will sweep away soils as well. Rising seas will, of course, inundate land, but can also ruin underground aquifers by seeping salt water into them.

Ecosystem destruction leads to species extinction. Ecosystems are themselves composed of various smaller ecosystems, some as small as a flower, which might contain water, spiders, and other creatures. As large ecosystems, such as forests, are decimated, there may be a minimal size below which the ecosystem, and the populations of the creatures that live there, completely collapse.

The economic benefit of having millions of different kinds of plants and animals is one of those long-term problems that it seems people are not good at solving. People are not going to forgo the gains from, say, cutting down a part of the Amazon to grow soybeans, because maybe there is a plant in that area that could eventually be used to cure a disease. People are powerfully attracted to zoos, but this doesn't seem to translate into enough support for saving rainforests and ocean hatcheries as one might hope. I think that the task of saving forests, grasslands, oceans, and even some deserts that are under siege will depend to a great extent on a shift to the cultural and spiritual ideas of the peoples, often called indigenous peoples, who have survived from the time before agriculture.

It would probably be helpful if these crises gradually ramped up in severity, with a certain pattern that people could understand, but it's unlikely that nature will be so kind, especially since there are so many positive feedback loops in operation. So it is likely that there will be a fairly small window—hopefully, of a decade or so—when the ecological tsunami is hitting, but society is still organized enough to understand and rise up to the challenge of the various catastrophes then unfolding. If that is the case, then it is imperative that there be a set of proposals floating around in global intellectual space that people can grab onto and implement, or else fear and loathing will subsume all other emotions.

CONCLUSION

There is a contradiction built right into human history—those civilizations and nations that achieve dominance through their technological mastery of the environment lead to their own collapse by destroying that environment; however, the civilizations and nations that can sustainably manage their environments have not had the technological mastery that they needed to defend themselves from the first group. This second group, indigenous peoples, hold certain cultural and ecological knowledge that the first group, the technological masters, must adopt or our global civilization will perish.

For hundreds of years, manufacturing competence has been the cause of the rise and decline of nations and empires. Environmental catastrophes have been postponed by the growth of manufacturing and its attendant characteristic, expanding agriculture. Now, the looming crises are global; nations will have to come together worldwide and cooperate to prevent the worst of the problems I have described above.

How can we reconfigure civilization to be sustainable, not destructive of its capital? To that task, we now turn.

PART THREE

A DESIGN FOR A GREEN TRANSFORMATION

The bad news is that if we continue with business-as-usual, we will warm up the planet, run out of oil, destroy ecosystems, and in the case of the United States, lose the middle class. The good news is that the technology and social systems exist to create a society that can avoid all or most of these problems. In fact, the solutions, like the problems, are all interconnected. Just as we can model reality as various systems to more clearly understand complexity, we can divide the solutions into four main categories: transportation, energy, cities, and government.

Chapter 9 lays out the case for a transportation system that is based on electricity. Such a system would replace much of the use of cars, trucks, and planes with electric trains of various kinds: a high-speed Interstate Rail System, regular rail from towns and suburbs to cities, and subways and light rail within cities. Some all-electric cars would be used. The use of oil could be virtually eliminated, thus avoiding the problem of the end of the era of cheap oil.

To use electricity sustainably for transportation, energy will have to be generated from free energy sources, that is, wind, solar, geothermal, and water, as Chapter 10 explains. An Interstate Wind System, with an Interstate Smart Transmission System, could provide the backbone for a renewable system. Besides transportation, buildings are the other big consumer of energy. They can become more energy self-reliant, particularly for their heating and cooling, and partly with electricity from solar photovoltaic panels. These changes will eliminate much of the sources of global warming and ecosystem destruction.

The way that buildings are placed in relation to one another, that is, the way cities, towns and suburbs are laid out, will determine if the transportation system can be electrified and if we can be efficient with energy. Chapter 11 shows how trains and all-electric cars will only be practical if there is enough density in urban areas; trains need a minimum number of people traveling on them to justify their use; and all-electric cars need to be based in homes that are close to town centers to justify *their* use.

All three chapters will show how manufacturing can be rebuilt by rebuilding various parts of the infrastructure, whether for train systems, wind networks, solar panels, or buildings. The coordination of this massive undertaking will have to be directed and financed by the government, as Chapter 12 explains, because the market is not up to such a large task. The important question then becomes, How do we make sure that government is controlled by the citizens and not by the chief executive officers of the most powerful corporations? How do we make the economy more democratic, both at the level of the individual business and for society as a whole?

CHAPTER 9
Making Transportation Sustainable

All of the niches of the economy fit together. The niches can create a system that will lead to the economy's collapse, or they can fit together in such a way that a sustainable economy is possible. Despite modern social science's obsession with stability, the recommendations emanating from the field of economics in particular will lead to extreme volatility and then collapse; only by understanding that the economy is an ecosystem that is driven by positive feedback loops can we create a society that is stable.

Everything affects everything else; this is the perspective of a systems-centered understanding of the world. However, we don't need to understand how everything about the constituent parts work before we can figure out how the system as a whole works. Because there simply isn't enough time, we create simplified models of reality in an attempt to deal with complexity.

THE BASIC INFRASTRUCTURE

If we divide society into a set of functional niches, we can look deeply into the various niches to more fully understand the underlying dynamics, without getting lost in complexity. Let's say that we consider the following categories of niches: transportation, energy, urban structure, manufacturing, agriculture, resource use, health and education, finance, and all other goods and services. If one agrees that manufacturing is at the center of the economy, then there are two main groupings here: manufacturing and everything else. Manufacturing creates the means by which all the other sectors exist.

We can then group transportation, energy, and urban structure together, and focus on how those three systems are interconnected. Agriculture and resource use can be considered as subsystems of urban structure. Because in our current civilization petroleum is a part of the energy system, then the social choice to base the transportation system on the internal combustion engine becomes possible. Petroleum plus the internal combustion engine enables an urban structure that can be spread out very sparsely because of the existence of cars and trucks.

Note that the existence of a natural resource, oil, enables the widespread use of a particular technology, in this case internal combustion engines; it does not make that choice necessary. Society chooses to take a certain path according to its wishes; that choice is a combination of what individuals choose through the market, what government enables by building infrastructure and otherwise structuring the economy, and how private companies influence both governments and individuals.

Agriculture has been profoundly affected by the choices of petroleum, internal combustion engines, and sprawl. Modern agriculture is dependent on tractors and other forms of agricultural machinery that use petroleum, on pesticides derived from oil, on fertilizers derived from natural gas, and on trucks to carry everything anyplace. A significant amount of resources have gone into finding and mining oil, and oil itself is being used up. The financial system, as in the case of the banks established by Rockefeller, for example, was to a considerable extent built on petroleum. The health system is affected by the annual death tolls on the roads and the lack of walking. We can understand quite a bit about the structure of the civilization if we concentrate on just transportation, energy, and urban structure. Let's call these three niches together the *basic infrastructure*.

The current basic infrastructure of the civilization is unstable and will lead to civilizational collapse. Because fossil fuels are nonrenewable, the characteristics of the basic infrastructure will self-destruct, and because other sectors depend on fossil fuels as well, the basic infrastructure will contribute to the collapse of the rest of society. The basic infrastructure is a major contributor to global warming, although certainly not the only one (agriculture, resource use, and manufacturing being the other main ones).

The basic infrastructure also undermines ecosystems, mostly because sprawl destroys them. Agriculture also destroys ecosystems and leads to deforestation (as does sprawl), while manufacturing pollution and the lack of recycling of resources are also critical factors.

On the other hand, a system that relies on indefinitely renewable sources of energy for generating electricity, relies on various forms of electricity-using trains for transportation, and places its energy-efficient, large buildings close together is a basic infrastructure that can be indefinitely sustainable, if the agricultural system does not destroy ecosystems and if the manufacturing and resource sectors are based on recycling. In this chapter, I will assume that the energy for a sustainable economy comes in the form of renewable electricity, and that the buildings and people in cities, towns, and suburbs are close enough together to justify the construction and use of electrified trains.

THE RISE OF TRAINS

The first major transportational technology of the Industrial Revolution was the train. Trains became possible because the technologies of making iron had vastly improved. But they were also made possible because of an energy-converting breakthrough, steam engines powered by coal. Because of the state of the art of machine tools, steam engines had to be fairly large, so that only something as big as a train could use them; steam engines were never really small enough to use in individual transportation, that is, the automobile.

When Daimler invented the internal combustion engine, he used peanut oil to create an explosion from within the engine, which pushed the piston. But for this to happen, he also needed steel instead of iron, because steel is lighter and stronger than iron, and he also needed better machine tools to create the holes and impressions that make an internal combustion engine possible.

By the time mass production of internal combustion engines became possible, cities and towns were adapted to the train—which wasn't that much different from the basic plan of cities for thousands of years. For most of history (which is the history of cities), cities had been compact enough that they were walkable, because the only other technology of transportation was horses. Trains tied together these walkable cities and towns, so that it was not necessary to take a slow horse trip between cities.

Trains also made it possible to begin to build suburbs, that is, towns that were accessible enough to the city that people could live outside of the city but still go into the city every day, mostly for work. Even today, there are dozens of towns outside of older cities such as New York City and Chicago that are serviced by commuter rail, which were originally steam-powered trains.

However, as electricity generation became more widespread, intra-city trains, or trolleys and subways, became possible, fed by overhead wires on the street or by a third electrified rail underground. This enabled the city itself to expand beyond simply what was walkable; the "outer" boroughs of the Bronx, Brooklyn, and Queens became more residential than before, sending their residents to work in Manhattan.[1]

This combination of coal and hydropower-generated electricity, plus coal-generated steam engines, in combination with dense but growing cities, provided the foundation for a sustainable basic infra-structure. A renewable way had to be found to generate electricity, the subject of Chapter 10.

By the 1930s at least, trains could move across the United States at 100 mph. There was an almost unbroken string of trolleys all the way from New York City to Chicago. The same was true in Europe. Trains were also the primary means of moving freight, which was, and continues to be, extremely efficient. The siting of agriculture in the fertile middle of the country was made possible by trains.

Rail lines were generally monopolistic in nature, because it is very inefficient to lay more than one rail between two destinations. Be-cause rail lines were private, the rail companies would do what any firm will do if it can get away with it, and virtually enslaved anyone completely dependent on it. In particular, the farmer class, which was disorganized and usually of modest means, was exploited. The consequence was one of the biggest progressive movements in U.S. history, usually described under the general umbrella of the "Popu-list" movement of the late 1800s.

According to Alfred Chandler,[2] train companies were the first truly modern corporations, because they had to create a level of coordi-nation and control that no other company, or even government, had ever attempted. But because train transportation is inherently monopolistic, the train companies become larger and larger, gener-ally monopolizing a particular region—somewhat like the phone and cable companies of today—which really means that the govern-ment could just as well have run the railroads, even in the 19th century, which might have prevented some of the depressions that followed in the wake of speculative bubbles.

It might also have led to a national rail system that did not go into decline and fall apart, the way the American system did—including tearing down the old Penn Station, one of the great tragedies of New York City life, as anyone who has had to endure the basement-like conditions of the current Penn Station can attest. In the 19th and for much of the 20th century, however, the government did not have the financial resources to run the rail system, and only began to think in terms of large-scale capital investments in the 1930s and then most decisively during World War II.

Alfred Chandler spends a good part of his groundbreaking book, *The Visible Hand*, tracing the development of the railways, because transportation is such an essential part of an economy. The ease of water transportation has often given cities that are next to heavily used waterways a big advantage: New York City's harbor has been called the best in the world, and the maritime nations, such as England, Holland, and Japan, were often in the forefront of commercial development. Ancient Rome built itself partly on its road system, which served both to bring agricultural and other goods into the center but also to allow troops to move out. Before rails, the biggest transportational infrastructural systems had been canals, for instance, in Imperial China, or in the antebellum United States. By World War I, the United States had the makings of a very efficient transportation system, with centralized cities, compact towns, manufacturing close to the city or actually right in the city, and agricultural deliveries centralized on rail networks.

DESIGNING A RAIL-CENTERED SOCIETY

The most efficient structure of a transportation system is as a hub-and-spoke system. That is, you have a central point, and all other points go through that central point, instead of being able to travel from any point to any other point. This is because you can achieve economies of scale, that is, you can create a transportation system in which the most people or freight can be carried for the least expenditure per distance traveled. In the spread-out system that we now have, usually only one person travels in a car, and so an entire vehicle must be outfitted, with an engine, while one train can easily move 1,000 passengers with one engine. Although that engine is obviously bigger and costlier than a car engine, it also needs much less maintenance per passenger.

The airlines have adopted a hub-and-spoke system, which is much easier to coordinate, although their systems are so centralized that it is very inefficient in terms of energy use. The United States could be restructured on a hub-and-spoke system, composed of, say, 30 major cities, with the rest of the towns surrounding the central city connected by what is now called commuter rail, that is, an electrified rail line into and out of the city. It might also be possible to run some rail lines, perhaps light rail, in circles outward from the city, so that it would be possible to move among suburbs without having to go into the city first. A hub-and-spoke-with-circles system would only work if the suburbs and towns surrounding the city had a dense city center that contained the main train station.

The most efficient economy-of-scale transportation equipment is rail, because steel wheels rolling on steel track generates much less friction than rubber on road—and uses less energy than airplanes, which need a huge amount of energy to get airborne, and slightly less to stay aloft.

Freight trains are currently about four times more efficient in the use of fuel than trucks, and freight trains have doubled their fuel efficiency since 1980. They emit about 75 percent less greenhouse gases than trucks—and that's using diesel fuel.[3] Transportation expert Alan Drake estimates that electrifying the freight rail system would cut the amount of energy needed (in British thermal units [BTUs]) in three[4]; that is, an electrified freight train system is at least 12 times more energy efficient than a truck-diesel-based system. Drake further estimates that the electricity required to put all intercity truck freight and current diesel-based train freight on electric freight trains would require about 25% of current national electrical output. If that electricity was generated from renewable sources, then such a system would emit no greenhouse gases during its operation, and if manufactured in a zero-carbon manner, would be completely greenhouse-gas free.

A piece of transportation equipment that is powered by electricity is much more efficient than one that is powered by an internal combustion engine, as are cars and trucks. In an electric system, the motors are located right next to the wheels, while in an internal combustion system, the motor has to transmit the energy through the drive shaft, that is, a rigid piece of steel that is turned by the power of the engine, and that in turn turns the wheels. This system is quite similar to the pre-electric factory, in which a steam engine drove a shaft that drove rubber and leather loops that spun something on the factory machinery. The introduction of electricity into the factory was a great boost for factory productivity because it allowed for a much easier way to control the speed at which different parts of the machinery would move.

So ideally, a transportation system would have a centralized, highly dense core, with outlying factories and farms and dense suburbs ringing it, served by large, electric trains. This would be the most efficient system, and would require reorganizing the spatial placement of our buildings and activities within a city. In other words, it would require changing the urban structure of our society.

We can get an idea of the minimal amount of electricity that might be needed for travel by looking at New York City (NYC), where much of the population uses subways almost exclusively. The NYC subway system uses about 1.8 Twhrs of electricity per year,[5] out of a total of 4,119 Twhrs used in the United States for all electrical needs in 2008.[6] New York City has about 8 million people; even if we increased subway service (and included, say, some light rail and rapid bus transit) by more than five times in NYC, with more service and more subway lines, thereby eliminating the need for any cars in the city at all, this would still only increase the electricity requirements for transportation in NYC to about 10 Twhrs of electricity per year. If we covered the needs of, say, 240 million people in this way, that would be 30 times the 10 Twhrs needed for NYC, and thus would be about 300 Twhrs; even if we increased this by 33 percent, 400 Twhrs are still only 10 percent of all electrical use for one year in the United States.

I am not advocating forcing everyone into a Manhattan-type living situation. I am simply pointing out that, judging from our best evidence, it would be theoretically possible to fulfill the intra-urban region transportation needs of the U.S. population very efficiently, in terms of energy, if living arrangements were densely structured and well-designed subway and light rail systems were built.

Even Manhattan could probably be more efficiently structured if roads were set up to encourage bicycle riding, including some human-powered vehicles that could carry some freight. But it is the trips taken by walking that probably account for the greatest

efficiencies in urban living, including NYC, because walking eliminates the need to use vehicles. Before 1920, cities were heading toward a sustainable basic infrastructure, much like NYC.

Then came the automobile.

THE AGE OF THE AUTOMOBILE

Many, if not most, animals value speed and power for their
obvious evolutionary advantages of conferring on the most powerful
and fastest animals the ability to either avoid being eaten or catching
more prey. The flip side of more speed and power, though, is that
more resources are needed to feed this large and fast machine; that
is why most animals are pretty small.

The automobile is like a large prosthetic device that confers on its
owner greater power and speed. However, it too needs more resources; in other words, it is much less efficient than the technology
it replaced, trains and walking. The bicycle, which immediately
preceded the automobile and was responsible in the course of its development for many of the technological advances that made the
automobile possible, is the most efficient land-based technological
device developed by human beings, because they weigh only a fraction
of the person who rides them, while cars, trains, and other equipment
weigh much more than the people they carry.

Automobiles are inherently risky and dangerous, as the statistics
bear out—over 37,000 people are killed per year in the U.S. alone.[7]
For the U.S., that's almost an entire Vietnam War of deaths every
year; or at over 3,000 people per month, a World Trade Center
attack every month; at over 100 per day, a big plane going down every two days. Yet the lure of power, speed, and control of one's
means of transportation has made this public health disaster seem
like a necessary part of our life.

According to the National Highway Safety Administration,

In 2005, motor vehicle traffic crashes were the leading cause of
death for every age 3 through 6 and 8 through 34. Because of
the young lives consumed, motor vehicle traffic crashes ranked
third overall in terms of the years of life lost, i.e., the number of
remaining years that the person is expected to live had they not
died, behind only cancer and diseases of the heart.[8]

According to another report, the total cost of automobile crashes in 2000 was $230 billion, including $32 billion in medical bills.[9]

Besides overloading the health system, the automobile encouraged a complete change in the urban structure, that is, the urban structure has changed from an efficient hub-and-spoke model, in which compact cities and towns were linked together by an efficient rail line, to a sprawled-out system, which still contains a central city business district, but in which there is no structure to speak of in the rest of each urban system.

The entire U.S. road network is now worth over $2.6 trillion, and the consumer automobile fleet is worth about $1.4 trillion.[10] It would take $4 trillion to replace the entire road and car system (there are 4 million miles of roads, 3 million of which are "rural"). All of these roads have to be paved with asphalt, made from oil. Trucks seem to be worth about $700 billion. Railroad equipment is only worth a little over $300 billion now, but exactly because rail is so efficient, we have an overcapacity of transportation equipment factories. If most transportation occurred by rail, the trains could be produced in a fraction of the factories that now make cars. Vehicles, including cars, are not being used 96 percent of the time.[11] If factory equipment was not being used as much as cars are not being used, most economies would implode, because the factories would not create enough output to justify the cost of the equipment. But because people are so committed to the automobile, this socially expensive technology continues.

The only thing more inefficient than a parked car is a car that is being used. Oil is very explosive, very easy to control, and very easy to transport. On the other hand, internal combustion engines are very inefficient. If you are driving a one-ton car—which is quite small (a sport utility vehicle [SUV] by law, to get a tax write-off, has to be over 6,000 pounds, or three tons)—if a person weighs 200 pounds, then about 90 percent of the energy that the oil and internal combustion engine is carrying is just to push the car, not to carry the person. The internal combustion engine only has, at best, 25 percent efficiency. This means that about 75 percent of the energy produced in a car engine is completely wasted in the form of heat. A person is only using about 2 percent or 3 percent of the energy of the oil to move him- or herself. Amory Lovins actually estimates that the number is less than 1 percent[12]—it depends on the size of the car and how many people are being moved.

Besides the roads that take up at least 20 percent of the land area of cities, parking seems to take up in the vicinity of 12 percent,[13] although the data are not particularly good. Let's conservatively assume that one-third of cities are taken up with roads and parking. Parking is by definition storage of a piece of machinery. Because the storage facilities for rail equipment is trivial, and subways and elevated trains account for virtually no surface space used in cities, this represents a huge waste of land within cities, which thrive because of the density and compactness, which leads to the innovation and wealth-generating qualities of proximity.

Cars are very wasteful of human life, space, production capacity, and energy. An enormous amount of the production potential of society goes into maintaining a car-based system. The resources needed to maintain this system will go through the roof when the price of oil does.

WHERE DOES ALL THE OIL GO?

As we can see in Table 9.1, 47 percent of petroleum dollars in the United States are spent on gasoline for automobiles, 10 percent for trucks, almost 6 percent for government vehicles, and about 5 percent for planes. We should also add the 2 percent used for paving; that means that 70 percent of petroleum is used for transportation, and because 5 percent of oil is used in the refinery process, we could add a few more percent to the percentage of oil that transportation uses. Including shipping, three-quarters of petroleum use is for cars, trucks, planes, and ships. Most of the rest is for raw materials (feedstocks) for the chemical industry, with some oil in this country still being used for heating and generating electricity; there are also a few more percent used for agricultural machinery, mining machinery, and military equipment.

In other words, cars use about half of our petroleum. Let's say that electric cars could replace the 3 trillion vehicle miles traveled in a typical year,[14] and let's say that the average miles per kilowatt for an electric car would be about one-third of a kilowatt hour (kwhrs) per mile, meaning we would need 1,000 billion kwhrs—assuming electric cars could go the long distances that people use cars for now, which electric cars cannot currently do. But compare 1,000 billion kwhrs with the 400 needed for an augmented NYC-style efficient

Table 9.1 Oil Use by Category, Dollar Value, and Volume

Oil Consumption (by dollar)	Percent Total (%)	Oil Consumption (by volume)	Percent Total (%)
Personal Transport	46.80	Cars (includes SUVs, Minivans, Pickups)	40.70
Government Transport	3.58	Recreational Vehicles	1.00
Trucks	9.41	Trucks (> 8500 lbs)	12.70
Transit, Sightseeing	2.09		
School Buses	2.46		
Chemicals	3.00	Raw Material for Plastics, Chemicals, etc.	10.30
Air Transport	4.33	Passenger Air Travel	6.70
		Air Freight	1.10
Manufacturing	1.52	Process Heat for Factories	5.00
Waste Management	0.89		
Services	3.73	Heat + hot water for homes, offices, stores	4.90
Home Heating	4.03		
Petroleum Refineries	5.00	Energy to Run Oil Refineries	3.03
Pipelines	1.35		
Asphalt, Machinery Lubrification etc.	1.89	Road Pavement	2.80
Water Transport	0.27	Waterborne Freight	2.50
Agriculture	2.19	Agriculture (Drying Crops, Farm Machinery, etc)	2.20
Power & supply	1.48	Electricity generation	1.60
Construction	3.09	Construction Machinery	1.60
Mining	1.02		
Military	0.80	Military (mostly jets)	1.50
Rail	0.48	Rail Freight	1.20
Total	99.40	Total	99.13

Sources: For oil by dollar value, Bureau of Economic Analysis, Department of Commerce, Benchmark Input-Output Accounts, 1997, Standard Make and Use Tables at the detailed level, http://www.bea.gov/industry/io_benchmark.htm#1997data.
For oil by volume: Charles Komanoff, *Ending the Oil Age: A Plan to Kick the Saudi Habit.* New York: Komanoff Energy Associates, 2002, 8. Available at http://www.right ofway.org/research/newoilage.pdf.

subway system—and we know the technology definitely exists for subways. Many people are now touting the benefits of plug-in hybrids, that is, cars that use both gasoline and electricity. But this could simply lead to what is called Jevon's Paradox,[15] that is, sometimes making something more efficient actually increases its use. A plug-in hybrid will make it cheaper to travel great distances because the first 30 to 50 miles will use electricity, which will be much cheaper. After that, the gasoline engine will kick-in, which will be just as expensive as any all-gasoline car. If everyone has a plug-in hybrid, they could do the right thing and simply drive the same number of miles as they have always driven, thereby drastically cutting back on gasoline. Or, they could do the not-right thing and drive even more, perhaps giving another boost to living 100 miles from work, as happened in the 1990s when an equivalent phenomenon took place, the plunge in the price of gasoline.

Plug-ins are more expensive than "regular" cars. It will in effect require two engines, which is why a Prius is so expensive. The Prius must be the world's all-time most neglected consumer superstar in history, because only now is Toyota setting up another factory to produce them, even though they have been selling out for over a decade. In the meantime, Toyota built enough SUV capacity to easily outproduce their Prius. One must assume that Toyota can't make much money from a car with two engines.

In fact, Toyota has been "vocal about the drawbacks to plug-in hybrids," as *The New York Times* put it.[16] Putting a set of batteries in a car adds about $15,000 to the price of the car; Toyota's will only allow the car to drive for 14 miles on the battery. *The New York Times* reported from an interview with a Toyota executive about electric vehicles (E.V.s):

> That limited range means that E.V.s work best as "very small commuter-type vehicles" for use in major metropolitan areas (he used Europe and Japan as examples). Asked if longer-range E.V.s were possible with current technology, he said that could happen only "if we forget about battery life and if we forget about the cost incurred for replacement of those batteries."[17]

In other words, electric batteries are not up to the task of replacing long-distance, fast, large, internal-combustion, engine-powered cars. Batteries can convert at something like 80 percent efficiency, but that still leaves the waste of moving around a large vehicle that needs to be heavy to be "safe." The injuries from a crash are very dependent on the speed at which a crash occurs. We pay for going faster, and we get more and more inefficient by doing so.

TRANSPORTATION ELECTRIC

It is proving very difficult, if not impossible, for a battery to generate anywhere near the power of liquid gasoline exploding. The batteries, so far, are also extremely expensive. The safest, most efficient thing to do would be to produce cars that don't go much above 20 mph, which would decrease the weight needs, and drastically decrease the injury rate. At 20 mph, only 5 percent of accidents result in fatalities, whereas at 30 mph the figure goes up to 45 percent, and at 40 mph it's 85 percent.[18] It just so happens that most electric vehicles can't go much above 20 mph anyway, but the big push is on to increase the speed of all-electric cars.

In addition, the charge in batteries is such that distances are low as well—probably around 50 miles on a decent charge. The average daily traveled distance is about 40 miles.[19] So an electric vehicle should be able to handle most of the trips that Americans take, which are often driven at around 30 mph anyway. For most urban and even perhaps a majority of suburban driving, an all-electric car, using current technology, would be adequate.

But that wouldn't work well on the highway. To travel long distances, you would either have to drive your all-electric vehicle onto a train, or park the vehicle at a station and then take the train as a regular passenger. In any case, the number of train stations would be limited, and would make the most sense if placed in the middle of a town. Thus, there would have to be a town center, which many suburbs don't really have. If one didn't exist, either the suburb would have to be abandoned, which might be a good thing, particularly when trying to make agriculture sustainable by reclaiming farmland lost to suburbs, or the suburb would have to be "infilled," that is, a place would have to be created that could serve as a town center.[20]

Again, I am not advocating that the government force people to get into electric cars, although the government could work proactively and encourage the creation of town centers, which some local governments are doing. The market will move everyone in this direction, if chaotically, but it would be nice to anticipate and reconstruct communities to accommodate the new reality before it becomes painful.

If cars need to be light weight to go 50 miles per charge, long-distance trucks will be impossible to move economically in an oil-constrained world. Short-haul, all-electric trucks within a major metropolitan area would be a possibility, but long-haul freight will have to move by freight train. However, a shift from a truck-based freight system to a hub-and-spoke type rail-based system would mean, just as much as in the case of cars, that the urban/suburban structure of the society would have to change.

Manufacturing plants would have to move, perhaps literally, so that they could be within convenient distance of a rail line—ideally, right on the rail line. Agriculture would also have to be within easy access to trains, as they were until the truck became ubiquitous after World War II. Some agricultural goods still move by train, but not enough.

The retailing of goods would have to become more centralized. No more huge Walmarts, Home Depots, and Costcos in the middle of nowhere. These "big box" stores depend on a fleet of trucks spread out all over the country; retail, just like manufacturing and agriculture, will have to locate near rail tracks and stations, and will have an advantage if they are closer to the city, which will have many stations in relatively close proximity.

If trucking will be problematic, the economics of air travel will be catastrophic. According to Jeffrey Stein, flights shorter than 350 miles will cease once gasoline reaches $8 per gallon; at $10 per gallon, 500-mile flights will stop.[21] At that price, long-distance flights will be very expensive.

Currently, Amtrak has the annual ridership equivalent to that of Jet Blue, a reasonably successful carrier. But Amtrak's long-distance routes, beyond 500 miles, are once-a-day, and they don't have the reserve stock of trains necessary for expansion. As it is, the route from Chicago to NYC takes about 20 hours, and snakes through upstate New York before heading south to NYC. The train from Chicago to Los Angeles or Seattle takes 48 hours. If the airline industry collapses, so will most long-distance passenger and business travel, unless the rail system is upgraded.

There are two main strategies for upgrading the system. The easiest would be to optimize the rail system that is currently on the ground, and to make it possible to go as fast as possible on the current routes. This would probably require, at the least, laying new tracks to shift the freight traffic to its own rail line. Currently, Amtrak trains are poor second cousins to any freight train on the track; even though the freight train companies agreed to give passenger trains the right of way. Because the freight trains own the tracks, they reneged on the deal.

If routes were made more direct, trains didn't need to wait for freight, the locomotives and passenger cars were properly maintained, and the tracks upgraded, we could probably see speeds of up to 100 mph on much of the long-distance system in the United States. If many trains per day were to run, this would be a decent alternative to air travel, particularly when medium-distance flights stop.

However, to be sustainable, rail has to be electrified. Currently only about 1 percent of U.S. rail is electrified, whereas in Japan all rail is electrified (Japan also has the highest transportation share of rail use, at 27 percent). To electrify a rail system costs as much as building the rails in the first place. In the 1980s, John Ullman, professor of industrial engineering at Hofstra, estimated that electrifying the rail system in the United States would cost $100 billion. On the bright side, the efficiency of an electric locomotive can surpass 90 percent.

The other main strategy for upgrading the rail system would be to create a world-class high-speed rail system. The recently approved high-speed rail system in California, which will eventually link Sacramento with San Francisco, Los Angeles, and San Diego, is expected to cost about $50 million per mile.[22] If the current approximately 40,000-mile Interstate Highway System were paralleled by an Interstate High-Speed Rail System of the same length, such a system would cost about $2 trillion. Spread out over 10 years, which would be rather quick, such a system would cost an average of $200 billion per year, or $100 billion per year if spread out over 20 years.[23]

Electric trains are much more efficient than any other kind of powered vehicle; human-powered bicycles are the most efficient vehicles. But the reason diesels are still popular worldwide is that electric trains require a large upfront capital investment for overhead wires for long-distance trains, or third rails for subways. However, the operating costs for an electric locomotive are much lower than for a diesel; electricity is much cheaper, the locomotive itself is much simpler and requires fewer moving parts that can fail so maintenance is much cheaper, and the locomotive is lighter. As we will see with renewable energy, our society must become more focused on creating capital upfront, and less focused on indicators of flows, like gross domestic product (GDP), or on taking the short-term route, as in building diesel systems instead of electric ones, or coal-powered electrical-generating plants instead of wind farms.

A complete train network would include high-speed rail and optimized regular rail for intercity travel, electrified regular rail for lines from towns and/or suburbs into city centers, and subways, elevated systems, light rail, and electric bus rapid transit for intracity travel.

Bus rapid transit has become quite popular recently. It was first implemented in Curitiba, Brazil, where it was accompanied by large bus stations in which the riders pay their fare, easing entry onto the buses; an entire lane is reserved for them; and the buses are rather large. The advantage is that the infrastructural work is much cheaper than light rail or subway. On the other hand, the main problems are that it isn't as efficient as having those more expensive rails, and for an oil-constrained world, buses will be impractical unless they are electrified. That will require, in the most efficient implementation, overhead wires, because it is less efficient to drag batteries with the vehicle, which increase the weight, and batteries are less efficient than whatever large-scale generating plant is used. If bus rapid transit has electric wires overhead and if the capital is available, it will be an easy step to convert to light rail or trolleys (which I define as being a single car, instead of a set of two or more with light rail). Light-rail and bus rapid transit advocates often fight each other, but they are both very similar options in an urban situation that is not dense enough to support a subway. A subway is the most efficient of all, both land and energy-wise, but can be very expensive in terms of upfront capital, as the most efficient solution often is.

Water travel is perhaps the biggest technological challenge when oil becomes expensive. For land travel, the switch to rail will actually mean moving to a more efficient electrical, rail-based system, even if it will be culturally traumatic. For water travel, there is no clear alternative to oil or coal, because it is not possible to run electric lines over oceans. It may be possible on rivers, so that barge and small ship traffic along waterways might actually expand in such a scenario. But globalization will receive a mighty blow if there are few ships on the open ocean. Currently, most cruise ships use electric motors in their propeller systems, so it might not be too large of a leap to install very large batteries, along with some wind turbine and solar panel technology, but much research will be necessary to see if this is possible.

REBUILDING MANUFACTURING BY
BUILDING TRAINS

Transportation technologies use all of the various parts of the core of an industrial system. They use copious amounts of steel and other materials, they need machine tools and other shaping and assembly technologies, and more and more, they incorporate advanced computer technology. Their production uses electricity almost completely. Although the first rail systems in many countries were entirely built with private investment, by World War I at the latest, most national systems were owned and controlled by the government, so it is not too controversial to give the government a clear role in developing rail systems, something that is not as obvious when it comes to energy. Even the World Trade Organization allows for "general infrastructure" to be not only subsidized by government, but also restricted to domestic manufacture.

The United States faces various hurdles to a complete rail network. Most of the critical parts of the industry no longer reside in the nation of their creation. For instance, there is no domestic subway industry; when NYC put out bids for its most recent multi-billion-dollar acquisition program, it only received bids from foreign firms, and wound up awarding contracts to Alsthom (France) and Kawasaki (Japan). Although much of the assembly will take place in the United States, assembly is the least skilled part of the construction of most manufactured products.

However, General Electric (GE) and the former locomotive-building division of General Motors (GM), Electro-Motive Diesel (EMD), are the two largest builders of diesel-electric locomotives in the world, and have been for the last 50 years. Motive Power (Wabtec) manufactures diesel-electric locomotives, spun off from Morrison-Knudsen, in Idaho, and Brookville in Pennsylvania rebuilds trains. All Amtrak diesel-electrics are American made, as best I can tell.

However, GE produces only one engine that can use an electric third rail, P32AC-DM; the last time it built an electric locomotive, the e60, was in 1983, and soon after EMD stopped producing an all-electric locomotive (the AEM-7). All electric locomotives for New Jersey (NJ) Transit, for instance, come from ABB (Swiss/Swedish) or Bombardier. Many of Amtrak's rail cars were produced by Budd, which no longer exists. Many of the cars that were previously built

by Budd and Pullman in the United States are now built and supplied to agencies such as NJ Transit by Bombardier and Alsthom,
who sometimes build the exact same passenger cars as the now de-
funct American companies.

Bombardier (Canadian/Swedish/German), Alsthom (French), Sie-
mens (German), Kawasaki (Japan), Rotem (South Korea), and
Hitachi (Japan), in about that order, are the major producers of electric locomotives. None of these is American, and one would have to
guess that the last American engineers who helped design an electric
locomotive have retired. However, there is plenty of human capital in
locomotives. This is a perfect opportunity for the government to step
in and work with the diesel locomotive manufacturers to prepare for a
world in which oil is very expensive, diesel sales are declining, and the
world is making a switch from diesel to electric, just as almost 100
years ago the world moved from steam locomotives to diesel ones.

Throughout history, countries have attempted to learn new technologies from other countries. It often took guile, because countries
often tried to keep their innovations to themselves to maintain the
political and economic superiority that technological superiority confers. At the beginning of the Industrial Revolution, England actually
banned machinery exports; engineers stowed themselves in barrels or
other contrivances to make money abroad.

The historian Alexander Gerschenkron[24] argued that the further
away a country is from industrialization, the more heavily the country
has to rely on the government to catch up to the leaders. The United
States and United Kingdom, although they used a significant amount
of governmental help, did not need as much as the French, who established industrial banks that directly loaned to companies attempting to
industrialize. The Russians started their industrialization push even
further behind, and by the 1920s they needed to industrialize so
quickly that they instituted a centrally planned economy.

Having forged ahead of the United Kingdom by the second half
of the 19th century in railroad technology and systems, the United
States allowed its rail system to decline. Indeed, it positively pushed
it down a slippery slope. Railways had to pay taxes on all of their
tracks (and they still do to some extent), and they had to build the
tracks themselves, while roads for cars were built by the government
and never pay taxes (it is ironic that conservatives decry subsidies to
railroads, when the transformation from a rail- to car-centered society was one of the more "socialist" processes in U.S. history). The

government built and maintains the airports that doomed much of intercity rail and provide air traffic controllers.

Rail systems thrive when cities thrive and decline when cities decline. This is because trains are the most efficient method of moving large numbers of people, but if cities are not able to congregate dense numbers of people in one area, then trains no longer make economic sense. Not only did government not help to rebuild the cities before World War II (and after), thus dooming rail, it encouraged the development of the suburbs by laying infrastructure such as water and electricity, while creating institutions to make home ownership easy in the suburbs and more difficult in the cities, as I describe in Chapter 11.

The coup de grace was probably the effort by General Motors and other companies to buy up municipal transit lines, mostly trolleys, rip up the tracks, and transform them into bus systems.[25] Buses are inherently less efficient because tires use up more energy in friction than rail; in addition, most buses are bumpier for riders than rail, and their diesel exhaust has led to asthma and other diseases because of their pollution. Now, with oil set to go up, up, and away in price, diesel buses, like diesel trains, will become uneconomical.

Governments at national, state, and local levels will have to engage in a coordinated effort to rebuild the rail networks and the train manufacturing industry. The first task will be to guarantee a long-term, stable market for rail manufacturers, so that they can be sure that there will be a market for a long time to come, which will allow would-be engineers and skilled production workers to be assured that if they embark on a career of engineer or train skilled worker, they will be able to support themselves and their families for decades. In addition, a stable market will allow rail manufacturers to survive the ups and downs of the business cycle, which can devastate makers of machinery, as well as the ups and downs of cities and other governments. Therefore, it will be necessary to have a plan, of a flexible nature, showing how the train network will expand over at least the next 20 years. Such a plan will be dependent on a plan to create a renewable electricity network and a plan to make cities and towns compact and dense enough to use rail efficiently.

The second requirement to create a viable rail network is to create the manufacturing competence to make world-class locomotives, cars, and track.[26] This will require creating entire new engineering departments for rail technologies or expanding existing transportation technology departments; creating or expanding vocational schools to create a pool of skilled technicians; and establishing incubators linked to universities to help entrepreneurs create new technologies and understand current ones. It will also mean sending engineers and skilled production workers abroad to work in factories or schools to learn foreign technologies, and to contract out with foreign producers and academics to come to the United States to learn closer to home.

The third requirement will be to create, or help existing companies create, a company or company division that would have the competence to act as the prime contractor to build subways, regular rail, and high-speed rail. The prime contractor is the company or agency that coordinates the building of the product, subcontracting out to others to do the pieces. Thus, in the case of a train, subcontractors might be selected who would produce the air conditioning units, the electric engines, the wheels, the chassis, etc. It may be that subcontractors would also have to be created or expanded within existing companies in the United States.[27]

Finally, the government should provide financing and technical support for companies to gain or regain the needed competence and to put together the factories that will supply the rail networks planned by governments at all levels. This could take the form of a bank that helps companies from start-up plans to major financing to expansion. It would take several years to set up new, competent factories and companies, and during that time they would have no orders to bring in revenue—the cost of their entire operations, even for a time after they begin manufacturing, would have to be financed. It might be the case that private investors would provide some of this capital, but the government would have to step in to provide the rest, or at least guarantee it.

Foreign companies could play an important role in all of these steps, both as advisers and as partners in jointly run factories and companies, until the U.S. companies became competent to stand on their own. Although it might seem in the long-term interest of the foreign companies to keep U.S. expertise stunted, in reality it is in the long-term interest of foreign companies and trading partners to have a wealthy United States to trade with and produce in. It won't help foreign subway manufacturers to produce subway cars that the United States can't afford because it can't produce enough wealth to pay for the subway cars.

Train production in particular has the capability of increasing the long-term wealth of the United States because the foundation of the manufacturing sector, the industrial machinery sectors, can be revived by building for train production. Train production requires machine tools to make the parts, steel for the raw material, instrument control systems to make the trains run, and myriad other machinery and equipment technologies. For the last 50 years or so, the automobile industry has been providing the market for the industrial base, but that industry is now seizing up, and train production can step in and take up where automobiles left off.

Transportation is intimately interconnected with energy, the next system to be explored.

CHAPTER 10

Making Energy Sustainable

Transportation and energy are inextricably linked, since vehicles require energy to move. The energy system also requires a dependable transportation system for its operation, since the process of creating energy involves moving energy resources and machinery from one point to another. In the case of transportation, the world has, for the most part, made the great mistake of building a global system that is dependent on oil. Even in the course of human history, much less geologic time, the age of oil will be rather short-lived, at most 150 years. Hopefully by the time oil becomes scarce, transportation will have shifted to the modern form of energy—electricity.

SINGING THE NATION ELECTRIC

The great thing about electricity as an energy source is that it can be used to turn a motor. The electric motor revolutionized manufacturing, because it became possible to control the machinery in factories very precisely, which made it practical to apply motors anywhere they were needed. Before electricity, power was distributed in a factory by means of belts hanging from the ceiling. The belts were rotated by an axle, as in a car—that is, a rod was rotated by the big steam engine in a separate engine room, and the rotation of the rod in turn rotated the big belts, which were in turn attached to machine tools and other production machinery, not only creating a great deal of noise and safety hazards, but making it very difficult to control the machinery and to apply power where and when it was needed.[1]

It is also very inefficient to have a separate power source in a transportation vehicle such as a car and truck, and have that internal combustion engine power an axle that powers the wheels. In fact, it is inherently more efficient to take the power source *off* the vehicle, because the extra weight of the power source requires a large percentage of the energy used to power the vehicle. The provision of power outside a vehicle is straightforward with electricity, as you can lay down power lines or put them in the air; the train or bus can attach to the power lines and draw electricity, directing the electricity straight to the motors that are right next to the wheels.

Electricity is currently used for heating and cooling, but ultimately it might be better if most heating and cooling came from devices attached to the buildings themselves. For instance, by attaching buildings to the earth 5 to 100 feet underground, using technology called geothermal heat pumps, all of a building's heat and cooling needs can be met, using about one-quarter of the electricity ordinarily needed. Israel mandates that every roof must have a solar hot water heater, and China has been installing millions of these devices as well. Electricity is best used for what it is good for, electronics and turning motors, and solar and geothermal heat is best used directly for heating and cooling.

Almost all electricity is now generated using coal, natural gas, and oil, and most heating and cooling is provided by electricity and natural gas. Those who would disregard the possibility of a renewable energy sector throw up their hands at this point, and claim that because such a small percentage of renewable energy is being generated now, we can't possibly generate a large percentage later. History is full of large-scale shifts in energy usage, most prominently in the case of electricity and oil. If someone had said at the turn of the 20th century that eventually virtually all transportation would be based on oil, the skeptic would have said that that's ridiculous, most oil was being used for lighting, and oil would never replace coal-powered steam travel. One could also have claimed, quite rightly at the time, that virtually no one was using electricity, so it would be preposterous to assume that virtually all households and businesses would be completely dependent on it within 50 years.

In fact, enormous resources were poured into creating electricity and oil infrastructures; the electricity network has been called the world's biggest machine.[2] There is no reason a similar feat of capital construction could not be achieved in the case of renewable energy. But this green transformation will have to be designed and financed by the government.

The definition of *renewable energy* should be the following: energy generated without permanent damage to an ecosystem, or energy that does not consume net natural capital. By *net*, I mean that any decrease in natural capital would be filled by an increase in natural capital somewhere else. This follows Herman Daly's criteria for ecological sustainability: renewable resources should provide a sustainable yield (the rate of harvest should not exceed the rate of regeneration); the use of nonrenewable resources should be offset by the equivalent development of renewable substitutes; and waste generation should not exceed the assimilative capacity of the environment.[3] In other words, the system must be able to regenerate itself, indefinitely.

Wind energy uses free wind energy. Ninety percent of the material, by weight, of a wind turbine is metal, which means it can be recycled. Most of the rest is fiberglass of some kind, which is mostly glass, that is, it comes from sand. Some of the components of wind turbines may be plastic, which currently is made out of petroleum. Enough plastic could come from sustainably harvested biomass to produce plastics for critical applications like wind. There are also some rare minerals used for wind turbines, but these are not crucial.[4]

The biggest environmental problem for wind is the tendency for birds and bats to be killed by fast-spinning blades, although as turbines become larger, the blades slow down. Wind manufacturers are becoming better at siting and building wind turbines that minimize such damage. In any case, wind energy is responsible for a miniscule amount of bird and bat deaths compared to coal pollution,[5] and much less than the effects of global warming.

Any form of long-distance electrical transmission has disadvantages. Long-distance transmission lines require building and clearing paths. If a forest is in the way, for instance, one might need to cut a path right through it. In addition, it can be expensive to maintain and build these lines. It would be better to put the lines under the ground, but that is much more expensive than putting them in the air. Also, about 7 percent to 10 percent of electricity is lost when electricity flows across the country in transmission lines, although this loss decreases when newer, high-voltage direct current lines are used. In general, the closer one can generate electricity to the destination, the better.

Solar energy, because it can be sited right on the building that is using it, does not have the same problems as a remotely generated electrical source. Solar energy is free, and the main ingredient used for solar panels is silicon, which can be obtained from sand. The manufacturing of solar panels can involve many toxic chemicals, but those chemicals are not critical to their manufacture.

Concentrated solar power (CSP) may or may not be a practical part of a renewable solution. The idea is to place a large array of mirrors in the desert (for example, in the U.S. Southwest), concentrate the sun's rays on a tower, and boil water in the tower to generate electricity. It is a very efficient way to generate solar power, and because some of the heat can be stored and used after the sun goes down, CSP may get around intermittency, the biggest problem with renewable energy.

Intermittency is the problem that renewable power—like any power source—can be intermittent, that is, it can stop flowing at any time. In the case of solar, this is obviously because the sun goes down at night. In the case of wind, sometimes the wind does not blow. Geo-thermal energy does not have this problem, since the temperature of the crust, after even about five feet down, tends to stay the same, and becomes hotter the further down one goes. Fossil fuel plants can have intermittency problems if the fuel source is cut off—and the entire grid can suffer a "blackout" if there is a total collapse of the system. Even coal plants are only operational about 88 percent of the time.

FOSSIL FUELS

Part of what makes fossil fuels so attractive, and what has made the shift to renewables difficult, is that oil, coal, and natural gas can store energy very easily. Oil, in particular, is very easy to store in huge oil tanks, and to put into pipelines to ship hundreds of miles at very little cost. The oil can then be pumped into a car or truck's fuel tank, with virtually no leakage, for a very long time, with no special effort needed.

By contrast, hydrogen, the smallest atom in the universe, loves to leak out of anything but the most solid containers; it explodes; and it doesn't like to be compressed, so that storing it takes huge amounts of space. A pipeline for hydrogen would be like constructing a pipe-line out of matches, and about as practical.

Both coal and natural gas have volume issues, in different ways. Because coal has much less energy potential per volume, it takes a lot more of it to get the same amount of energy as oil, and it's not as easy to burn in small quantities, which is why there aren't any coal car engines. Half of the U.S. freight rail capacity is used to move coal. But coal is very polluting and wasteful; if the society was worried about deaths and injuries caused by coal, it would have been banned long ago.

According to the Union for Concerned Scientists,

> A typical 500-megawatt coal-fired power plant draws about 2.2 billion gallons of water each year from nearby water bodies, such as lakes, rivers, or oceans, to create steam for turning its turbines. This is enough water to support a city of approximately 250,000 people.[6]

According to the European Commission, the external costs (that is, the costs in terms of health, crops, buildings, global warming, and ecosystems) of coal are about twice the price charged for coal-generated electricity, and often more than three times the price.[7]

Studies have shown that coal is responsible for up to 24,000 deaths annually in the United States, and that coal emits mercury, arsenic, sulfur dioxide, and other toxic elements. Coal, and any other centrally produced electricity that uses heat to produce steam to produce electricity, wastes about two-thirds of the fuel it uses. And the United States is efficient and clean, compared to rapidly industrializing countries such as China. As Grist.org's David Roberts is fond of declaring, "Coal is the enemy of the human race."

Natural gas is easy to transport via pipeline, but not by ship, as oil and coal are. To be used as a fuel for transportation it must be compressed, which is only practical in large vehicles like buses. To move large amounts of natural gas across oceans, it must be transformed into liquified natural gas (LNG), requiring a large amount of energy to be cooled down and then pumped onto specially constructed ships, which use specially constructed terminals. If one of these was to explode, the entire terminal, at the least, would go with it. The United States is poorly equipped to bring in LNG at this point. Recently, in the eastern United States large amounts of natural gas have been found and we have gained the technology needed to bring it up; however, the amount of water that would have to be used and polluted, plus the use of other toxic chemicals, might mean environmental catastrophe wherever these techniques are attempted.

In all cases of fossil fuels, there are significant transportation expenses in moving the fuel from where it is to where it will be used. In the case of oil, 5 percent of petroleum is used to refine it into gasoline, and 1.35 percent is used to power the pipelines that transport it. So the overhead, particularly when one includes the environmental and health damages, is quite high. The main problem with fossil fuels, from an economic point of view, is that they are not renewable; in fact, they are either presently peaking or will peak in a few decades, as I discussed in Chapter 8. Biofuels, that is, fuels derived from plants, are not renewable except in small quantities. However, we don't have many good examples of creating biofuels or biofeedstocks, that is, biological inputs for chemical manufacture. One example of sustainable harvesting of biological products is the practice of the Menominee Indians of Wisconsin. They have been sustainably harvesting trees from their forest for well over 100 years. Their forest ecosystem is thriving,[8] while most of the forest outside their management area is gone, or at best, exists as sterile plantations. The Menominee have an ethic of sustainable harvesting; that is, they only take out just as much lumber as the forest can handle without permanently damaging it. In other words, they do not destroy the capital of the forest.

On the other hand, there is currently a great deal of effort to use wood to burn in electricity-generating plants, but according to recent studies, wood used in this way is actually a worse greenhouse-gas emitter than fossil fuels, and forests are also destroyed as a result.[9] Sometimes it is claimed that we could use the "unneeded" dead wood and underbrush in forests, but it is very difficult to tell what is truly needed and what isn't. In a normal forest, all of the material is recycled and used. Some forests have been allowed to "overgrow" because fires have been suppressed, but this shouldn't be used as a blanket judgment to take underbrush from all forests.

It is almost always the case that wind, solar, and geothermal are more efficient sources of power than biofuels because the amount and intensity of use of the land to obtain enough biofuels to be useful for energy generation are prohibitive. For this reason, biofuels will never be able to replace oil to a great extent. Even the relatively low percentage of biofuels being used to replace oil is devastating grain supplies worldwide.[10] This means that plants, including trees, should be used to replace oil for chemical feedstocks, or simply as lumber, not as a source of energy.

Nuclear power provides 20 percent of U.S. electricity. At least up until now, it can be argued that coal has been much more destructive of life and health than nuclear power, but nuclear power is as expensive as it is to a great extent because so many precautions have to be made with its radioactive fuel and radioactive waste. A sustainable society should not tolerate a substance that will be dangerous for hundreds of thousands of years. As it is, many uranium workers and other workers are overexposed to radiation. The fuel must also be mined and transported, and uranium supplies will not last forever.

Wind power is being added to the electrical generation system faster than any other source. Nuclear power requires a huge upfront investment, something that generally only governments are good at, which is why France gets 80 percent of its electricity from nuclear power; Charles De Gaulle, who ruled France with as close to an iron fist in the early 1960s as can be done in a democracy, shoved nuclear power down France's throat. Nuclear energy advocates don't seem to understand that the construction of nuclear power plants has always required massive government subsidies and an unlimited, free government-supplied insurance policy, and creating a significant number of new nuclear plants would be a government directed effort. If the government is going to construct a new electrical system, wind has proven itself, and wind can also be added incrementally, that is, a turbine at a time, while nuclear plants require at least 10 years and billions of dollars for each installation.

MAKING RENEWABLES CONTINUOUSLY AVAILABLE

Renewable power, by which I mean wind, solar, geothermal, and some forms of water sources, has none of the problems of mining or transporting, future availability, health, or environmental impacts of fossil fuels and nuclear power. The technology is available and known, and gets better year by year (I won't discuss the enormous potential of wave and tidal power because it is not actually being used at a large scale). The big problem is that the supply of power in the case of solar is obviously limited to daytime, and in the case of wind, can be rather unpredictable and intermittent; in addition, solar energy potential can decrease on cloudy days.

So how do we get around the intermittency problem? There are a few main ways: constructing geographically diverse wind systems, using stationary batteries and other storage systems, and using geothermal as much as possible.

Wind power should designed to be used as part of a national system, not as individual turbines, because a system can be constructed which is made up of turbines that are placed in such as way that, through time, a predictable and significant number of them will always be supplying power. That is, if a wind system is built which has a set of wind turbines such that there are always a certain number that are working because the wind is blowing, then the intermittency problem can be solved.

Mark Jacobson, an engineering professor at Stanford University, along with Christina Archer, have produced an important set of papers showing that world wind power potential is several times the total of energy use today.[11] The solution to the problem of intermittency is to diversify the siting of the wind turbines, as they found when

> the benefits of interconnecting wind farms were evaluated for 19 sites, located in the midwestern United States . . ., it was found that an average of 33% and a maximum of 47% of yearly averaged wind power from interconnected farms can be used as reliable, baseload electric power. Equally significant, interconnecting multiple wind farms to a common point and then connecting that point to a far-away city can allow the long-distance portion of transmission capacity to be reduced, for example, by 20% with only a 1.6% loss of energy.[12]

"For a typical power system, the rule of thumb is that base load power is usually 35–40 percent of the maximum load during the year,"[13] so wind systems could be used as a baseload system. A *baseload system* is one that provides a reliable supply of electricity, 24 hours per day, 365 days per year. It does not mean that, in the middle of summer, when everybody has their air conditioners going full blast, that the baseload system can provide enough electricity; "peak" power is needed for those extraordinary times when demand skyrockets. Generally, peak power has been provided by natural gas generating plants, which can start and stop easily, and are generally low cost. It might be necessary to use natural gas "peak" plants, at least until air conditioning can be powered from geothermal units and can be augmented by better building design.

How much would a baseload wind system cost? There has been quite a bit of variability in cost of wind turbines, particularly in 2007 and 2008, when commodity prices increased rapidly due to Chinese industrialization, in particular. Using what I think is a fairly conservative number of $1.5 million per mega watt (million watts, or MW),[14] let's assume that wind turbines convert, on average, 33 percent of their potential; that is, if 100% of potential was the case that a wind turbine was always running full-blast, then 33% potential means that one-third of this maximum potential is being realized. Let's also assume that the United States continues to use 4 million gigawatt hours per year (or 4 million watt hours, or 4,000 Terawatts), then to install the raw power needed to fill U.S. electricity needs we would have to spend about $2.2 trillion to build wind turbines. The American Wind Energy Association points out that in the 20 years prior to 2005, costs of wind power declined by 90 percent, and although that rate of decrease may no longer be possible, the size of wind turbines keeps increasing, which makes them much more efficient. The huge 6-MW and 7-MW turbines being installed in Estinnes, Belgium are so big that an entirely new kind of crane, the largest in the world, had to be built.[15]

However, if an Interstate Wind System was going to provide half of the electricity currently used then the system would more likely cost about $1 trillion. Over 10 years, that would only require expenditures of about $100 billion per year. These costs would not be volatile, because wind turbines are built with very common materials, in particular, steel.[16] The blades have been some form of fiberglass, which is a form of glass, whose main ingredient is sand.

Wind turbines are made up of about 8,000 parts. According to the European Wind Energy Association, the cost breaks down this way: the huge tower (26 percent), made mostly of steel; the long blades (22 percent); the hub, shaft, bearings, and frame for the blades (6 percent) that bring power to the gearbox (13 percent); the yaw and pitch system that shifts the blades to optimally face the wind (4 percent); the systems to put the electricity on the grid (9 percent); and various other parts (5 percent).[17] Many of these parts are the basic output of much of the production and reproduction machinery sector, as explained in chapter 3. These parts require very precise, reliable, durable manufacture, using high-skilled labor and advanced engineering. Currently, very little of this engineering is being done in the United States. Eleven companies produce 96 percent of medium to large wind turbines in the world; only one, General Electric (GE), is based in the United States, with a 16 percent share of the global market.[18]

Thus a large-scale, government designed and financed wind power construction program could, if properly conceived, serve to rebuild the manufacturing sector of the United States. A program of constructing a wind-centered energy system would complement the construction of a rail-centered transportation system, because they would both provide a market for many of the same kinds of critical manufacturing firms.

ELECTRICITY AS A NATIONAL SYSTEM

To take full advantage of wind energy and any other long-distance transmission of energy, you need a transmission network, that is, a set of wires and other electrical equipment that string together the electrical generating plants with the final destinations that use the electricity. The U.S. transmission system, the first and for a very long time the best in the world, is falling apart. According to the American Society of Civil Engineers:

> The U.S. power transmission system is in urgent need of modernization. Growth in electricity demand and investment in new power plants has not been matched by investment in new transmission facilities. Maintenance expenditures have decreased 1% per year since 1992. Existing transmission facilities were not designed for the current level of demand, resulting in an increased number of "bottlenecks," which increase costs to consumers and elevate the risk of blackouts.[19]

According to Philip Bane, the cost of upgrading the national grid, and making it smart enough to handle the variability of renewable electricity, would cost about $165 billion over several years.[20]

The market can't create an Interstate Wind System and Interstate Smart Transmission System, anymore than it could have created the Interstate Highway System: the market doesn't have enough resources to construct a complete, national system, and there is no way for the market to indicate to producers where to put the turbines so that they create a reliable baseload, nonintermittent system. The government has to plan, design, and finance the construction of the wind turbines and national grid, and private firms will need to produce the turbines. Because there are no large systems integrators in the United States, with the exception of GE, foreign wind manufacturers could be encouraged to form joint ventures with U.S. firms, and to sub-contract to U.S. firms. The construction and installation of wind turbines would have to be mandated to be carried out within the United States, so that U.S. labor would benefit and learn from the production process, and so that the United States could encourage the revival of its manufacturing base.

Besides constructing wind turbines, solar panels, and transmission networks, a renewable electricity system would probably require a certain amount of storage, even with an Interstate Wind System serving as baseload. Because the input into the grid would be more variable than by using fossil fuel plants, a reliable system of storage would make the system as a whole more reliable.

Research for the efficient storage of electricity has not received the amount of support it should have, so we know much less about how to store renewable electricity than we know about how to create it. CSP can heat up large amounts of salt, which retains heat well and could provide up to 7 hours of energy for electrical generation after the sun sets. The problem with CSP is that it destroys any eco-system it is sited on and requires long transmission lines.

Some have proposed using stored water; that is, solar or wind energy can be used to pump water up into something, either a water tower or even a cave, and then when power is needed, the water is released back down and run through a turbine, generating electricity. It seems to be hard to find really large areas that can serve as water storage areas, but it might make sense, say at a neighborhood or city level, to build one or a set of water towers for this purpose.

The other obvious way to store electricity is in batteries. There has been an enormous amount of research, much of it seemingly in a vain attempt to develop batteries that might be used for cars. It seems to be easier to construct efficient batteries if they are closer to the size that might be useful, say, for a large building. Sodium sulfur batteries[21] seem to be the almost-perfect choice for this task—they are made from very common materials (sodium and sulfur) and are relatively cheap. The big problem with them is that they need to be carefully made because pure sodium explodes if it comes into contact with water, and only one company in Japan now makes them.

According to the National Energy Technology Laboratory, sodium-sulfur batteries cost from $350 to $500 per kWh (1000 watt hours).[22] If the United States uses 4,000 billion kWh of electricity per year (4,000 Terrawatts), it uses about 10 billion kWh per day, on average. If we spent $1 trillion over 10 years to create 3 billion-kWh capacity of sodium-sulfur batteries—conservatively assuming mass production would lower costs to the low end—then we would have about one-third of a day, or about 8 hours, on average, of storage for a national grid, distributed across the country. If the Interstate Wind System is providing one-third of the power, constantly, then wind plus batteries would probably provide at least 16 hours as a backup system—plenty to smooth over rough spots in the provision of solar and wind power, particularly if buildings were hooked up to geothermal units, a subject to which we now turn.

THE EARTH'S ENERGY

Geothermal energy has perhaps the greatest potential of any renewable technology, since the energy is continuous—the Earth won't cool down for a few billion years. Although there are several power plants that use deep geothermal power for electricity generation, the research into this form of energy has been pathetic. A geothermal "Manhattan project" type effort should be initiated. Whereas solar and wind power would certainly benefit from large-scale research efforts, geothermal might achieve breakthroughs if given enough resources.[23] Much of the problem is simply drilling far enough down to get access to large amounts of heat, and since these heat sources are at different depths, it is unclear how far one would have to drill. The basic technique is to inject water down the holes and let the earth generate hot steam, which then is used to turn turbines, which then generate electricity; we need to make sure that the water can be recycled and not pollute ecosystems, although it seems that the amount of water used is miniscule compared to fossil fuel electricity-generating plants.

There is another important geothermal technology, called geothermal exchange units, or geothermal heat pumps. As of 2004 there were about 600,000 in the United States alone.[24] Depending on the building, pipes can be installed from 10 feet or so to 400 feet below the surface, because the temperature at a certain depth stays very constant, even in very hot or very cold climates. The geothermal units can take advantage of this heat constancy to heat or cool a building, depending on the need; the units use some electricity to move energy to and from the ground.

If buildings could produce all the space and water heating, air conditioning, and ventilation that they need, using geothermal heat pumps or other technologies to make a building self-sufficient for heating and cooling, the United States could shut down all of its coal-powered electricity-generating plants. This is because heating and cooling buildings and water now consume 30 percent of our electricity and 32 percent of our natural gas.

If geothermal heat pumps were installed under all buildings, we wouldn't need to burn 60 percent of our coal because we would not need 30 percent of our electricity (half of our electricity comes from coal). We could, as a bridge until an Interstate Wind System was built, redirect our natural gas from warming and cooling into electricity generation, allowing the United States to replace the remaining coal with natural gas.

In other words, buildings could both destroy electrical demand and free up natural gas, until renewables come online and replace natural gas in turn. If we did this within a 10-year time frame, we could generate millions of green-collar jobs making buildings self-sufficient in heating and cooling, create millions more jobs manufacturing geothermal systems, and help the rest of the world kill off the rest of coal.

To understand how geothermal heat pumps could accomplish this task, and to be "electricity literate," let's take a tour of how electricity is used in the United States, shown in Table 10.1 (sort of a "natural history" of electricity use). The U.S. Energy Information Administration (EIA) divides energy reality into four main areas of use: residential; commercial (which seems to include government); industrial; and transportation. Residential air conditioning, space heating, and water heating use up about 14 percent of all electricity and about 18 percent of natural gas; for commercial buildings such as malls and schools, 13 percent of our electricity is needed for heating and cooling and about 11 percent of our natural gas. Industry only uses a few percent of each for heating and cooling their buildings.

There are other heating and cooling needs that take up quite a bit of electricity, and as far as I know, the possibilities of using geothermal heat pumps to replace electricity for these other uses has not been investigated. Refrigeration, for instance, is a huge consumer of electricity, taking up 6 percent of all electricity in homes, 3 percent in commercial buildings, and 1 percent in industry. Household washing and

Table 10.1 The Distribution of Electricity Demand in the United States in Residential, Commercial, and Industrial Sectors

Distribution/Use	Percent (%)
Residential, 2001	
Air Conditioning	5.68
Space Heating	5.37
Refrigerators and Freezers	6.07
Other Kitchen Appliances	3.39
Water Heating	3.23
Lighting	3.12
Home Electronics	2.56
Washers/Dryers	2.36
Other Uses	3.63
Total Residential	35.41
Commercial, 1999	
Space Heating	1.70
Water Heating	0.41
Cooking	0.71
Cooling	8.71
Lighting	7.86
Office Equipment	6.09
Refrigeration	2.92
Ventilation	2.48
Other	3.16
Total Commercial	34.05
Industrial, 2002	
Process Heating	2.85
Process Cooling and Refrigeration	1.71
Machine Drive	14.04
Electro-Chemical Processes	2.37
Facility HVAC (g)	2.25
Facility Lighting	1.70
Other	1.58
Total Industrial	26.50

Note: Distribution accounts for about 96% of electrical use; transportation accounts for less than one-fifth of 1 %.

Sources: For the distribution among residential, commercial, transportation and industrial sectors, Table 7.2, Retail Sales and Direct Use of Electricity to Ultimate Customers by Sector, by Provider, 1997 through 2008, from *Electric Power Annual*, U.S. Energy Information Administration, 2008, using the row for the year 2006, for the section "total electric industry"; available at http://www.eia.doe.gov/cneaf/electricity/epa/epat7p2.html. For percentages for residential use, Table US-1, Electricity Consumption by End Use in U.S. Households, 2001, from the U.S. Energy Information Administration, Household Electricity Reports, available at http://www.eia.doe.gov/emeu/reps/enduse/er01_us_tab1.html.

For percentage for commercial use, "Preliminary End-Use Consumption Estimates," *Commercial Buildings Energy Consumption Survey*, U.S. Energy Information Administration, http://www.eia.doe.gov/emeu/cbecs/enduse_consumption/intro.html. For percentage for industrial use, Manufacturing Energy Consumption Survey, "Manufacturing and industrial uses and costs," Table 5.3, End Uses of Fuel Consumption, 2002, available at http://www.eia.doe.gov/emeu/mecs/mecs2002/data02/pdf/table5.3_02.pdf.

drying use over 2 percent, and process heating in industry, almost 3 percent. Again, these would probably have to be redesigned to accommodate heat pumps, but it would seem to be more efficient to use heat pumps than to create the electricity that then is used to mimic heat pumps.

Geothermal heat pumps use electricity to move the water around, but retrofitting buildings to retain as much heat as practical would probably cut down on the size of the geothermal unit needed. There are other ways to decrease the use of electricity, for lighting, electronic equipment, and industrial processing.

Residential lighting accounts for 3 percent of total electrical use—and commercial lighting *almost 9 percent.* So, Walmart might offer compact fluorescent light (CFL) bulbs, but they're probably wasting all of the saved electricity by lighting the huge buildings that they sell the CFLs in.

For a time, it seemed that the media had come to the conclusion that replacing luminescent light bulbs with CFLs, or driving a fuel-efficient car, or buying a more efficient refrigerator would solve the climate crisis. There is still quite a bit of information on how YOU can help solve the climate crisis by cutting down on consumption. Although individual actions are certainly important, the focus of this book is on the systemic, national, and international efforts that must be made to make our society sustainable. Al Gore and others have pointed out that no matter how much we do as individuals, it will not be enough. As we can see from the example of light bulbs, we can certainly make a difference, but it is a rather small one, particularly when compared to building Interstate Wind, Rail, and Transmission Systems.

Kitchen appliances, home electronics, and that researcher's nightmare, the "Other" category, account for almost 10 percent of American electrical use. Most of these items could be made more efficient, saving probably a few percent of electrical use.

In the commercial sector, office equipment uses up 6 percent of our electricity. Industrial machinery uses up a whopping 14 percent; no doubt much electricity is wasted in both sectors.

Finally, we have industrial heating and processing, which uses up 23 percent of U.S. natural gas consumption, and 5 percent of electricity. Much of this energy is concentrated in just a few industries, in particular, chemicals, plastics, petroleum, primary metals, glass, and some food processing. These industries use almost 20 percent of all electricity, and 80 percent of industrial use. Petroleum and chemicals use nearly 15 percent of all of the natural gas; so if we stopped using petroleum, cut back on chemicals and plastics, and recycled our metals, glass, and paper, we could reap a huge reward in electricity and natural gas saved and ensure that coal was not needed.

There are still many unknowns concerning the cost of carpeting the entire country with geothermal heat pumps. For instance, according to the *San Francisco Chronicle*,[25] a 2,000-square-foot home would require $20,000 for a geothermal installation. And how much electricity would that take? According to a Department of Energy study,[26] a 25,000-square-foot building required about 33,000 kWh to operate for a year; if the typical household uses 2,500 square feet, then 3,300 kWh per year would be needed, or about 9 kWh per day. Again according to the Department of Energy,[27] "1 kilowatt [of solar photovoltaic] will produce about 1,800 kilowatt-hours a year," so we would need about 2 kWs for a typical household, or about $10,000 worth of photovoltaics, to provide the electricity needed to operate the geothermal heat pump.

With 100 million households, times $10,000 for photovoltaics and $20,000 for geothermal, that runs to about $3 trillion for the whole country; if we assume commercial buildings use about the same amount of electricity for geothermal, then we would have to double the national bill to $6 trillion. Over 20 years, this would cost $300 billion per year. I will assume that there would be enough electricity from the Interstate Wind System, or from the national network of sodium-sulfur batteries, to provide the electricity for the geothermal units at night.

If the government simply paid for these systems, then every building could use a base amount of electricity for free. Above the base level provided by the free geothermal heat pumps and Interstate Wind System, people would have to pay extra; otherwise, people would go back to wasting electricity because it was so cheap. With base electricity paid for, businesses would have much lower costs, obviously, as would residents of buildings. Maintenance of these units is pretty minimal, but the expense could be covered by a governmental corps of building energy technicians, for example.

MAKING SOCIETY ENERGY EFFICIENT

It is quite possible that the total bill for universal heating and cooling would be far under $6 trillion. First, mass production would probably cut the cost, as it has for wind power and solar photovoltaics. Second, as I argue in Chapter 11, people may choose to live in smaller units in cities, and multifamily dwellings are much more efficient than single-family homes because there is only one roof for many households. There should also be economies of scale for larger buildings in terms of insulating them, and for larger geothermal heat pumps.

Third, it might be more efficient to expand the Wind System to provide the electricity for the heat pumps, and use less of the expensive roof-based photovoltaics, except that photovoltaics on everyone's roof provides another, decentralized source of electricity and provides for resiliency. In fact, the government could bring the price of photovoltaics down drastically—if market forces don't do it instead—by financing the construction of many silicon purification plants. Pure silicon is generally the price bottleneck with photovoltaics, because refining silicon is a very energy-intensive and high-tech process. If the energy for silicon processing came from CSPs or wind, the factories could be sustainable, because the main material for pure silicon is sand.

Third, our commercial buildings are often much larger than they need to be, with all of the attendant heating, cooling, and lighting.

Finally, the most cost-effective way to decrease energy use for heating and cooling is to make buildings energy efficient. In other words, the heating/cooling needs described above could be drastically reduced if the buildings were simply better insulated. The fact that most buildings aren't is a major example of the market not working the way it is supposed to. Virtually any building efficiency work pays itself back, at most, in 10 years; yet the market has not responded.

The main reason seems to be that the financing is not available for energy retrofits, as they are sometimes called. How can we have a huge financial system for financing home purchases and virtually nothing for a sure-fire return on investment in efficiency? The answer is that the government created the entire home-financing industry during and after the Great Depression, as I relate in more detail in the next chapter.[28] The financial and real estate industries then used this government-created system to make themselves fabulously wealthy, and then they detonated the entire economy in the recent financial meltdown. The government will have to intervene again to show the "market" how to make money. One advantage of energy retrofitting is that it is very labor-intensive; the government

can certainly use large-scale retrofitting programs to soak up burgeoning unemployment, particularly in the construction industry.
Van Jones and others have shown how green-collar jobs such as retrofitting buildings can be used to lift people, or even potentially whole
communities, out of poverty.[29]

There could also be legions of energy auditors, whose job it would
be to tell home owners how to retrofit their buildings. It might also
be wise to require that owners of rental buildings would have to have
energy audits and retrofits, or else renters would have no recourse
(this would apply to commercial buildings as well). Since energy retrofits always save money, we just need the capital to do it.

Eliminating fossil fuels from our society is eminently doable. All it
would take is trillions of dollars of financing from the government
over about 10 years, and an intelligently designed set of national and
local systems. An Interstate Wind System, which could provide baseload plus part of the rest of electrical needs, could cost about $220
billion per year. An Interstate Smart Transmission System might cost
$200 billion, and could hopefully be built within five years, to give
time for the other systems to connect to it; that would be about $40
billion per year. An Interstate Battery System, made up of sodium-
sulfur and other storage systems, could cost around $1 trillion over
10 years, adding another $100 billion per year. A $6 trillion system
of geothermal heat pumps and solar photovoltaics for all residential
and commercial buildings could be extended over 20 years, at $300
billion per year, assuming it was that expensive. Finally, a national
program of energy retrofitting surely wouldn't cost more than $100
billion per year. Add them up, and we have $760 billion per year to
make our energy system completely sustainable.

Once these systems were constructed, the cost for a base amount
of electricity and heating and cooling services would be virtually
free, raising the standard of living for most people and giving a
boost to businesses. These systems could be paid for with money
printed by the Treasury Department, instead of the Federal Reserve.
That way, spending would not increase the federal debt, and would
not require the expense of paying interest. It is prudent to print
money to reflect a real increase in wealth, which building a sustainable energy system would certainly be.

Because the systems would be so cheap to maintain, without capi-
tal-related interest charges or debt, any revenue from them could be
used by the government to replace income taxes, thus stealing away

one of the conservatives' favorite talking points—and relieving pressure on the middle class, all at the same time.

People or firms could conceivably trade the electricity they don't need with people or firms who need more, thus creating a whole new market.

This program of green transformation assumes that the transportation system will use only electricity. There would probably be enough capacity left over in the Interstate Wind System to power the rail systems and the use of small electric cars. However, to make the transportation system work, and drastically reduce the amount of energy that the country needs as a result of a drop in the need for travel, we will have to redesign our urban areas.

CHAPTER 11

Rebuilding Urban Space

Cities are where all of the production systems of a society should come together. The transportation, energy, and water infrastructure networks, the spatial placement of buildings, agriculture, manufacturing, finance, and governmental policy, all have cities as their focal point.

Because human society is so complex, it is most efficient to have people physically close to each other so that they can produce, exchange, discuss, and play. Even though a majority of Americans live in suburbs, most still work and entertain themselves in cities. Cities are simply the most efficient way for humans to organize themselves.

As Jane Jacobs[1] pointed out, cities are the centers of innovation and specialization that are required for the division of labor that is needed in a complex society. A city is a system—its main elements are buildings, and the single most important definition of a city is that it has a physical structure that is dense. Cities, at the simplest level, are sets of buildings that are closely positioned next to each other.

CITIES AND DENSITY

Usually, people think of cities as being full of people, but the reason they are full of people is because they are full of buildings, often quite tall, usually tightly packed together, accompanied by an infrastructure that services those buildings. Human beings are a "buildings" species; most of our energy is used in buildings, and most of the rest is used to move from one building to another. Manufacturing

occurs in buildings, and the biggest industrial activity outside manufacturing is construction, which is mostly about making buildings.
Agriculture is the largest activity that takes place outside of buildings
on a regular basis, and even that could conceivably be moved into
buildings. Wars are the great building destroyers, and the largest activity that takes place "outside," that is, outside of a building.

Where buildings are placed in relation to one another has a profound
effect on how the buildings are used, and on the potentialities of the
urban system. *Sprawl* means that buildings are placed far from each other,
too far for walking and too sparsely populated to make transit usable.

There is a "tipping point" or "critical mass" of density that cities
need to "ignite." Because an economy is made up of so many functions, most of which need to interact with most of the others at any
particular moment in time, the city must be able to hold all of these
functional units within a small area at the same time—in other
words, buildings must be densely placed.

Not only the production system but the distribution system and
the political system must have a presence in cities—for instance,
there should be enough lawyers around when deals are going down
or new production lines are being set up. Financial and retail services must be available for the production processes, as well as marketing and advertising services, and city governments are needed to
provide protection and myriad services.

In fact, a city has to be pretty big and very dense to accumulate all of
these functions at once. The first city in a country to achieve this density
tipping point may build up enough positive feedback loops among its
various industries that it dominates the entire economy. New York City
(NYC) first achieved this role, and used it to become the headquarters
for many firms and industries, although there are now many cities that
reached a tipping point of diversity of service and manufacturing niches.
NYC is still the top city for many American industries, as London is in
the United Kingdom, Paris in France, or Tokyo in Japan.

Density is a very efficient structure for providing infrastructure
such as transportation. Walking is the most efficient form of transportation, because there is no need to store, provide energy for, wait
for, or start up a piece of transportation machinery. Before trains,
cities were basically only as big as could be walked in a reasonable
amount of time; transportation by horse didn't improve the situation
too much, but trains allowed for the first suburbs to form, albeit
suburbs that had houses within walking distance of the rail station.

Subways and elevators allow for a very quick transfer of a daily working population from outlying districts and within the city into dense commercial districts with very tall buildings, as in Manhattan. Both of these very efficient modes of transportation use electricity, unlike almost all other current forms of transportation. Subways are only worth the very large investment if the city is dense enough. Only NYC and the center of Washington, D.C. seem to have the required density in the United States; Chicago's system, the second largest, has a mostly elevated system, and Chicago would probably have to become a good deal denser to be a good candidate for an underground system.

Automobiles were, in a sense, a step backward, showing that technological change is not always beneficial, in the long run. Because automobiles take up so much space and transport so many fewer people compared to ground transit such as light rail, buses, or underground subways, they burst cities apart, much like cracks in pavement let in water, which when it turns to ice, create potholes. Or as Kenneth T. Jackson put it, "cities began to 'come apart' economically and functionally."[2] Because cities such as NYC that were built before cars couldn't widen their streets or provide much in the way of parking lots, they were able to maintain their density—at least, as in NYC, where the center of the city was successful enough to avoid being condemned and paved over.

Robert Moses attempted to destroy NYC by paving it over with highways, like some bureaucratic Godzilla running amuck. Much of the South Bronx was wiped out, and eventually became synonymous with urban decay, forced on it by the automobile. Jacobs and others managed to save much of downtown Manhattan, such as Greenwich Village, and those areas are still thriving. It is exactly because NYC, and Manhattan in particular, make driving such a brutal experience that it is able to retain its wealth-generating potential. I remember moving to Manhattan in the winter, and between the lack of parking, traffic jams, snowstorms, and ease of moving around on foot or by subway, I decided to leave my car in California. Eighty percent of the residents of Manhattan don't own a car.

Space is at premium in cities, and cars use up too much space. For the movement of people, they are unnecessary. For moving packages and goods, trucks of some sort are necessary; and within a dense city, small trucks that are powered by electric batteries would suffice (UPS is experimenting with electric brown trucks). Bicycles are much more efficient in terms of space than automobiles, so bike lanes that have barriers should be encouraged. In a very dense city such as New York, it probably would make sense, ultimately, to put subway lines down all the major avenues, as was proposed in the 1930s; the Second Avenue subway is the remaining remnant of that idea, and that is going to cost $20 billion. Light rail would make sense in the east-to-west direction, since Manhattan is narrow, and there are less people moving in an east-west direction.

CITIES AND WALKING

But before we can think about extensive, electrical transit systems, we have to plan for creating more density in the cities, and that means building more and taller buildings in the centers of cities. Assuming we would like to minimize the need for transportation and energy, the best urban structure would be one in which the city is not only dense, but *mixed use*, that is, residential, commercial, cultural, office, and even some manufacturing are all mixed together. In other words, the ideal city center is very functionally diverse.

Ideally, many people would be able to live, shop, work, and recreate all within a walkable area. Chris Leinberger uses the term *walkable urban* to describe such an area:

- at least five times as dense as drivable sub-urban (floor-area-ratio of between 0.8 and upwards to 40.0),
- mixed-use (residential, office, retail, cultural, educational, etc.),
- compact (regional-serving walkable urban places, as defined below, are generally between 100 and 500 acres in size),
- generally accessible by multiple transportation means (transit, bike, car and walking), and
- walkable for nearly every destination once in the place . . .
- Regional-serving places provide uses that have regional significance, such as employment, retail, medical, entertainment, cultural, higher education, etc., and generally integrates residential as well. (p. 1 and 2)[3]

Floor-area-ratio refers to the total area in a building, in relation to the parcel of land it occupies. Thus an 80-story building that occupies half of a piece of land would have a floor-area-ratio of 40; a single-family home with two floors might be below the .8 ratio that Leinberger describes as a minimum for a walkable area.

Leinberger estimates that only about 5 percent of the country can be described as walkable, and thinks that upward of about 30 percent would like to live in one. I think it's probable that if one-third of the country was living in a walkable community, a tipping point might be reached in which a majority of the country would come to want to move to or change their community to a walkable community; the living ideal might move from suburban dreams to urban dreams.

Density leads to transit—buses, light rail, and subways, in that order of increasing density—and transit can lead to greater density, because businesses sprout up along new transit stops, and then residences do too. Urban planners seem to think that if there are about 4 or 5 people per acre living in an area, that a bus stop will be justified. In NYC, with over 20,000 people per square mile, transit ridership is over 50 percent[4]; Manhattan's density is over 66,000 per square mile.[5]

The only way to build a society that does not rely on oil is to build one that is mostly composed of walkable communities. If Leinberger is correct that a large percentage of Americans would like to live in one, then the real estate market is not doing its job (although Leinberger believes that, with the right incentives and eliminating existing disincentives, the market could accomplish most of the work). A large-scale program of energy-efficient building construction would provide millions of good jobs, as well as provide the density cities and towns need.

Cities can make it difficult to create more density. Generally, people in a neighborhood don't like to increase density; they mistakenly think that it will ruin their quality of life, even when that quality of life is made possible by density. For instance, Richard Register writes about how difficult it has been to try to construct even incrementally denser building arrangements in Berkeley because of local opposition to "development."[6] Density and walkable urbanism will be needed to avoid the worst of our ecological problems and maximize the potential of a manufacturing-based economy.

THEN CAME THE SUBURBS

One of the reasons the suburbs were able to expand as fast as they did was because developers were able to use undeveloped land and build an entire community from scratch, without worrying about whether the residents and powers-that-be would object. Another reason was that cities, particularly by World War II, had entrenched political machines that made progressive change very difficult. The school and infrastructural systems were neglected, particularly by the end of the Depression, and these systems weren't upgraded during World War II either,[7] so that by the 1950s, it seemed easier to just build whole new communities, based on what seemed the technology of the future, the automobile. In addition, governments at all levels provided plenty of money to build long chains of roads, water and sewage lines, and electricity and oil infrastructure outward.

From the 1930s through the 1950s, the federal government essentially created the modern mortgage industry, which the private financial system used to build up their own wealth, as well as the wealth of the real estate sector, which now accounts for one-eighth of gross domestic product (GDP), as we saw in Chapter 2. According to Kenneth Jackson, "No agency of the United States government has had a more pervasive and powerful impact on the American people over the past half century [since the 1930s] than the Federal Housing Administration [FHA],"[8] which guarantees mortgages that private financial institutions provide. However, "the corollary to this achievement was the fact that FHA programs hastened the decay of inner-city neighborhoods by stripping them of much of their middle-class constituency."[9] This included the practice of "red-lining," following practices pioneered by the FHA, to rate neighborhoods by a letter and a color, "red" being the worst, which inevitably meant that it was either the area where African Americans lived or an old section of the city, or both.

Thus the federal government used its financial power to affect the shift from the cities to the suburbs—with the willing help of much of the middle class. What the federal government and the middle class wrought in one direction, they could both now do in the other.

The federal government also built the Interstate Highway System, one of the largest, if not the largest, infrastructure projects in world history. To get the project through Congress, I was told by former Speaker of the House Jim Wright, the authors of the bill had to show how it could be used by tanks in case of a national emergency. The Interstate System was critical to the spread of the automobile and particularly trucks, and gave them both a big leg up on railroads.

While in the 1960s a debate raged about whether we could afford, in Lyndon Johnson's words, "guns and butter," that is, a huge military budget along with money to keep the civilian society running, few were wondering whether we could afford both suburban and urban "butter" at the same time. James Howard Kunstler calls the construction of suburbia the biggest waste of resources in history,[10] although the construction of the military and nuclear arsenals certainly would give suburbia a run for its money.

Meanwhile, the 1960s were the era of the "urban crisis" and "urban renewal," which often meant urban destruction à la Robert Moses and large, isolated housing projects that were all density and no mixed use; a sort of vertical suburbia for poor people. This was also the period when deindustrialization started to have very deleterious effects on cities such as Newark, which had been a major manufacturing center, the second pole in the NYC metropolitan area. In 1963 the NYC area was the major manufacturing center of the United States,[11] which was the major manufacturing nation in the world. Inbred city politics which tried to keep African Americans from any power, plus a declining manufacturing job base, resulted in a lethal brew that exploded in the riots of 1967 in Newark, one of many in those years that helped burn out once-thriving industrial centers.

By the 1970s, people weren't worrying very much about the "urban crisis," as suburbanization went on its merry way, and cities like New York were told to "drop dead" by the federal government, as the *New York Daily News* headline famously put it in 1975. By the 1980s, it started to occur to people that maybe there was something nice about being able to enjoy a diversity of cultures and activities in a walkable environment; in addition, NYC started to make a comeback, with a still declining manufacturing base, by concentrating on finance and services. Services can maintain a few big cities in a large country, but they can't maintain an entire country. The "Rust Belt" emerged as a common term to describe the factory heartland of the country in the Midwest that has shut down its factories, and with them, many of its cities.

The downtowns of many cities, under assault by the automobile, finally collapsed along with manufacturing, as did many towns. The rise of big box stores such as Walmart, which in turn were dependent on the Interstate Highway System, trucks, and container cargo ships to move goods from low-wage countries, wiped out most remaining downtown retail centers.

Some of the American cities, such as Pittsburgh, Cleveland, and Buffalo, had a certain amount of success in pulling in industries and buildings that were associated with services instead of manufacturing.

Chicago still retains much of its industrial base; Richard Florida has speculated that large city regions like Chicago and New York will thrive in the future, while smaller ones like Cleveland will continue to decline, if current trends continue.[12]

THE IMPORTANCE OF BEING URBAN

Cities, like the countries that they anchor, are dependent on manufacturing for the production of wealth. As Jacobs pointed out, a city that has had a diverse set of industries, like Birmingham in Britain, has been much more resilient than a single-industry town, as Manchester was with textiles.[13] When the textiles leave, so does the job base. When one industry gets into trouble in a diverse area like Birmingham or Chicago, there are plenty of other industries ready to replace the declining one. In addition, the proximate location of so many different industries leads to cross-fertilization and the grafting of technologies from one industry to another.

For instance, the emergence of Silicon Valley resulted from universities such as Stanford and Berkeley, which are part of the greater San Francisco urban region. New companies were created from old ones, with a potpourri of innovative professors and engineers from many different fields. However, Silicon Valley grew during the era of cheap oil and plentiful automobiles. Silicon Valley will have to construct several town centers to make transit a realistic possibility.

Manufacturing has been outsourced to different continents from the United States now, but the exodus first began when factories moved out of cities such as Newark and into suburbs or rural areas such as the South. The need to move pollution-belching factories out of cities like Pittsburgh helped lead the exodus, but now technologies are available to avoid most or all pollution from manufacturing processes. If factories were arranged in circles around major cities, it would rebound to the benefit of both the city and the manufacturing. The city would gain a base of jobs for its residents, and the manufacturing firms would gain the educational and skill base with which to improve and expand.

Jacobs looked at cities as import replacement and exporting centers because of their ability to innovate, a process that was in turn dependent on the easy interaction among a diversity of people with many different talents and skills. People need to see and even feel and touch the machinery that makes goods by visiting the factories and talking face-to-face with the managers, engineers, and skilled production workers who are actually doing the work. Engineering is very much a visual, and even tactile, profession.[14]

The city also possesses a political advantage for society. When people are living close together, it becomes much easier for them to become involved in political processes and political activism. The diversity of the different cultures in the city breed a tolerance based on familiarity and less fear of the other, which in turn makes it easier to bring people together. Manufacturing also makes political activity easier because factory work brings a large group of people together in one building, particularly if the workers are unionized and the union is politically active. When most people were living in cities and the manufacturing work force was closer to 30 percent, it was much easier to organize people in favor of progressive policies. When people are spread out in culturally monolithic communities with little interaction and few opportunities to congregate, politics shifts toward fear and loathing.

Diversity means difference in building function, and it also means enjoying and taking advantage of the multiplicity of racial, ethnic, religious, gender, orientation, or myriad other differences among a large group of people. By providing a place for people to meet and interact, sometimes by chance, cities have always been cauldrons of artistic and cultural activity, and the innovations thrown up by this mixture benefited the political and economic aspects of the city.

A thriving, dense, mixed-use city that is based on manufacturing, therefore, should ideally possess the positive feedback loops within it that maintain its wealth-generating capacity. Manufacturing provides the basis of wealth creation, and the different functions within the manufacturing system all easily interact in an urban environment because it is easy for people and machinery to get from building to building, in a relatively short time span, and back again. The speed of innovation is increased as a result of the city; the increase of random, serendipitous meetings and insights serves a similar function as the random changes in DNA do for evolution, that is, density and diversity increase the likelihood of what Darwin called "variations." Variation is the raw material for evolution, and cities constantly create new technologies and opportunities.

For example, let's take clothing, still one of the strengths of NYC. The clothing industry requires textile making, which requires textile machinery, which requires all kinds of reproduction machinery such as machine tools and steel factories. New York City was never a center of machine tool manufacture but it had a great number of machine shops, and was one of the centers of the expansion of electricity early in the 20th century. The textiles, once made, have to be put together by apparel manufacturers, which tend to congregate in the "fashion district," which means that fashion designers are close by so that they can quickly try different designs and ideas. In fact, there are still some apparel makers in the fashion district whose main clientele are the fashion designers. The Fashion Institute of Technology provides a set of skilled workers and designers. Meanwhile, the marketers, advertisers, lawyers, and financiers are readily available; then there are the retailers like Macy's, which provide instant feedback on the consumer response to the industry's products, while fashion shows in the city serve as meeting places for everyone in the industry, offering more opportunities for positive feedback loops.

Printing is another example of a great many interconnections. Although newspapers are generally in trouble now, there used to be dozens of newspapers in NYC, and there are still more newspapers there than in any other city, partly because people can read on the subway or bus. Printing requires journalists, of course, many of whom become book authors, and New York has always been the center of the book industry as well, so that printing presses have plenty of business, along with magazines. Then there are the various commercial printing needs and the graphics business, which is partly supported by the needs of the corporations that are headquartered in NYC. And connected to the previous example, fashion magazines are an important part of the fashion industry and the printing industry.

In turn, the various printing and fashion industries are heavily unionized, which means that their members are both active politically and well paid. It was certainly easy to print up activist literature when manufacturing was thriving, and easy to call a large number of people together in one place to rally behind various demands.

Perhaps the classic example of a city fomenting civic participation is Paris. Every time a new administration comes to power in France, the Prime Minister tries to cut back on various parts of the safety net, and thousands or even millions of people come out into the streets to protest even the smallest infractions. Paris is also the center of a manufacturing system.

Thus for economic and political reasons it is important that manufacturing and cities go together. They both need to be strung together by infrastructure, which is in turn dependent on manufacturing for its parts. The manufacturing sector produces the trains, buses, cars, and trucks that allow the various parts of the manufacturing system to communicate and move, and manufacturing creates the machinery that allows the roads and rail tracks to be created and maintained. The water infrastructure provides the water that is used by industry, as well as enabling the dense packing of buildings and people that makes manufacturing innovative. Communications and energy networks can be efficiently installed throughout a dense area, particularly underground, with a much higher usage per person than in sparsely populated suburbs or rural areas. Indeed, one of the great achievements of the New Deal was to electrify rural areas, which were uneconomic to wire without government help. In turn, cities create the wires and telecommunications equipment and develop the electricity-generating machinery, as in Thomas Edison's first Pearl Street electricity-generating station in NYC, that power manufacturing and the rest of the city.

STARVING CITIES OF RESOURCES

The problem, as the rural electrification project demonstrates, is that the market is not willing to undertake the upgrading of the various infrastructure systems. If private firms have the political power to avoid being taxed to pay for these upgrades, then the rebuilding won't happen; and in the last several decades, infrastructure projects haven't been undertaken on the scale required to keep U.S. cities equipped with an adequate infrastructure.

Instead, huge amounts of capital have been expended on building a military system that contributes nothing to the future wealth-generating capacity of the country. The military industrial complex, to use Eisenhower's term, is very well organized, while the infrastructure-industrial complex is very disorganized. The Pentagon has created a very elaborate quilt of congressional districts and states that are dependent on Department of Defense contracts for thousands of very well-paying factory and engineering jobs. There are a few main prime contractors for the Pentagon, that is, large companies that organize the construction of jets, tanks, and other military equipment, with thousands of other firms being subcontracted to make the parts of the military equipment; meanwhile, for infrastructure, there are thousands of local jurisdictions that are individually responsible for roads, water, electricity, or any of the myriad other infrastructural projects that are generally the responsibility of a welter of states, counties, and cities, often in overlapping districts.

The Pentagon also figures that it will get better support from more conservative regions of the country like the South and Southwest than from the more liberal urban regions of the Northeast or Midwest, and so most military factories are in the "Sunbelt," causing a large-scale, long-term movement of capital, in the form of government revenues, away from the "Rust Belt," which is rusty partly because of the diversion of resources to the military. Newt Gingrich, the former Speaker of the House and general Republican strategist and leader, hailed from the district centered in Marietta, Georgia; that's Marietta as in Martin-Marietta, one of the largest defense contractors. No wonder he likes large defense budgets; but he certainly is not a fan of infrastructure investments in the cities; those we "can't afford."

If the Pentagon was devoted to creating world-class urban infrastructures instead of a world-dominating military, a political machine would be created that would support a green transformation and a built-in lobby for maintaining and improving the infrastructure.

We will have to upgrade these urban infrastructures if we want to weather the storms of the end of cheap gasoline, global warming, and ecosystem destruction, and we will need to reorient the cities to become the foundations of a manufacturing economy.

MANUFACTURING AND AGRICULTURE

Manufacturing is not the only part of the production system that should be recentralized around cities. At some point in the future, humanity will have to produce its food without the help of fossil fuels and without destroying the soil. In the well-researched essay, "What Will We Eat as the Oil Runs Out?,"[15] Richard Heinberg lists the main crises facing the global agricultural system:

The direct impacts on agriculture of *higher oil prices*: increased costs for tractor fuel, agricultural chemicals, and the transport of farm inputs and outputs[,] . . . the *increased demand for biofuels*[,] . . . the impacts of *climate change and extreme weather events* caused by fuel-based greenhouse gas emissions . . . [, and] the *degradation or loss of basic natural resources* (principally, topsoil and fresh water supplies) as a result of high rates, and unsustainable methods, of production stimulated by decades of cheap energy.[16]

His solution:

The idea is not new. The aim of substantially or entirely removing fossil fuels from agriculture is implicit in organic farming in all its various forms and permutations—including ecological agriculture, Biodynamics, Permaculture, Biointensive farming, and Natural Farming. All also have in common a prescription for the reduction or elimination of tillage, and the reduction or elimination of reliance on mechanized farm equipment. Nearly all of these systems rely on increased amounts of human labor, and on greater application of place-specific knowledge of soils, microorganisms, weather, water, and interactions between plants, animals, and humans.[17]

To make the agricultural system fossil fuel-free, the transportation of food will have to be minimized; in other words, agriculture will need to be relocalized or transported on electrified freight trains. Let's look at the United States: could organic, local farming feed everybody? I thought that as a first approximation of an answer to this problem, I would make a set of very simplified assumptions:

First, assume that 80 percent of the population lives in a city the size of NYC, which covers 786 square kilometers of land (323 square miles) and contains 8.2 million people. Thirty New York Cities would hold 246 million people and cover only three-tenths of 1 percent of the 7,900,000 square kilometers of the lower 48 states.

Let's drop the assumption that most people live in a Manhattan-style urban structure, and instead assume that myriad towns would have a similar level of density; in other words, instead of 30 more New York Cities, you might have 10 more NYCs and 200 very dense towns, for example.

Assumption number two: all farming acreage would exist in a belt around each urban region, which would include several towns in addition to the main city. And how much land would this require? According to John Jeavons,[18] inventor of the Biointensive farming system, the average American currently needs at least 15,000 square feet for food production. Jeavons claims that a vegetarian diet with vegetable sources of protein can be produced for one person using biointensive techniques on 4,000 square feet. Let's assume, however, that we will add an extra 2,000 square feet to allow for some fish and to raise some chickens, and that we will even make room for red meat lovers by letting the prairie reassert itself and culling a certain sustainable percentage from the millions of bison that again roam the plains (without industrial agriculture using up all the prairies, and no sprawl, the prairie can grow back).

So we can envision each city region being surrounded by an area that could feed 8 million people with 6,000 square feet set aside per person, or 48 billion square feet of farmland, or 1,722 square miles. This would equal about 6 times the area of the 300 square miles of the city. Each city region would have 8 million people in the city area, and 2 million people in the farming area, of which perhaps half would be adults, who would do the farming. So instead of about 1 percent of the population doing all the farming, about 20 percent would be, or around 60 million people. Heinberg estimated that a farming population of about 50 million might be necessary in a fossil fuel-free future.[19] So 2 million people times 30 regional city systems would yield about 60 million people, plus the 240 million for the cities themselves as calculated above, and we have modeled the 300 million people of the United States.

If we added about 1,000 square feet per person for a manufacturing corridor around the city, each regional city system would be composed of one-eighth city, one-eighth manufacturing corridor, and six-eighths farms. So only about 2 percent or 3 percent of the land area of the continental United States, theoretically, could feed, house, manufacture for, and employ the U.S. population (see Figure 11.1).

I'm not advocating that everybody be dragged into a NYC-styled area, sort of like a reverse-Pol-Pot scenario; NYC offers a convenient statistical and actually existing example of what is possible.

There is another sustainable alternative to industrial agriculture that is only in the planning stages. Since I am trying to restrict myself to proven technologies to map out a sustainable strategy, I wouldn't suggest this as a core solution. But a professor at Columbia, Dickson Despommier, has been developing a concept of a "vertical farm," basically a big building up to the size of a skyscraper that would grow food—light would come from windows and from

Figure 11.1 Model of an urban region incorporating agriculture and manufacturing

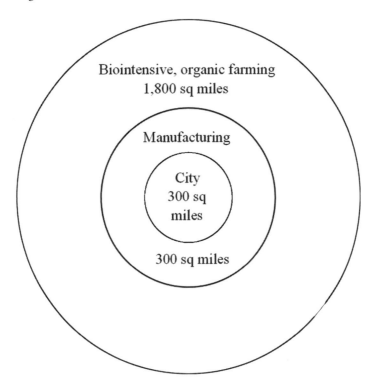

Biointensive, organic farming
1,800 sq miles

Manufacturing

City
300 sq
miles

300 sq miles

artificial lighting, the energy would come from solar panels on the building and from burning the building's agricultural waste. Instead of soil, he advocates spraying nutrients on roots or using hydroponics, that is, suspending nutrients and plants in water. Essentially, the idea is to have "super urban gardens."[20]

Urban gardens have throughout history provided quite a bit of the vegetable content of urban residents. There were the "victory gardens" in the United States during World War II that accounted for up to 40 percent of the vegetables eaten, or the tiny vegetable plots in the Soviet Union that accounted for most of the vegetables eaten there. In Havana, Cuba, 90 percent of fresh produce comes from urban gardens, as the Cuban agricultural system had to be quickly transformed when their patron, the former Union of Soviet Socialist Republics (USSR), collapsed.

Of all agricultural products, vegetables should be grown as close to the consumer as possible, because vegetables lose their nutritional value the longer they are stored before being eaten. Vegetables tend to be more expensive than grains and bulk foods like soybeans, partly because it's harder to mechanize their harvesting, so bringing vegetable gardening into the city makes them more accessible. City residents often have a hard time getting vegetables, particularly the poor. Eating your vegetables can help improve health.

Grains and bulk goods, like soybeans, may be another matter. Permaculture and biointensive gardening weave grains into the ecosystems that they create, but it might make sense, at least as a bridge system from an unsustainable to a sustainable society, to keep some form of the mechanized grain farming where it is in the Midwest, albeit with no pesticides, artificial fertilizers, or water use from non-replenishable aquifers.

Meat is the great conundrum of the agricultural system. Much of the destruction of rainforests occurs to provide pasture for raising livestock. Livestock eat most of the grain made in the world, even though, for cattle in particular, it is not a natural part of their diet. Ten calories of fossil fuels are used to produce one calorie of meat; one pound of meat, in our industrial agricultural system, necessitates the use of at least 5,000 pounds of water. Livestock—cattle, pigs, and chickens, mainly—are confined in huge factory-like areas, wallowing in their poop, which instead of being used to fertilize the farms, becomes a huge public health problem.

Can the culture adapt to less mammal meat, in particular? Can the culture adapt to less long-distance, powerful automobile driving? Eating lots of mammal meat, like long-distance car driving, is a cultural decision, not related to what the human organism needs to survive. Yet the particular modes of transportation and agriculture that we have adopted actually threaten the long-term survival of the species.

A sustainable meat system would involve, first, growing the meat sources closer to the cities, resulting in the breakup of factory farms. The second requirement would be to allow livestock to roam around farms, as they used to do, fertilizing the farms, and in turn eating some of the less usable agricultural material grown there.[21] Third, we would probably have fewer cattle and pigs, in particular, since they would roam around and not be penned up; but they would be much healthier, and they wouldn't contribute to ecosystem destruction. Or we could cull buffalo from the liberated prairies.

The fourth element in a sustainable meat system would be to encourage the production of freshwater farmed fish such as tilapia and catfish, which can actually be used to recycle garbage and wastes. This can all be done with current technology; indeed, much of it has been done for thousands of years, the recent addition being to integrate these methods with organic and permaculture farming. In much the same way that the United States was moving toward a sustainable basic infrastructure before cars arrived on the scene, much of our agricultural system has actually devolved.

All agricultural activity, to be sustainable, would have to be compatible with sustainable cities, transportation, and energy. In other words, the materials needed for farms would have to be delivered to the farms from the cities, and the produce from the farms would have to be moved from the farms to the cities. Since farms would be close to the cities, we could have an updated version of the pre-petroleum system: small electric trucks, instead of horse-drawn trucks, would take the produce to a rail station, where it would be efficiently and quickly moved into the city, and where farmers could pick up supplies.

City-based farming would be much more labor-intensive than current farming, because it would be more complex; the farmers and/or gardeners would have to understand ecological theory and practice to raise food. Much of the machinery now needed probably wouldn't be; farms would be more like gardens, particularly as you move toward the city, meaning food and materials wouldn't have to be moved as far within the farm and/or garden, and whatever processing did take place would be based on electricity. This expanded farmer population would also depend on a town center, just as the old towns often serviced the surrounding farmers.

THE CITY AS A SYSTEM

The general form of an urban region, which would be different for every area, would have a city center in the middle, where services, education, government, and other centralized activities would take place, and where the great bulk of the population would live. This small center would be surrounded by a larger ring of suburbs, which would contain town centers that had been built to create density. Most people, eventually, would probably live in the walkable neighborhoods of the cities, but suburbs that are close to rail stations and can maintain functioning centers would remain. The exurbs would not.

Surviving suburbs would have homes, ranging from single-family through apartment buildings, within 5 to 10 miles of the town center, close enough to drive with an electric car or bike. Each town center could have a train station; Manhattan is in some respects a set of town centers, each with several train (subway) stops, flowing into two huge, intercity stations, Grand Central and Penn Station. A suburb or town might be large enough for a central station that could then be linked to other stations outside the city center, but most stations would run directly into the central city's main train station.

This mainly residential and service production area would be surrounded by factories, and I'm assuming the factories would not pollute but instead would be efficient recyclers. Around these factories, and perhaps in a ring after them, would be wind farms and perhaps solar farms for energy; and then the biggest ring would be for farming and gardening, with connections from the rings into the cities using a sophisticated train network, as shown in Figure 11.1. Recycling, instead of garbage collection, would be a major activity. Each city region would be linked to other city regions by high-speed rail.

Are cities too big for an oil-free world? Big cities, because they are so dense and diverse, are actually more efficient than towns. To depopulate a city the size of NYC would require many times the acreage as now needed. For instance, Montclair, New Jersey, at a density of 6,100 people per square mile, is a relatively dense suburb (Los Angeles county has a density of about 2,000 per square mile), with some small town centers and good commuter rail. But if NYC as a whole had that density, it would spread from around 300 square miles to 1,350 square miles. The efficiency of land use is much better in large cities.

David Owen sums up the logic of big cities:

> Every house, office building and appliance, no matter where its power comes from or how many of its parts were made from soybeans, is just a single small element in a civilization-wide network of deeply interdependent relationships, and it's the network, not the individual constituents, on which our future depends. Sustainability is a context, not a gadget or a technology. . . . Dense cities . . . prove that it's possible to arrange large

human populations in ways that are inherently less wasteful and destructive.[22]

A dense city of efficient buildings, transit, local agriculture, manufacturing, and renewable energy can be built and maintained in a sustainable way, that is, without using up the natural capital of the planet. Civilization depends on it. But this green transformation can only be designed and financed by governments that are being directly pressured by an informed citizenry. We will now explore the roles of government and democracy in the creation of a sustainable society.

CHAPTER 12

The Government Is Here to Help

There are two main ways to destroy a country: either conquer a country from the outside, steal all its assets, and prevent the people of the country from rebuilding; or conquer it from the inside, steal all its assets, and prevent the people of the country from rebuilding. If you destroy the power to create wealth, destroy the capital, you destroy the country; if you build up the capital, the country will thrive.

The government, or as it's called in the social sciences, the state, is expected by its population to prevent both paths of destruction and encourage the buildup of capital. The *state*, according to the German sociologist Max Weber's definition, is an organization that has a monopoly of the legitimate use of force within a particular territory. When a country conquers another country, such a conquest is illegitimate, because the territory has been taken in a way that the conquered people do not consider legitimate; therefore, when Iraq invaded Kuwait in 1990, the global consensus was that this conquest was illegitimate and should be stopped. Since the world is divided among more than 200 countries, there is no overarching world government that can lay down rules that all other states have to follow. Instead, there is a set of very loose rules that most states follow most of the time, and when one of these rules is broken, often many other countries will work to punish the transgressor, as in the case of Iraq.

On the other hand, when the administration of George W. Bush invaded Iraq, it went through a long dance with the international community in a vain attempt to achieve some sort of legitimacy for its invasion. When the invasion occurred without any global blessing, it was considered illegitimate according to international consensus. However, the territory of Iraq now seems to be under the control of a government, which seems to hold some sort of legitimacy, at least among the Shi'ite part of the population.

It has generally also been an international rule that other states should not interfere in the internal processes of a particular state. This is implied by the stricture against invasion—if a country shouldn't invade another country to augment its own power, it shouldn't be trusted to invade another country to improve it, as in George W. Bush's partial justification of his invasion of Iraq. This rule was first agreed to by a wide array of nations after the Thirty Years War in 1648, because that war was much bloodier and destructive than it should have been, partly because some countries decided that they had the right to invade a particular territory to change the official religion. It is now usually recognized that the people of a particular state have the right to decide for themselves how they are going to structure their own systems.

This hands-off approach leads to fewer wars, but it means that it is up to the people of a particular state to make sure that the elites of that nation do not destroy the country from the inside. As we have seen, the central contradiction of social existence is that a group of people who can grab a short-term advantage in terms of wealth and power can use this advantage to create a self-reinforcing, positive feedback loop of accumulation of power. One of the easiest ways to grab this initial power advantage is to liquidate capital, that is, machinery, human capital, or natural capital, and to turn that capital into wealth that allows for a short-term increase in power domestically.

INTERNAL CAUSES OF DECLINE

A country can conquer another country, liquidate its capital, and use the newly obtained wealth to conquer ever more countries. Internally, an industry, such as the financial industry, or a part of the government, such as the military, can do something very similar, and liquidate capital to grab even more control. Like a parasite, these institutions can hollow out the society and leave an empty shell, just as an outside power can take over a country and tax it into poverty.

The 18th-century philosopher Montesquieu seemed to think that this process of depletion is a problem of size:

> It is natural for a republic to have only a small territory; otherwise it cannot long subsist. In an extensive republic there are men of large fortunes, and consequently of less moderation; there are trusts too considerable to be placed in any single subject; he has interests of his own; he soon begins to think that he may be happy and glorious by oppressing his fellow-citizens; and that he may raise himself to grandeur on the ruins of his country.[1]

The problem Montesquieu illuminates is that if the political unit is small enough to avoid "grandeur" leading to "ruin," it will be too small to build up enough wealth to fend off the military or economic influence of its neighbors. This occurs because a system of production needs to be large in scope, not "only in a small territory."

The founders of the American republic paid attention to Montesquieu and attempted to construct a government of "checks and balances," one that would prevent too much grandeur while allowing for growth. The problem with checks and balances has always been that the U.S. government has been too weak to protect itself against power centers; what the founders did not quite count on was the rise of huge centers of economic power. The checks and balances made it easier for these power centers—corporations, mostly—to swallow the state and raise themselves on the ruins of the United States.

Even the name of the country—United States of America—underscores the attempt to deal with the problem of democracy within a large size. Each state, one might argue, would be a better foundation for a more direct form of democracy than a large country. The word "state" was used by the founders because it signified an entire country. The United States was supposed to be based on local democracy, but unified economically and militarily so that it could create both wealth and power, respectively, to survive as an independent entity.

As Alfred Chandler showed in his books, first the railroads, and then other large corporations, sought to span the entire country, both because it was more efficient to do so—because of economies of scale—and because those efficiencies brought more wealth and more market power. Most industries quite naturally turned into oligopolies; that is, they are controlled by a very few companies.

In many other countries, when something like railroads or phone systems had to be created, the economies of scale led to government takeover of the industry in question; but this didn't always take place, as in Germany, where cartels were formed that encompassed most of an industry. In the United States, the problem of corporate size led to antitrust legislation and the regulatory agencies of the Progressive era that were often captured by the very industries they were trying to regulate.

Now several industries have virtually taken over their counterparts in the federal government. Probably the first industry to do this was the agricultural industry, which basically owns the Department of Agriculture, but there is also the fossil fuel industry's Department of Energy and the financial industry's Department of Treasury. Because there is no Department of Health Insurance, the health insurance industry simply took over Congress, and exempted itself from antitrust legislation and virtually any other oversight.

THE LOGIC OF EMPLOYEE POWER

The logical, if not politically realistic, solution to the lack of checks and balances between the political system and corporations would be to make all large companies employee-owned-and-operated. To a certain extent, the Germans reacted to their pre-World War II era cartels and the very irresponsible way that their big companies cooperated with Hitler by mandating extensive employee control of most companies. Although not as complete as total employee control, "codetermination," as the Germans call it, between the management and employees, allows for enough influence by unions to avoid many of the problems of corporate-captured government that plague the United States.

Most people in Germany have gone through apprenticeship programs, even in the service industries, which build a high skill level among the citizenry, which translates into more power in the workplace. The apprenticeship programs are run by the government, business, and the unions, cooperatively.[2] German companies cannot simply pull up and move factories to another country, as they can in the United States, and this stability gives the employees much more say. The German metalworking union is the largest of its kind in the world, and always has a powerful voice in wage determination and other internal corporate policies.

Wouldn't employee-controlled health insurance companies and financial firms be just as greedy and self-centered as ones controlled by top managers? Probably not, because the vast majority of employees at most companies would have the great advantage of having a longer-term view than the current crop of top managers. Top managers want to become as rich as possible, as quickly as possible, which often means liquidating capital. By contrast, most employees would naturally seek to conserve most forms of capital.

Employee-controlled firms would want to preserve human capital, since that is what the employees are. Nobody is going to vote for a set of managers who will want to fire the voters. The more employees have control, the more they are going to want to upgrade their skills with training. Japanese workers and unions insisted on the lifetime employment policies of Japanese corporations; by retaining employees for their entire working lives, Japanese firms gain a large advantage in the human capital that they continually augment.[3]

Think how much better off the middle class in the United States would be if companies had been employee-owned-and-controlled these past thirty years. Millions of jobs would have been saved, and trillions of dollars more would have gone into paychecks. The middle class would not have had to indulge in the Faustian bargain of credit cards and home equity loans to make up for the gap in income growth that occurred in the 1980s, 1990s, and 2000s.

In the United States, on the other hand, we are often told that jobs will become more and more uncertain, that people will have to get used to moving from company to company, taking their "bundle of skills" with them, selling themselves as virtual entrepreneurs to the next employer who, in any case, will dump them as soon as it is minimally convenient. If this were the early 19th century when many of these theories were dreamed up, it might make some sense, but in the 21st-century world this wanton destruction of human capital simply impoverishes the firms that engage in it, and by extension the country as well.

Neoclassical economists often seem to think of the firm as some kind of early 19th-century textile factory, where the main problem was to try to prevent that great evil of neoclassical economics, "shirking." Because economists assume that technology doesn't change and that capital doesn't exist, the big problem in the firm is to make sure that all employees work as hard as they can. In reality, if the firm gives employees a certain amount of leeway in their jobs, and a certain amount of ownership over how their job operates, employees can create most of the innovation that even economists admit is the root of economic growth.

In addition, attentive and motivated employees will keep the physical capital, that is, machinery, running at a constant and reliable rate. The productivity of capital is much more important than the productivity of labor. The *productivity of labor*—how many people it takes to create a certain output—is an indicator of how rich people are, or should be if income is distributed fairly. Labor is productive for three reasons: the machinery (physical capital) that the labor uses, the skill of the people (human capital), and the way that the labor and machinery are organized to create the output (a combination of physical and human capital).

Machinery should ideally be constantly in use, that is, creating output. In service industries this principle might not make too much sense, because they service people and people sleep and rest. In factories, machinery can run 24 hours—if it is adequately maintained. If machinery stops working, nothing is output and so productivity goes down. If capital is less productive, so is everything else, including labor.

So how do you keep capital, that is, machinery, up and running? You give the workers who are running the machinery as much training and power over the machinery as possible. The more highly skilled they are, and the more they can control what they are doing, the more the machinery can keep going, and the better productivity is and the richer the society becomes. For instance, Bernard Nneji compared two machine shops for his dissertation. In one, the machinists had no control over their machinery; in the other, in which the machinists were able to program their machines and had a say in their operations, productivity and stability of production were much greater; machine utilization jumped from a range of 25 percent to 30 percent to a range of 70 percent to 90 percent.[4] When workers have decision-making power within the workplace, they simply perform better, and they keep the machines running more reliably and cooperate to turn the entire factory into an efficiently operating system.

The more sophisticated the machinery is, the more worker power yields higher productivity. This is why a factory that pays its workers in the United States 10 times the wage of a worker in China can make more money than if it was in China, if the U.S. workers are 10 times better at keeping the machinery running—which they often are. In addition, if the engineers who designed the machinery and the layout of the factory are a few minutes away from the factory, and the engineers can help to iron out bugs and help with enhancements, the factory can become more productive, more quickly, than one in another country with no engineers in sight.

Some firms are set up so that the engineers take a design they are working on, then "throw it over the wall" to the production department, never to deal with the design again. The Japanese and Germans don't have a wall, and by the 1980s they were outcompeting American companies in many product areas. Now, many American companies take their designs and "throw it over the ocean," letting the production team in China wrestle with a flawed design.

The third kind of capital, natural capital, would also be better preserved the more employees controlled their own workplaces. Any immediate loss of profits from installing pollution equipment or using recycled materials or not emitting carbon would be spread out over a much larger group of employees than in the case of top management, who are skimming the profit and distributing it among a very few people. The employees would appreciate the long-term savings from being more efficient. In addition, people in a factory live in the area of the factory (or the office) and would reap the benefits of an improved environment, while absentee owners who live hundreds or thousands of miles away wouldn't even notice the effects of less pollution, except for the size of their bonus.

If most firms were not only employee controlled, but also employee owned, the most profound effect might be that the stock market would virtually disappear. The stock market exists to trade shares of a company, that is, pieces of ownership. If firms were employee owned, there would be no shares that could be owned outside the company.

Sometimes employee-owned companies distribute their shares to their employees who are then free to sell it—even to people outside the company. Any employee-owned-and-controlled firm in which this happens is not an employee-owned-and-controlled firm in the long run, and thus, not considered so for the purposes of this analysis. The biggest and best known example of workplace democracy is the Mondragon system of co-ops in the Basque region of Spain, and the shares that all workers own there are not tradeable.

The economic justification for the stock market is that it serves to provide financial capital to firms. In most other countries, the main method of providing capital is through the banks, a difference that was the subject of a book by John Zysman.[5] He argued that economic systems that are financially centered on banks, such as Germany and Japan, perform better in the long term and do not suffer from the same sort of short-term problems that the American stock-market-centered system does. We see that German and Japanese machinery industries are trouncing American ones.

In the American stock-market-centered system, quarterly profits become the focus of economic performance, because stocks can go up and down in milliseconds, and firms can profit from those ups and downs. But trying to maximize performance every three months is about the worst way to run an economy; it's a system designed to liquidate capital, thus undermining long-term performance. Certainly routine maintenance of machinery would be "shirked"; who cares if a $100 million boiler has to be replaced a few years earlier than necessary, if you can save a few thousand dollars in a quarter? This actually happened in a firm studied by Shoshana Zuboff.[6]

Any investment is suspect if performance is judged every three months. Employee training (much less raises), or hiring new engineers, or installing equipment to prevent carbon emissions or energy loss is put off or eliminated in such an environment even if it would lead to greater profits in the future.

Worst of all, if some companies are increasing their profits in the short term and raising capital from the financial system as a reward for doing so, they can get a jump on their competitors who are doing the right thing and becoming more efficient and sustainable in the long run. The firms that are doing the right thing have to start doing the wrong thing or risk being taken over or losing market share.

Short-term obsessed firms come to control the *state* to ensure that the state will stay out of their way as they dismantle as much capital as possible and destroy the country from within. If these firms *use* the state to grab even more wealth, they can pick up the pieces after disasters; this is what Naomi Klein calls "disaster capitalism."[7] No conspiracy theory is needed; people with large piles of wealth and power at their disposal can simply sit around and wait for disaster to strike, much like a bunch of vultures will sit in a tree waiting for an animal to die—not to disparage the essential work of vultures.

Firms in which employees have a good deal of power will try to preserve the various forms of capital at their disposal, and will tend to act and invest in a more long-term manner. Because the state controls the legal framework of a country, it also controls the governance of the firm. Currently, it considers a corporation to have the same rights as an individual, but does not extend liability to the actual individuals that control the firm.

The state could also control how employees control part or even all of the decision making within a firm. The easiest change would actually be to require that all companies above a certain size have a union or unions representing all the employees. This could be accomplished with one piece of legislation, and would ensure that employees had some kind of organized voice vis-a-vis the management, as well as encouraging high wages and the attendant innovation incentives of higher wages.

The state could also require, as Germany does, that almost all firms have a supervisory board in which half of its members were elected from all employees; or the state could require that all members of the board of directors be elected by the employees.

The state could even require that all firms follow the Mondragon model I alluded to earlier. In the Mondragon system, each employee gives the co-op system a certain amount of money when they enter, in return for a share of the system.[8] This investment capital is lent to new employees if they don't have the money available when they are first hired. When the employees leave or retire, they get the investment back plus a percentage of all profits accumulated since they were hired. The financial capital of the firm thus acts as a kind of retirement account, as well as equitably sharing the returns of the system. All employees elect the equivalent of the chief executive officer (CEO) and board of directors.

There are almost 100,000 people working in the Mondragon system—how would an entire society be constructed using Mondragon principles? Validating Montesquieu and Rousseau, it would seem that economic democracy really needs to take place at a fairly local level. The biggest individual unit in Mondragon is around 500 employees. Above that number, they have found that democracy becomes much more difficult. Besides a systemwide board that is composed of representatives of all firms, the unifying institution in Mondragon is their bank, the Caja Laboral, the Working Peoples' Bank.

The Caja Laboral is controlled by all of the firms in the system and by the employees of the bank. The bank is funded from profits of the system and by consumer deposits from the workers and even local residents, and provides the finance capital needed for the various firms. In addition, it serves as a venture capital and/or management consultant agency, helping new companies to form and helping established ones expand. Not only does it help the companies think long term, it encourages those stars of the neoclassical universe, entrepreneurs.

There is a system of local, municipally owned banks in Japan that serves a similar supportive service. These Shokoka[9] loan small amounts to the myriad small machine shops and small manufacturing businesses in many districts of Japan, and have been an important reason for Japan's rise to manufacturing leadership.

The Emilia-Romagna region of Italy is home to networks of thousands of high-skill, entrepreneurial firms, most of which are co-ops. The region's government helps these firms financially and technically.

In a large region such as the United States, it is conceivable that one might want to have an Employee Bank in, for example, every Congressional district, which has about 500,000 people apiece. Putting the congressperson on the board of directors would be one way to ensure political support for a national network of banks, sort of a super-military-industrial-congressional complex; that is, a workplace-democracy-financial-congressional complex.

Economic democracy could be encouraged short of a full-scale Mondragonization of the country. Besides making unionization much easier (if not mandatory), one could also raise minimum wage laws, or make the government the "employer of last resort."[10] As employer of last resort, the government could replace minimum wage laws by guaranteeing a job for anyone who wanted one, with a certain minimum wage, such as $10 per hour. As I have explained in the last few chapters, there is plenty of work that needs to be done to make the society economically and ecologically sustainable.

If employees could leave a bad employment situation, the employer would have to make the workplace more attractive to keep employees; one of the best ways to make a workplace attractive is to give employees more decision-making power. One of the great motivating factors for companies moving offshore has been exactly to threaten employees and take away whatever decision-making responsibilities they have gained over the years.

In studying factory off-shoring over several decades, Seymour Melman could find no instance in which a factory was actually losing money. In other words, the factories that closed down were always making profits, which meant that had those factories been employee-owned-and-controlled, virtually no factories would have been offshored, and there would be millions more good jobs in the United States. Besides the short-term increase in profits for the companies that resulted from the offshoring of factories, the other effect was to weaken unions and the general ability of working people to control their work lives.

Governments all over the world count factories as a part of the country in which they are located; they don't allow factories to simply be closed down and their equipment moved. In the 1980s there were proposals to at least give a certain warning period before closings took place in the United States, but those were shot down in the heady days of the Reagan administration. Making the shutdown of factories difficult would increase employee power; despite warnings of the horrors of decreased "flexibility" that conservative economists decry concerning restrictions on factory shutdowns, their relative rarity in Europe and Japan does not seem to be hurting their overall industrial competence.

Another avenue is to pursue what might be called "labor policies," or simply move more toward a "Nordic Model," both being proposed by James Galbraith.[11] There are many possibilities here. For instance, in Sweden about 85 percent of the workforce is unionized, and 80 percent receive some sort of training throughout the year. Since the unions negotiate the wages and salaries, companies can't lower wages. A universal, affordable health care system not only increases health, but allows people to move from jobs they don't like without fear of losing health insurance. A well-run pension system gives people the option of retiring, which decreases labor supply, which pushes up wages. Child care support by the state makes entry into the workforce easier, as well as helping the long-term development of children.

One result of greater employee power is that the Nordic countries are actually more open to free trade and in many cases have less regulation of business than in countries that have less employee power. If firms were employee-owned-and-controlled, there would be less need for regulation, because firms would be less likely to abuse their workers, their communities, consumers, and environment.[12]

The more power businesses have over the state, ironically the less able the state is to protect those businesses' long-term future and the future of the great majority of its people. In a modern economy, because of modern transportation, energy, and communications technologies, economic enterprises obtain the advantages of economies of scale by forming oligopolies, which enable the dictators of those firms, the CEOs, to wield enormous power over the state. If firms are made more democratic, the power of the CEOs is diminished, the incentives toward short-term behavior are minimized, the productivity and maintenance of capital is encouraged, and the capability of the government to look out for the general welfare, in the long-term, is increased.

The consequence of these processes is that the middle class would become both richer and more powerful within companies. The process of democratic decision making or at least having a certain amount of control and permanence in one's job, would give the middle class an almost daily chance to experience democracy firsthand.

SNOWBALLING POWER

Why is it so easy for large companies and concentrations of power to form and influence government? Mancur Olson[13] tried to explain why nations become "sclerotic," as he put it, that is, they became controlled so tightly by the powers-that-be that they can't move or act to fix the problems that they face. He begins with the basic problem of "collective action," an area that he pioneered. He points out that it is easier for a small group of people to act collectively than for a large group. Thus, even though a majority of Americans would like to see a single-payer health insurance system like Medicare, a handful of health insurance CEOs can get together and decide on a particular strategy that wins in a confrontation in Congress.

Olson noted that World War II cleared out much of the sclerosis from Western Europe, in countries such as Germany where the elites were almost completely overthrown. Hopefully we don't have to wait for a World War to move against the entrenched interests that are slowly choking the United States and the whole planet.

The large corporations, along with the military elites, are trying to extend their power, as power elites have been trying to do for thousands of years. C. Wright Mills referred to this combination of power, along with other government elites, as the "power elite."[14] They are caught up in the rush of holding power; they can't help themselves. John Kenneth Galbraith hypothesized[15] that there are various forms of "countervailing" power, in particular unions and the government, that can form a balance of power, a negative feedback loop, against the snowballing accumulation of power that besets any society after a certain amount of time. In order to prevent countervailing power from forming, it has been part of the corporate strategy to extinguish the unions and to convince the public that the government can't help economically.

One of the primary motivations behind the offshoring of factories in the United States has been to break the power of the unions. Manufacturing is very heavily unionized, because manufacturing gives workers a large amount of potential power. Because they physically control the means of production while they are working, they can easily take over a factory and shut it down if their demands are not met. As I explained previously, competent management will improve the machinery and processes of production in response to successful demands for a share of the productivity gains of the enterprise. By contrast, a management that depends more on control than technological innovation can move the factory to an area in which the government can be counted on to prevent unions from forming and operating, such as Mexico and, ironically, Communist China.

As manufacturing has declined, so has unionization. In 1975, the unionization rate in private industry was 25 percent, in 1985 it was 15.9 percent, and in 2008 it was 8.4 percent.[16] In the same period, the percentage of the economy devoted to manufacturing declined from 20.6 percent to 17.5 percent to 11.5 percent.[17]

The government can't democratize the economy if it has been taken over by market forces. Ronald Reagan, the hero of the conservative movement of the last 50 years, used three lines over and over: "Government is not part of the solution, government is part of the problem"; "get the government off our backs"; and "the nine most dangerous words in the English language are 'I'm from the government and I'm here to help.'" Microeconomics courses teach their students to believe these things, with different words; the government, except in those occasional moments of "market failure," can only make things worse, because competitive markets will naturally move back into an optimal equilibrium, if only they aren't interfered with. If the economy is heading in the wrong direction, then, it must be the government's fault, because markets are self-correcting, or so goes this line of reasoning.

Many centrists and progressives, who don't necessarily buy this conservative-economist line, see that the government is controlled by huge industries, and conclude that the government can't be trusted. For instance, many environmentalists are justifiably concerned that one of the federal government's main forays into the economy has been to encourage the production of corn ethanol, which is not only destructive of the environment, takes food away from poor populations, and costs a lot of money, it might actually wind up putting more greenhouse gases into the environment than oil.

With the government and unions checkmated instead of fulfilling Galbraith's roles as countervailing forces, the current power elites have little to challenge them except the reality that their preferred policy prescriptions will lead to the collapse of the country that is the base of their power. But like any addict, the power elite are not too concerned with the long term, and in any case they convince themselves—or in the case of the power elite, pay a lot of people a lot of money to convince themselves and everybody else—that whatever they are doing is the best of all possible worlds. So much of the public is convinced, or has a tendency to believe, that the government shouldn't intervene in the economy. An explicit argument needs to be made that the government does, indeed, need to intervene.

A THEORY OF GOVERNMENT INTERVENTION

Currently, the state of the art of the ideological justification for state intervention is not very useful, for a number of reasons. First of all, the dominant economic paradigm, neoclassical economics, is partly based on the idea that the government shouldn't intervene. Second, and worse, there is no alternative paradigm that people can turn to. Marxism used to be an alternative and still is, but central planning has been rightly discredited. Most of the current Marxist writing is concerned with analyzing capitalism, not an alternative.

Third, most advanced and developing countries practice a good deal of governmental intervention, but they don't try to intellectually justify their actions. Industrial policy is simply described, as when the Japanese government uses the Ministry of International Trade and Industry to "guide" the economy to become a more sophisticated manufacturing power than the United States, or China uses very high trade barriers to help in its industrialization, or Germany mandates that employees elect the members of the board of directors and supports apprenticeships for nearly the entire population. All of these countries have properly trained economists who produce analyses that would be very well accepted in the United States, even though their governments pay no attention to such analyses.

The result is that even enormous global problems, like global warming, spawn the advocacy of market-based solutions like cap-and-trade that can't solve the problem and are very obscure to almost the entire population. Countries that know better, like Japan, don't advocate the direct construction of wind farms and trains to prevent global warming; instead they go along with market ideology, even hosting the largely toothless and ineffective Kyoto Protocols. This all occurs while climate change leaders such as Al Gore call for a "World War II"-type effort, not seeming to realize that a "World War II"-type effort means that the government would have to take over one-third of the economy.

If we actually look at what governments do, however, we see a completely different picture. South Korean history offers an excellent example of a government-controlled development process that was also market based. The government very carefully controlled, and still mostly restricts, all investment money coming into the country, and controls most of Korea's financial institutions. It can therefore direct funds in the way it thinks most appropriate, which, since 1960, has meant more and more advanced levels of manufacturing.

The Korean government determines that a certain sector needs help, and then goes about finding foreign companies that are willing to come to Korea, set up a joint venture—that is, create a company that, in the Korean case, is usually majority-owned by a Korean company—and then arranges for the skills and technologies of the foreign company to be transferred to Korean engineers and companies. Finally, in most cases, at the end of a number of years the firm is actually required to become totally Korean. Perhaps incredibly for American sensitivities, numerous firms, including American ones, have participated in these joint-venture-becomes-Korean-venture deals, because the foreign company does make a good profit—in fact, the profit is often guaranteed. More incredibly, no domestic firm is allowed to be taken over by a foreign one.

This is the way Russell Mardon puts it:

Once a foreign firm enters into a joint venture with a Korean firm, technical and managerial expertise begins to be transferred. As agreed on in the terms of the joint venture, the foreign partner is required to train the Korean partner's personnel in managerial, technical, engineering, accounting, and other related production techniques and skills. Several foreign managers in Korea related that a joint venture with a Korean firm involves a high level of personnel rotation. Korean personnel assigned to joint venture projects are often transferred to other subsidiaries of the Korean partner after they have acquired the necessary knowledge to perform their tasks. New personnel must then be trained by the foreign partner while the original employees apply their knowledge to other production processes of the Korean firm. After the Korean personnel have learned the technology necessary to operate the joint venture enterprise, expansion in that sector is carried out by the domestic partner exclusively, and that sector is closed to further foreign investment. Eventually, production thus becomes dominated by Korean producers.[18]

What the Koreans have done is to make sure that their human capital is *expanded quantitatively* and *improved qualitatively*. They did this by controlling finance capital, and in particular, foreign finance capital in the form of foreign direct investment, that is, financial purchase of a piece or all of a company. The Koreans might have the lowest level of direct foreign investment in the world, yet they are often held up as an example of the success of a market economy by neoclassical economists, because they attained what most government-directed industrial economies attain—the competence to produce manufactured goods that can be successfully traded in international markets.

As Erik Reinert points out,[19] all economies that have thrived in the global economy have done so after instituting trade barriers, industrializing, and then gradually bringing down those trade barriers, so that ironically the best way to increase trade, in the long run, is to decrease foreign imports in the short run. In the same way, the best way to increase the military potential of a country in the long run is to decrease one's military size in the short run, and for the same reason: it is human and physical capital associated with civilian manufacturing that must be encouraged, by transferring foreign knowledge if necessary, and by transferring capital from the military to the civilian economy, if possible.

Instead of assuming that the economy is self-correcting, we can assume that the economy is like an ecosystem, made up of functional parts. Every part is necessary and all the parts are interdependent. If one part robs the others of resources or declines, then the whole system can decline. Firms compete within an industry, but they cooperate across production niches. Furthermore, in a loosely interconnected functional system such as an economy or ecosystem, there is no automatic stabilizer present that can save the system as a whole. But humans can save a system by understanding how it works.

The scariest words in the New Testament are Jesus' last words, "Forgive them, Lord, they know not what they do," because people should collectively know what they are doing, and use their government to do what the situation requires. We have the advantage of large, complex brains.

For instance, by the turn of the 20th century, Americans seemed to be on the verge of destroying every possible ecosystem, but citizens came together and established a national parks system, which eventually became a system for managing the ecosystems within the national parks. A wolf population was reestablished in Yellowstone, which helped various plant species. After all, plants need carnivores to control the plants' mortal enemies, herbivores.

A few decades later, the national government intervened to save the national economy in the form of the New Deal, overcoming the neoclassical economic doctrines of letting the market, that is, the most powerful economic actors in the country, from doing whatever they will. Now we are in a position where many of the functional subsystems in the economy—manufacturing, transportation, energy, urban, financial, health, education—are moving in the wrong direction, and will make the problems of each worse as they themselves worsen.

We can look at a machine, say a car or a TV, and we know that it is not working because one of its parts is broken, or perhaps there is a more systemic problem at work. We can look at an ecosystem, and know that it is declining because of outside factors, such as climate change or resource exploitation, and figure out ways to fix the

problem. If a person is sick, a doctor figures out the best intervention. In all of these examples, we are looking at a system as a whole,
and quite consciously changing the system because we know how
the system works. We know how each piece works, and how the
pieces should affect and impact the other pieces.

An economy, and particularly a global economy, is about the most
complex system we encounter, with the exception of the global climate and ecosystems. We can never achieve the same sort of exact
knowledge and prediction as, say, with a human body or machine.
Like an ecosystem, we are dealing with a dynamic, unpredictable,
constantly evolving system. But also like an ecosystem, we know at a
system-wide level how the parts should fit together, and we have
some idea about what kinds of technologies would work better than
others.

For instance, since we've never used wind and solar energy as a
basis of an electrical system we don't know exactly how the parts of
a renewable energy system would all fit together and replace coal,
oil, and natural gas, but we have a pretty good idea of how to do it,
and we know (or should know) that we have the resources to do it.
We know we can put together cities and systems of cities that use
electric trains, because we've been doing that, in various ways, for
decades. We have dozens of examples of policies that have helped
countries develop manufacturing systems.

Government intervention is the only way to consciously fix the
economy, and we need to design a new economy before it's too late.
Effective government intervention has to be holistic, not the result
of a multitude of power-extending industries trying to squeeze more
wealth out of the capital of the economy and the environment.

The various sectors of the economic and political systems cannot
fix the system by pursuing their individual short-term interests. For
example, legislatures tend to create fragmented policy, because they
reflect the particular interests of their district.

The top elite, such as the president of the United States, tends to
think of extending his power militarily, sometimes by limiting civil
liberties. The military also extends its power by engaging in imperial
wars like the ones recently in Iraq and Afghanistan, or previously in
Vietnam; in the United States the military has bought influence by
placing military equipment factories in most congressional districts,
so that the military has an inordinate amount of control in both the
executive and legislative branches.

For the financial sector, Marx's injunction that the capitalist must, before all things, "Accumulate!" is doubly powerful. Because financial accumulation of power can be very fast, every company must continually maximize its short-term wealth, or else it will be left behind. There is no market-based solution to being under the control of out-of-control institutions. The citizenry of the United States, and every other nation, has to understand how the various pieces of the political, economic, and environmental systems have to fit together and cooperate to be sustainable. Once they understand the global and national systems as a whole, they can debate how best to change the system to be sustainable, and then they will have to elect legislatures, presidents, and prime ministers who will put the pieces together. Without popular pressure, the government will keep doing what the wealthiest and most powerful institutions want. Without government and popular pressure, corporations will keep destroying ecosystems, warming the globe, liquidating economic and ecological capital, and using government institutions to expand their power.

THE GLOBAL IMPERATIVE

All around the world, we need to democratize, unify, and industrialize all the world regions of the planet. A world of democratic industrial continents and subcontinents would yield many benefits. First, the likelihood of war would dramatically decrease. Since each world region would have an independent capability to produce arms, each would be very difficult to conquer. Because all countries would be joined to a powerful region, no aggressor would be tempted to pick off weak countries. Global peace would free up trillions of dollars in military spending and prevent untold suffering.

A world of 10 or so economically integrated regions would create greater technological progress than we now have, because there would be 10 or so centers of innovation. Each region could trade their best innovations with one another, instead of beggaring one region by exporting from their own, as China is now doing with the United States. The threat of worldwide recessions and depressions would be lessened if all regions pursued intelligent policies of manufacturing support; at any one time, most regions would be able to provide a market for the exports if one other region did experience an economic dip.

The North American Free Trade Agreement (NAFTA) envisions a free market among the United States, Canada, and Mexico, but without the free flow of people that is possible in the European Union. The income difference between the United States and Mexico is the greatest between two neighbors. A real North American Union would have to involve the industrialization of Mexico, so that it could be integrated without massive disruption. Integration now would only destroy what is left of Mexico's economy, and encourage an even greater wave of people desperate to find jobs in the United States.

The European Union has its own problems, but it has encompassed most of the subcontinent of Asia, which we call "Europe." China and India are natural economic and political units; Afghanistan and Pakistan will probably only become stable if they are integrated into an India-centered South Asian region (without being exploited, of course). South America and Africa, or at least sub-Saharan Africa, would seem to be natural units; perhaps the Caribbean and Central America could eventually be folded into a larger North American economy.

The rest of Asia is a little more difficult to carve into natural regions, but the Middle East is generally considered as a unit; it might or might not include North Africa, or North Africa might eventually be part of an African region or even a European one. The former Soviet Union as an economic region has a certain logic, as it had when the Mongols controlled a similar area. Southeast Asia, in some form, including Australia and New Zealand, might make sense as part of a larger area including Japan and Korea.

However one draws the regions, the peaceful generation of wealth and power can only be brought to the entire planet if the economic region is large enough, the set of governments intelligently designs their economies to be centered on sustainable manufacturing, and democracy is spread through as much of the political and economic systems as possible. The regions will then have to work together to make all of their component systems, such as in transportation, energy, cities, and agriculture, as ecologically benign as possible.

The UN could be restructured to help move toward this world. Each of 10 or so regions could appoint a member of the Security Council, the central security decision-making body; the General Assembly, now composed of all members, could have two chambers, one that elected representatives according to party by region, the other that elected representatives by district by region, and together they could elect a global prime minister to replace the general secretary. The UN could then help to enforce the protection of the world's ecosystems, and help nations move to greenhouse-gas-free economies, based on clean manufacturing, using recycled goods.

Manufacturing green prosperity will not be easy. It will be a long-term process that we must build toward, city by city, nation by nation, and region by region. We will all have to participate in the great experiment called democracy to ensure that the human species thrives with the rest of the inhabitants of planet Earth.

CHAPTER 13

Conclusion: Beginning the World Over Again

What will our civilization look like in 50 years? If we continue as we are now, with business as usual, chances are that our civilization will be in the process of collapsing. If we follow the path I have been exploring in this book, a program of economic reconstruction, centered on building a sustainable manufacturing sector, democratizing firms, and reorienting finance, and encompassing a green transformation of urban, energy, and transportation infrastructures, then chances are that our civilization will flourish. My path is certainly not the only possible successful one; what is most important is that we paint a picture of what a sustainable civilization will look like, and then form a global consensus to move in the agreed-on direction.

Human beings think in visual terms. When someone says, "A picture is worth 1000 words," it is because the human mind understands the world as a system, that is, as a set of elements with a certain structure. A picture shows how things are positioned relative to each other, and the mind can process this information instantly as a "gestalt," that is, as a whole. All of our problems and their solutions are connected together; they must all be addressed at the same time, or the problems will not be resolved.

ALL TOGETHER NOW

The progressive public, on the other hand, tends to be broken up into little pieces. There are those who are focused on health care reform, some on global warming, some on union organizing, some on problems of the African American community in the cities, some on issues of concern to gay people, some on renewable energy, some on what the Republicans are doing (including almost all of the progressive media), some on electing good candidates, and many progressives are simply focusing on survival. All of these issues are very important and the work done on their behalf is to be encouraged. The problem is to link all of these issues together. Without this linkage, I fear, very little can be accomplished. With a common vision, I predict that most progressive policies could be realized.

Back around 1991, when the Soviet Union collapsed, many of us thought that the time had come to seriously shift resources from military to civilian needs. After all, the entire military had been built with one major purpose, to contain the Soviet Union. Surely, with the Soviet Union gone, the military would not need so many resources. This would be an opportunity to unite the various progressive movements; surely, everyone needed more money for their causes.

However, organizations only have so many resources, and cutting down the military budget seemed like Don Quixote tilting at windmills—that is, a lost cause. Meanwhile, the military was busy justifying their huge budget, although they needn't have worried too much, as the political machine they had built up, putting factories and bases in most congressional districts, plus a decades-long campaign of spreading fear and empire, was enough to keep them well-endowed until the next big foe, terrorism, allowed them to build up even larger budgets than when the Soviet Union was the big threat.

When the conservative movement was, seemingly, at a similar moment of loss of influence in the late 1960s, their response was to take a long-term view. They established various think tanks and media, engaged in wide-ranging discussions, and tried to work slowly to build up a set of ideas that would make for an attractive story about why the ills of society were the way they were, and how to fix them. With Ronald Reagan's ascendancy into the presidency in 1981, this strategy came to fruition.

Conservative efforts have always had more resources behind them than progressive efforts, because the very wealthy and very powerful wish to justify their wealth and power, and conservative ideology has usually (if not always) been based on the idea that the most wealthy and most powerful should be left to do what they will. As we have seen through the course of this book, the wealthiest and richest sectors of a society benefit from a positive feedback loop—their wealth and power increase their chances that they will be able to gain even more wealth and power. That means that if government can stay off their backs, they can generally accumulate more and more. This might collapse the entire economy, but very powerful people can hire other individuals to convince both other people and themselves that their actions aren't the problem, even if they obviously are.

The major institution that is always in a position to constrain the richest and most powerful is government, which is why it is an essential part of conservative ideology—enshrined in the dominant economic paradigm, neoclassical economics—that government is the problem, not the solution. When the richest and most powerful can turn the government to their own bidding, *then* government is seen as useful, at which point the society tilts down steeper and steeper, in a process reminiscent of ancient Rome, in which the ruling class took more and more from the empire and contributed less and less, until Rome fell.

Therefore, progressive movements should try to form a long-term project of understanding and explaining how we can get out of our various messes. The most important task is to paint a picture of what a sustainable society would look like. Currently, particularly in the progressive media, the focus is on the terrible things that the conservatives and Republicans are doing and have been doing, at least since Reagan. This is necessary work, but it is not the most critical work. The critical work is to elaborate a vision of where the society will be, with a perspective of at least 10 years in the future.

CONSTRUCTING AN INCONVENIENT CONVENTIONAL WISDOM

How can one think about long-term visions and futures when so much is going wrong right now? The carbon-equivalent in the atmosphere is currently 385 parts per million (ppm), and going up, while many scientists argue that we need to be at 350 ppm, if not less, to avoid the worst effects of global warming. The manufacturing system is going down in the United States, and the rest of the economy will not be far behind. Millions of people are suffering without jobs or are soon to be without jobs. Who knows what kind

of right-wing demagogue will rise up ready with false answers?
When oil prices spike permanently, the vast majority of Americans
will have no recourse because they live in areas where there is no
alternative to driving a car.

The list could go on, and meanwhile, as of this writing, the media
are in a panic because someone ignited a device and burned himself
on a passenger jet on Christmas, 2009. Perhaps this is a good time
for the nation to consider a poem by the famous Persian poet, Rumi,
that ends this way: "Just be quiet and sit down. The reason is you're
drunk. And this is the edge of the roof."

Surely, we can work on the problems of the here and now while
discussing and formulating a vision of sustainable systems. But proposing new ideas can be problematic, as John Kenneth Galbraith
explained in his famous essay, "The Concept of the Conventional
Wisdom":

> A "good" liberal . . . is one who is adequately predictable. This
> means that he forswears any serious striving toward originality.
> In both the United States and Britain, in recent times, American
> liberals and their British counterparts on the left have pro-
> claimed themselves in search of new ideas. To proclaim the
> need for new ideas has served, in some measure, as a substitute
> for them. The politician who unwisely takes this proclaimed
> need seriously and urges something new will often find himself
> in serious trouble."[1]

As Galbraith further points out, it can take an enormous investment of time and thought on the part of an individual to understand
the current conventional wisdom. Conventional wisdom is similar to
what I described in the discussion of Thomas Kuhn about a scientific paradigm. A paradigm is adhered to by most scientists of a certain discipline most of the time—science could not be as efficient as
it is if every time a discovery was made, the entire edifice of theories
on which the discovery was based had to be reexplained. Kuhn called
the science undertaken within the confines of a paradigm "normal
science." One might also have called it "conventional science."

Kuhn argued that "anomalies," that is, contradictions between
what the theory hypothesizes should happen and what actually happens, motivate people to look for an alternative paradigm. In the
same way, Galbraith explains that

> Since [conventional wisdom] remains with the comfortable and familiar while the world moves on, the conventional wisdom is always in danger of obsolescence. This is not immediately fatal. The fatal blow to conventional wisdom comes when the conventional ideas fail signally to deal with some contingency to which obsolescence has made them palpably inapplicable. . . . At this stage, the irrelevance will often be dramatized by some individual. To him will accrue the credit for overthrowing the conventional wisdom and for installing the new ideas.[2]

Galbraith points to the overthrow of the idea that government must always balance budgets, most clearly elaborated by Keynes, as an example of the process of change of conventional wisdom. Perhaps we are in a similar time right now. Although people often think that their particular time is the pivotal one for world history, we certainly have enough environmental and economic warning signs to think that we may be entering such a time.

However, it may be that we will have to wait for things to get much worse before the conventional wisdom will be seen to be "palpably inapplicable" to the new realities. In which case, not only do we have some time to develop a more holistic vision, we are under a certain amount of pressure, morally, to forge a new set of ideas before the old conventional wisdom fails. Of all people, this was probably expressed best, or perhaps most famously, by the most conservative economist of the post-war era, Milton Friedman:

> Only a crisis, actual or perceived, produces real change. When that crisis occurs, the actions that are taken depend on the ideas that are lying around. That, I believe, is our basic function: to develop alternatives to existing policies, to keep them alive and available until the politically impossible becomes politically inevitable.[3]

He wrote those words in 1982, after his ideas had been picked up by Ronald Reagan.

Ironically, the ideas we should have lying around are in many ways the opposite of Friedman's. I'm sure that he would completely disagree that a competent government is absolutely critical for the long-term survival of a nation's economy and for the long-term survival of our global civilization.

THE MARKET IS NOT THE ANSWER

The market, if left alone, will virtually guarantee that the economic system will collapse. There are a number of reasons for this.

First, the economy is a system, similar to an ecosystem, composed of many parts, all of which must be present for the system to thrive. These niches exist because of the physical reality of complex societies. The market cannot guarantee that the economic ecosystem will stay complete, that parts of it will not disappear.

Second, the market cannot design and plan a national or international system. There is no reason that an economy left to run by itself will maintain a production system. Adam Smith's "invisible hand" operates in the short term and within one industry, allowing for the automatic operation of most of the uncountable transactions that occur in an economy from moment to moment. But Alfred Chandler's "visible hand" is needed as soon as systems become complex and encompass a large territory; Keynes' "macroeconomic hand" is needed if a liquidity trap happens, which it will; and Japan's and every other developed country's "competent governmental hand" is needed to keep a country on track in the long term.

The various parts of the economic system develop at their own rate, and have no regard for the health of their required fellow niches. In fact, the consumer goods and services niches are usually much bigger than the technologically more critical production and reproduction machinery, which means that governmental policy will lean toward nonmachinery sectors, and the nonmachinery sectors may even destroy their less powerful but more important fellow niches.

The third reason free markets lead to collapse is that, as we have recently seen, the financial system will warp the entire economic system because of the power that accrues to it. Or to put it more colorfully, as Matt Taibi said recently about Goldman Sachs, an unregulated, powerful private financial industry is "a great vampire squid wrapped around the face of humanity, relentlessly jamming its blood funnel into anything that smells like money."[4] This power accumulates because the surplus resources of an economy are passed through the financial system, which can control where those resources flow. As gatekeepers to financial capital, they can insist on corporate policies that are good for the speedy return on investment, but not for the long-term health of the economy as a whole.

The fourth reason markets tend to destroy themselves is that they consume their own capital, thus killing the goose that is laying the golden eggs. The market does not distinguish between profits that are made by increasing wealth and profit that is made by selling off or otherwise liquidating capital. Machinery, or physical capital, may be left to fall apart; human capital may not be given training or may be thrown out of work; natural capital may be consumed, leaving society as a whole with less wealth.

The fifth flaw is the one that Keynes gained fame for pointing out, the tendency for economic systems to get stuck in a low level of activity, or a depression. This can be caused by a capital-goods-led depression, as explained in the chapter about sustainable growth.

For all of these reasons, an economic system is not self-correcting and cannot design a system to operate in the long-run. Both manufacturing and ecosystems are not sustained during the normal functioning of a market system, over the long term.

IS A SUSTAINABLE GOVERNMENT POSSIBLE?

If markets can't sustain an economy, what can? Governments have a different set of problems. First, national government elites have a tendency to want to expand their power, internally by restricting the freedoms that can lead to economic innovation and growth, and externally by directing resources to a military that is more interested in empire than in the long-term power of the country. Second, governments can be taken over by the very economic interests that are leading the economy off the cliff. Instead of working as a "countervailing" power to powerful firms, as Galbraith hoped, governments can become part of what Naomi Klein calls "disaster capitalism," helping the firms to gut the economy.

The process of decline thus involves two basic processes within a national political economy. The military becomes too powerful within the government, and because of its influence on the economy as a large-scale purchaser of military equipment, it warps the competence of the economic system as a whole. The result is what Seymour Melman called *state capitalism*, that is, the state becomes intertwined with the economy via the military. On the other hand, because of the positive feedback processes of the accumulation of power within the economy, large-scale concentrations of power emerge that are able to take over the state, which turns to the processes of disaster capitalism. This is "state disaster capitalism," the combination of an unconstrained market and a government that is not controlled by its citizens.

A sustainable government is one that is competent to guide the market while remaining autonomous from it. Occasionally, as in the case of South Korea in the 1960s and 1970s, this can happen when there is a dictatorship, but then the performance of the political economy is dependent on the particular person who heads the government. More common in dictatorships is the case of the Soviet Union, in which the economy rises to great heights, but then the military brings it to the point of collapse and beyond.

In a democratic polity, on the other hand, the citizenry is able to elect a competent government that can avoid both state and disaster capitalism. This obviously is not easy. The citizenry has to understand how a political economy works, not how neoclassical economists describe how it works. The electorate also has to have a sufficiently long-term perspective, ideally as close to that of indigenous peoples as possible; that is, the citizenry should work toward an economy and environment that is sustainable, in perpetuity.

Not only will the people of the United States have to elect a competent set of public officials that are beholden to the long-term future of the citizenry and not the short-term power of the wealthiest and most powerful, but the people of most countries around the world also will have to do the same. Global warming is a global problem; any regional ecosystem is affected, one way or another, by the collapse of another one. The world has chosen a path of becoming dependent on nonrenewable resources like oil. If the poor regions of the world, including the failed states that breed terrorism, are to become wealthy and stable, they will have to build a green manufacturing sector. For the first time in history, governments all across the world have to competently, consciously, and cooperatively manage a transition from one form of civilization to another.

In order for a civilization to be sustainable, it will have to develop a production system that can function for the foreseeable future. Within the constraints of current technologies, a sustainable civilization will have to be designed so that it does not use up its nonrenewable resources, does not change the climate, and does not destroy its ecosystems. In other words, a sustainable civilization will maintain its natural capital, not destroy its natural capital at a rate that will eventually lead to a planet of deserts.

A sustainable civilization will also have a sustainable economy. The first prerequisite of a sustainable economy is the maintenance of natural capital. But the second is to manage the various niches of an ecosystem, as in a managed national park, so that the various parts of the manufacturing and, most critically, machinery sectors are supported and maintained. That manufacturing system must, in turn, use mostly recycled materials, not pollute, and create recyclable goods to maintain natural capital. To build, expand, and even grow this economy, the government will have to support and encourage the development of human capital.

Creating a sustainable civilization will require popular debates about what are the best technological alternatives. The broad technological design of a society cannot be left to a semiconscious interplay between short-term corporate interests and the government, as happened with the development of an automobile-and-suburbia-based system. That might be what most people want, ultimately, but at least the alternatives should be discussed. The design of a civilization should be a broad-based, citizen-centered undertaking, directly related to who is elected to serve in government.

A DAY IN THE LIFE

What would a sustainable civilization look like? We can speculate about what a typical day might look like of a person who wakes up in a sustainable society.

You would wake up in the center of a city or town, where most people live, in a spacious apartment in an apartment building. All the appliances communicate with the municipal electrical system to minimize electrical use; all of your heating and cooling comes from underground geothermal heat pumps, and most of the electricity for your daily use is generated from the solar panels installed on the sides and roof of your building, with battery backup. Your basic heating, cooling, and electricity are free, because the geothermal heat pumps, solar panels and wind-powered electricity from the grid have been financed by a government program, and are maintained by municipal and national building energy agencies.

You can hear birds chirping a few buildings away because the center of town has been blocked off from automobiles, which are small electric cars parked in structures at the end of the town or city center. They usually come from the ecovillages[5] and densely built single- and multiple-family homes outside of the center of the town or city. You can get around by walking, biking in a physically separated bike lane, or taking a light rail or subway around, depending on the size of the city.

This morning, you're using your free municipal high-speed Internet, connected to a high-speed national backbone, to plan your trip on a high-speed train. The 1,000-mile trip you're taking with your family to the National Prairie Park, that now covers most of many states, will only take five hours. You'll be traveling in large seats, with easy access to observation cars and a restaurant—and the fare will be less than air fare now, because the government has already built the Interstate Rail System and only charges enough for maintenance and labor. Most electricity for the rails is very inexpensive, because the government has built an Interstate Wind and Transmission System, which, again, only requires maintenance.

Today, most of your food for breakfast, and then lunch and dinner, will come from a 20-mile radius around your town or city, and it will all be organic and nutritious (and good tasting). In fact, any vegetables will be from nearby neighborhoods. You can eat very inexpensive local catfish, tilapia, or chickens, as those are subsidized by the local government, or buy more expensive meat that either comes from the prairie or local small-scale farms.

All of the waste from your plate will go down the building's compost chute, and that and your bodily wastes, collected by another building system, will be used to grow the food you're eating. City agencies will pick up all your nonfood garbage for you and recycle them to the factories that are situated outside the city region.

This morning you take a free electric commuter train to work, which arrives at a factory a few miles outside town. First you stop to get cash at the local municipal bank, which uses the funds you deposit there to loan to small manufacturing and service firms in town, helping them to get started and expand. Your factory also uses loans from a larger, regional governmental bank for its operations, and for expansion plans for its cell phone production lines. You'll be going to training today, which is a major part of everybody's life at the factory, from engineers to managers to factory floor workers. After most of the day at training, you'll attend a factory-wide meeting to elect a board of directors.

For raw material inputs and unused outputs, the factory contracts with governmental/business organizations that handle the recycling networks of your urban region, and coordinates with other recycling networks for materials that might be in short or oversupply. Using these recycled materials—except in the case of the cell phone factory, where some new silicon is made from sand, using the government-financed regional silicon purification plant—the production of the cell phones takes place with no pollution or toxic waste, and the cell phones are designed to be disassembled by robots you're helping to build that will allow the phones to be 100 percent recycled.

After work, you go back on the free commuter train and pick up your kids from school or free preschool, either of which has 15 students or fewer in all classes, with art, library, gym, and science classes every day. You can attend a local political meeting with your partner at the town hall, because you get free child care if you engage in civic events. It's easy to get back and forth to your apartment, what with all of the people out on the streets going to restaurants, movies, cultural events, or just walking around, and with easy, free transport back to your building.

Speaking of walking, people are healthier, and the town hall used to be a hospital. Fewer hospitals are needed now since there is no pollution, the food is actually good for you, there are almost no vehicle crashes, and health care is free. There are city-sponsored prevention activities, such as early-morning tai chi and exercises in the park in the town square.

You can afford to take many trips and enjoy the cultural life of your and neighboring cities because you need to spend very little or no money on electricity, heating, cooling, travel, health, or education, and your food and housing are inexpensive. Many of the new apartment buildings in the town/city center have been financed by the government, and people can rent-to-own or buy new apartments with very low interest rates.

Your taxes are low or nonexistent because the municipal, regional, and national public banks make enough money from loans so that only the wealthy and large businesses need to pay taxes; the government also receives revenue from extra electricity and transportation that people want. In addition, the military has mostly been converted into those neighborhood recycling and energy teams, and the maintenance teams for the national rail, transmission, solar, and water infrastructure maintenance operations. These were formed after the converted military employees helped build the systems in the first place. Since the dollar became legal tender printed by the government, there are no interest payments on the national debt, because there is no national debt, further decreasing taxes for the middle class.

The expansion of employment from the switch to organic farming and from the revival of manufacturing, plus the government's employer-of-last-resort policy, has virtually eliminated poverty, and this has also meant that there is less of a need for taxes. Any addition to the national wealth, for example, by building more infrastructure, is financed by new, debt-free money, which prudently adds more money to the money supply.

You go to sleep, after a relaxed, busy, and engaging day at work, in town, and with your family.

IT CAN HAPPEN HERE

You can describe or paint your own picture of a sustainable society; the important point is that envisioning a better civilization should become a social process, part of the political debate, even perhaps part of conventional wisdom. When Martin Luther King Jr. said, "I have a dream," he didn't stop there, he described his dream.

Envisioning the dream of a wealthy, sustainable, just society is one that everyone can engage in. In fact, it will be absolutely necessary to discuss, debate, and delineate many different varieties of dreams and designs if we are to have a political process that translates good ideas into good legislation. To move forward politically, the citizens of the United States—and around the world—are going to have to come up with a political plan that they can use to hold candidates for office accountable.

Too often, candidates can get away with lofty words or vague rhetoric. They can do this because there is no set of policies that the officials *know* that the electorate wants. Political parties used to have something called a "platform," but they have largely abandoned such efforts, and the policy positions in the platforms often didn't come from the grassroots in any case. Particularly when we are facing long-term problems, we need to champion a set of coherent, mutually self-reinforcing ideas that can easily be used to tell an elected official, "See, this is what we elected you to do, to move toward."

So I would suggest to anyone reading this book that you start with yourself, your friends, your neighbors, people you do organized

work with now, of whatever sort, to figure out what you think would
be a good vision for the future. Then, look out for others around
you, electronically or physically, who might want to expand the discussion. See if there are good forums for discussion—I will attempt to
create one at the Web site for this book, http://www.manufacturing
greenprosperity.com, but there are plenty of others. For example, I
started by commenting, and then blogging, at Grist.org.

ONE PERSON'S VISION

The civilization sketched out above, and throughout this book,
has been designed to avoid the crises that the current civilization is
doomed to exacerbate: the decline of manufacturing; global warming; the depletion of nonrenewable resources, particularly oil; and
the collapse of ecosystems.

To prevent the worst of global warming, humans need to stop
emitting greenhouse gases. Using wind, solar, and geothermal
energy to generate electricity, using geothermal power to heat and
cool buildings, and making buildings more efficient, in combination,
should eliminate the need for fossil fuels for electrical generation.
Converting the transportation system to electric trains and electric
cars, and industrial heat processing from natural gas to renewable
electricity should stop the rest of fossil fuel emissions.

Reconfiguring the agricultural system to build up the soil instead
of destroying it, by universally adopting organic techniques, and
halting the use of fossil fuel-based pesticides and artificial fertilizers,
will make agriculture a potential way to take some of the carbon
dioxide out of the atmosphere, and will make the food and soil more
healthy, not less. Recycling livestock manure and minimizing their
belching will also help.

Many greenhouse emissions can be avoided simply by stopping the
destruction of forests, which is partly the result of the spread of non-
sustainable agricultural practices, such as growing livestock or soybeans
on degrading grassland. Another important source of deforestation is
the need for heating fuel in poor countries; a sophisticated, renewable
electricity and heating infrastructure can be built in poor countries as
part of a plan to develop them.

An inclusive recycling system will eliminate the need for landfills,
another source of greenhouse emissions. The need for recycling is

essential to solve the problem of the destruction of ecosystems by eliminating or minimizing mining, pollution, and landfills. In fact, all of the policies needed to prevent global warming are also needed either to preserve ecosystems or prevent resource depletion, such as for oil.

Dense cities and towns, made possible by electrified transportation and necessary to make electrified transportation possible, also allows for the restoration of ecosystems and the prevention of further destruction from development, otherwise known as sprawl. Saving forests is essential for saving ecosystems; if countries don't manage livestock sustainably, then their rangelands will turn into desert, as is presently happening. Protecting the oceans is critical to keeping the planet's biosphere healthy, and the encouragement of farmed freshwater fish will help in that effort as well. Without coal, oil, uranium and manufacturing pollution, lakes and other areas might also come back to life, which would greatly increase the health of the human population.

The problem of resource depletion, the limits to growth that the biosphere and Earth impose, can be avoided by implementing programs designed to prevent global warming and ecosystem destruction. Electric transportation eliminates the need for three-quarters of our use of oil; even coal and natural gas have their natural limits. Sustainably harvested biomass can replace whatever oil is used for manufacturing, and if plastics and other products of the chemical industry are recyclable, not much biomass would be needed in any case. Recycling cuts down on the need for energy use, and eliminates the need to use up nonrenewable resources.

Thus the three large categories of environmental crises—global warming, ecosystem destruction, and resource depletion—can all be accomplished with the same set of policies. In turn, by implementing these environmentally friendly construction programs, we can turn the economy into one that is re-centered on manufacturing, which will make the *economy* sustainable.

Governments have long had many tools available to maintain and augment the manufacturing systems in their countries; Erik Reinert's book *Why Rich Countries Got Rich and Why the Poor Countries Stay Poor* is a long compendium of these techniques and literature. The United States and every other natural economic region around the world have the unique opportunity to rebuild the transportation, energy, urban, agricultural, and resource systems by rebuilding the manufacturing system at the same time. This will involve making the manufacturing sector environmentally sustainable by constructing recycling networks and producing without polluting.

But the other reason a green transformation will lead to a manufacturing renaissance is that governments at all levels can direct their financing of this transformation at *domestic* companies and labor. By making a program of economic reconstruction stable and predictable in the long term, and using various tricks that governments have learned over the centuries—training and educating workers and engineers, providing resources for research, and transferring technology from abroad—the government can create an economically self-sustaining manufacturing system. The government can also encourage the empowerment of employees, both with economic democracy in the firm and by supporting people with health care, social security, and well-funded education.

Manufacturing is the foundation of any economic system, but it must be protected from the other parts of the economic and political systems, or its wealth-generating capital will be looted to build up parasitic centers of wealth and power. This sclerosis then leads any country, even a Great Power, into decline.

A world that has overcome the immense challenges of the 21st century will be one with a higher standard of living for all—with higher income, lower prices for necessities, better and more job opportunities, travel, housing, health, and education. In such a world, with virtually no poverty, and a dispersed distribution of power, the middle class will not just be rebuilt, it will dominate our political and economic systems. We have the technologies, the policy tools, the democracy, even the international peace, to make the transformation.

Over 200 years ago, the United States stood at a fork in the road, and Thomas Paine penned these remarkable lines:

We have it in our power to begin the world over again. A situation, similar to the present, hath not happened since the days of Noah until now. The birthday of a new world is at hand . . .[6]

We *do* have it in our power, so let's begin the world over again.

Notes

CHAPTER 1

1. Robert Jervis, *System Effects: Complexity in Political and Social Life* (Princeton: Princeton University Press, 1997).

2. Seymour Melman, *Our Depleted Society* (New York: Holt, Rinehart and Winston, 1965).

3. Kenneth Deffeyes, *Hubbert's Peak: The Impending World Oil Shortage*, 2nd ed. (Princeton: Princeton University Press, 2008).

4. Friedrich List, *The National System of Political Economy*, trans. S.S. Lloyd (New York: Augustus M. Kelley, 1885), p.133.

5. Ibid., p. 46.

6. Paul Hawken, Amory Lovins, and L. Hunter Lovins, *Natural Capitalism: Creating the next industrial revolution* (Boston: Back Bay Books, 2008).

7. Chalmers Johnson, "Going Bankrupt: Why the Debt Crisis Is Now the Greatest Threat to the American Republic," *TomDispatch.com*, 1/22/2008, available at http://www.tomdispatch.com/post/174884.

8. Al Gore, address to New York University Law School, 9/18/2006, available at http://www.grist.org/article/more-on-gores-speech/.

9. Williams E. Rees, Mathis Wackernagel, and Phil Testemale, *Our Ecological Footprint: Reducing Human Impact on the Earth* (New Society Publishers, 1998).

CHAPTER 2

1. Bureau of Economic Analysis, Department of Commerce, Industry Economic Accounts, "The Use of Commodities by Industries before Redefinitions (1997–2007)," available at http://www.bea.gov/industry/index.htm#annual, then choose "Interactive tables: Input-Output," then choose "The Use of Commodities by

Industries before Redefinitions (1997–2007)," then click "Summary" in the "Level of Aggregation" section, then click "View Table."

2. Statistical Abstract of the United States 2010, Table 217, "Federal Funds for Education and Related Programs 2005–2008." (Washington, DC: United States Department of Commerce, Census Bureau), p. 7; available at http://www.census.gov/prod/2009pubs/10statab/educ.pdf

3. Ibid., Table 253, "Public Elementary and Secondary Estimated Finances, 1980 to 2007, and by State, 2007." 43.

4. Ibid., Table 281, "State and Local Financial Support for Higher Education by State: 2005 to 2008." 70.

5. World Trade Organization, "International Trade Statistics, 2008," p. 6, available at http://www.wto.org/english/res_e/statis_e/its2008_e/its08_toc_e.htm.

6. Statistical Abstract of the United States, 2009, Table 1250. "U.S. International Transactions by Type of Transaction: 1990 to 2008" available at http://www.census.gov/prod/2009pubs/10statab/foreign.pdf.

7. The Federal Reserve Bank, Federal Reserve Statistical Releases, H. 10, "Foreign Exchange rates: Historical data, Japan, 2000–2006," available at http://www.federalreserve.gov/releases/h10/hist/dat00_ja.txt.

8. Bureau of Economic Analysis, International Economic Accounts, U.S. International Transactions Accounts Data, Table 12, "U.S. International Transactions, by Area—Euro Area," available at http://www.bea.gov/international/bp_web/simple.cfm?anon=71&table_id=10&area_id=11.

9. The Federal Reserve Bank, Euro, available at http://www.federalreserve.gov/releases/h10/hist/dat00_eu.txt.

10. Bureau of Economic Analysis, International Economic Accounts, U.S. International Transactions Accounts Data, Table 12, "U.S. International Transactions, by Area—Japan," http://www.bea.gov/international/bp_web/simple.cfm?anon=71&table_id=10&area_id=45.

11. Statistical Abstract 2009, Table 1343: Indexes of Hourly Compensation Costs for Production Workers in Manufacturing by Country: 1980 to 2006, p. 43, available at http://www.census.gov/prod/2008pubs/09statab/intlstat.pdf.

12. Bureau of Economic Analysis, "The Use of Commodities by Industries before Redefinitions (1997–2007)," except click on "Sector," not Summary. Calculated by subtracting exports from total commodity output, then dividing that number into imports, for the years 1998 and 2007, for manufacturing.

13. Ibid., except click "Summary," and look at the row for "machinery," in the years 1998 and 2007.

14. Statistical Abstract, Table 1318: Indexes of Hourly Compensation Costs for All Employees in Manufacturing by Country: 2000 to 2007; p. 40, available at http://www.census.gov/prod/2009pubs/10statab/intlstat.pdf

15. Al Gore, *Our Choice: A Plan to Solve the Climate Crisis* (Emmaus, PA: Rodale, 2009).

16. Jane Jacobs, *Cities and the Wealth of Nations* (New York: Vintage Press, 1985).

17. Daniel Bell, *The Coming of the Post-Industrial Society* (New York: Basic Books, 1976).

18. Department of Commerce, *The Historical Statistics of the United States: Colonial Times to 1970* (Washington, DC: Government Printing Office, 1975), Series D, 152–166.

19. Ibid., Series D, 127–141.

20. Ibid., Series D, 116–126.

21. Statistical Abstract 2009, Table 600: Employment by Industry, 2000–2007; p. 26, available at http://www.census.gov/prod/2008pubs/09statab/labor.pdf

22. Statistical Abstract, Table 1308, available at http://www.census.gov/prod/2008pubs/09statab/intlstat.pdf.

23. Bureau of Economic Analysis, U.S. Department of Commerce, National Income and Product Accounts, Table 1.1.10, "Percentage Shares of Gross Domestic Product," for the years 1947, 1970, and 2007, Using "Personal Consumption Expenditure: Goods" and "Net Exports of Goods and Service: Imports: Goods" (rows 3 and 19). I'd like to thank Franklin Spinney for suggesting this measure.

24. John Darwin, *After Tamerlane: The rise and fall of global empires, 1400–2000* (New York: Bloomsbury Press, 2008)

25. Eamonn Fingleton, *In Praise of Hard Industries: Why Manufacturing, Not the Information Economy, Is the Key to Future Prosperity* (New York: Houghton Mifflin, 1999), p. 32.

CHAPTER 3

1. Imre Lakatos and Alan Musgrave, eds., *Criticism and the Growth of Knowledge* (Cambridge: Cambridge University Press, 197).

2. Thomas S. Kuhn, *The Structure of Scientific Revolutions*, 2nd ed. (Chicago: University of Chicago Press, 1970).

3. Kenneth N. Waltz, *The Theory of International Politics* (New York: McGraw-Hill, 1979).

4. Robert Jervis, *System Effects: Complexity in Political and Social Life* (Princeton: Princeton University Press, 1997).

5. Ilya Prigogine, *The End of Certainty* (New York: Free Press, 1997).

6. R.V. O'Neill, D.L. DeAngelis, J.B. Waide, and T.F.H. Allen, *A Hierarchical Concept of Ecosystems* (Princeton: Princeton University Press, 1986).

7. Philip Morowski, *More Heat Than Light: Economics as Social Physics, Physics as Nature's Economics* (Cambridge: Cambridge University Press, 1991).

8. E. O. Wilson, *The Diversity of Life* (Cambridge, MA: Belknap Press, 1992).

9. Aristotle, *Physics* (Oxford: Oxford University Press, 1996).

CHAPTER 4

1. Donella Meadows, Jorgen Randers, and Dennis Meadows, *The Limits to Growth: The 30-Year Update* (White River Junction, VT: Chelsea Green, 2004).

2. William Catton, *Overshoot: The Ecological Basis of Revolutionary Change* (Urbana and Chicago: University of Illinois Press, 1982).

3. See Carroll Pursell, *The Machine in America: A Social History of Technology* (Baltimore: Johns Hopkins University Press, 1995), pp. 56–58.

4. Nathan Rosenberg, *Inside the Black Box: Technology and Economics* (Cambridge: Cambridge University Press, 1982), pp. 56–59.

5. Donella Meadows, Jorgen Randers, and Dennis Meadows, *Limits to Growth*.

6. Based on Evsey Domar, in *Essays on Economic Growth and Planning* (New York: Monthly Review Press, 1957), "A Soviet Model of Growth," pp. 225–35.

7. Paul Hawken, *Blessed Unrest: How the largest social movement in history is restoring grace, justice and beauty to the world* (New York: Penguin, 2008).

8. Using number of production workers, from http://www.bea.gov/national/nipaweb/SelectTable.asp?Selected=N, "Full-time equivalent employees by industry," Tables 6.5a, and c for 1947 to 2008; using quantity index for manufacturing from http://www.bea.gov/industry/gpotables/gpo_list.cfm; Table "Chain-Type Quantity Indexes for Value Added by Industry" for 1947 and 2008.

9. Seymour Melman, *Profits without Production* (New York: Knopf, 1983), pp. 133–35.

10. Joel Mokyr, *The Lever of Riches: Technological Creativity and Economic Progress* (Oxford: Oxford University Press, 1990).

11. Eugene S. Ferguson, *Engineering and the Mind's Eye* (Cambridge: MIT Press, 1994), makes similar points about the visual nature of engineering.

12. Iddo K. Wernick, Robert Herman, Shekhar Govind, and Jesse H. Ausubel, "Materialization and Dematerialization: Measures and Trends," *Daedalus* 125, no. 3 (Summer 1996): 171–98, available at http://phe.rockefeller.edu/Daedalus/Demat/.

13. Dmitry Orlov has argued that Soviet Russia is actually better prepared for the loss of oil than the United States because the cities are dense and mostly served by trains. See http://www.energybulletin.net/node/23259.

14. http://www.euractiv.com/en/energy/analysis-efficiency-coal-fired-power-stations-evolution-prospects/article-154672.

15. Al Gore, *Our Choice: A Plan to Solve the Climate Crisis* (Emmaus, PA: Rodale, 2009), p. 286.

16. Statistical Abstract of the United States, 2009, Table 953. http://www.census.gov/prod/2009pubs/10statab/construct.pdf.

17. http://www.oneclimate.net/2009/03/24/a-cup-of-coffee-uses-just-a-cupful-of-water%E2%80%A6/.

18. Martin C. Heller and Gregory A. Keoleian, Life Cycle-Based Sustainability Indicators for Assessment of the U.S. Food System, available at http://www.imamu.edu.sa/topics/IT/IT%206/Life%20Cycle%20Based%20Sustainability%20Indicators%20for%20Assessment%20of%20the%20US%20Food%20System.pdf.

19. Stockholm International Peace Research Institute, *SIPRI Yearbook 2009*, Executive Summary, p. 11.

20. Franklin C. Spinney, *Defense Facts of Life: The Plans/Reality Mismatch* (Boulder, CO: Westview Press, 1985).

21. Seymour Melman, *After Capitalism* (New York: Knopf, 2001), pp. 176–83.

22. David M. Gordon, *Fat and Mean: The Corporate Squeeze of Working Americans and the Myth of Managerial "Downsizing"* (New York: Free Press, 1996), Chapter 2, "The Bureaucratic Burden."

23. Ibid., Part Four.

CHAPTER 5

1. Paul Kennedy, *The Rise and Fall of the Great Powers: Economic Change and Military Conflict from 1500 to 2000* (New York: Random House, 1987).

2. William Catton, *Overshoot: The Ecological Basis of Revolutionary Change* (Urbana and Chicago: University of Illinois Press, 1982).

3. Lance H. Gunderson and C.S.Holling, eds., *Panarchy: Understanding Transformations in Human and Natural Systems* (Washington, DC: Island Press, 2002).

4. Richard Manning, *Against the Grain: How Agriculture Has Hijacked Civilization* (New York: North Point Press, 2004).

5. Riane Eisler, *The Chalice and the Blade: Our History, Our Future* (Gloucester, MA: Peter Smith Publishers, 1994).

6. William McNeil, *The Rise of the West: A History of the Human Community* (Chicago: The University of Chicago Press, 1963).

7. Janet L. Abu-Lughod, *Before European Hegemony: The World System A.D. 1250–1350* (Oxford: Oxford University Press, 1989).

8. Eliyahu Ashtor, "Underdevelopment in the Pre-industrial Era: The Case of Declining Economies," *Journal of European Economic History* 7 (Fall1978): 285–310.

9. Thomas Homer-Dixon, *The Upside of Down: Catastrophe, Creativity, and the Renewal of Civilization* (Washington, DC: Island Press, 2006). See Chapter 2, "A Keystone in Time."

10. Paul Kennedy, *The Rise and Fall of the Great Powers*.

11. Jared Diamond, *Guns, Germs and Steel: The Fates of Human Societies* (New York: W. W. Norton, 2005).

12. William H. McNeill, *Plagues and Peoples* (New York: Doubleday, 1976).

13. Alfred Crosby, *Ecological Imperialism: The Ecological Expansion of Europe, 900–1900* (Cambridge: Cambridge University Press, 2004).

14. Max Weber, "Politics as a Vocation," in *The Vocation Lectures* (Indianapolis, IN: Hackett Publications, 2004).

15. Immanuel Wallerstein, *The Modern World System I* (New York: Academic Press, 1974).

16. Denis Diderot, *A Diderot Pictorial Encyclopedia of Trades and Industry* (New York: Dover, 1959).

17. Clive Ponting, *A New Green History of the World: The Environment and the Collapse of Civilizations* (New York: Penguin, 2007). See section on wood in Chapter 12, "The Great Transition," pp. 275–80.

18. David S. Landes, *The Unbound Prometheus: Technological Change and Industrial Development in Western Europe from 1750 to the Present* (Cambridge: Cambridge University Press, 1969).

19. Hernando de Soto, *The Mystery of Capital: Why Capitalism Triumphs in the West and Fails Everywhere Else* (New York: Basic Books, 2003). See Chapter 1, "The Five Mysteries of Capital."

20. Adam Smith, *The Wealth of Nations*. Edwin Canaan edition (London: The Modern Library, 1994).

21. Ibid., pp. 305–307.

22. David Ricardo, *The Works and Correspondence of David Ricardo*, ed. P. Sraffa (Cambridge: Cambridge University Press, 1970).

23. Erik S. Reinert, *How Rich Countries Got Rich and Why Poor Countries Stay Poor* (New York: Public Affairs, 2007).

24. David Ricardo, *Principals of Political Economy and Taxation* (London: G. Bell and Sons, 1919), p. 114.

25. Alexis de Tocqueville, *Democracy in America* (New York: Penguin Classics, 2003).

CHAPTER 6

1. Ellen Hodgson Brown, *The Web of Debt: The Shocking Truth about Our Money System and How We Can Break Free* (Baton Rouge: Third Millennium Press, 2008). See Chapter 3, "Experiments in Utopia: Colonial Paper Money as Legal Tender."

2. H.J. Habakkuk, *American and British Technology in the 19th Century: The Search for Labour-Saving Inventions* (Cambridge: Cambridge University Press, 1967).

3. Thucydides, *The Peloponnesian War* (New York: W.W. Norton, 1998).

4. Brown, *The Web of Debt*, Chapter 8, "Scarecrow with a Brain: Lincoln Foils the Bankers," pp. 81–87.

5. Barrington Moore, *Social Origins of Dictatorship and Democracy: Lord and Peasant in the Making of the Modern World* (Boston: Beacon Press, 1993).

6. Peter Kolchin, *Unfree Labor: American Slavery and Russian Serfdom* (Cambridge, MA: Belknap Press, 1990).

7. David Kaiser, *Politics and War: European Conflict from Philip II to Hitler* (Cambridge, MA: Harvard University Press, 1990). Kaiser's focus is the rise and unification of Germany through war, as well as other European states.

8. L.T.C. Rolt, *A Short History of Machine Tools* (Cambridge, MA: MIT Press, 1965).

9. Nathan Rosenberg, "Technological Change in the Machine Tool Industry, 1840–1910," *The Journal of Economic History* 23, no. 4 (Dec. 1963): 414–43.

10. Alfred D. Chandler, Jr., *The Visible Hand: The Managerial Revolution in American Business* (Cambridge, MA: Belknap Harvard, 1977). See Chapter 3, "The Railroads: The First Modern Business Enterprise," and Chapter 4, "Railroad Cooperation and Competition."

11. T.K. Derry and Trevor I. Williams, *A Short History of Technology: From the Earliest Times to A.D. 1900* (Oxford: Oxford University Press, 1960). See Chapter 12, "Machine Tools and Their Products," pp. 343–363.

12. *American Machinist*, various issues in the year 1900.

13. Erik S. Reinert, *How Rich Countries Got Rich and Why Poor Countries Stay Poor* (New York: Public Affairs, 2007). See Chapter 4, "Globalization: The Arguments in Favor Are Also the Arguments Against."

14. Ludwig Dehio, *The Precarious Balance: Four Centuries of the European Power Struggle*, trans. Charles Fullman (New York: Alfred A. Knopf, 1962).

15. Michael W. Doyle, "Kant, Liberal Legacies and Foreign Affairs," *Philosophy and Public Affairs* 12 (1983): 205–35.

16. David Calleo, *The German Problem Reconsidered: Germany and the World Order 1870 to the Present* (Cambridge: Cambridge University Press, 1980). Calleo explores the idea that the Germans were expanding for reasons other than blind desire for conquest.

17. John Keegan, *The Face of Battle* (New York: Penguin, 1983).

18. Bruce Porter, *War and the Rise of the State: The Military Foundations of Modern Politics* (New York: Free Press, 1994).

19. William McNeill, *The Pursuit of Power: Technology, Armed Force and Society since A.D. 1000* (Chicago: University of Chicago Press, 1984).

20. Warren D. Devine, Jr. "From Shafts to Wires: Historical Perspective on Electrification," *The Journal of Economic History* 43, no. 2 (June 1983): 347–72.

21. John Kenneth Galbraith, *The Great Crash of 1929* (New York: Mariner Books, 2009 ed.).

22. John Maynard Keynes, *The General Theory of Employment, Interest and Money* (New York: Harcourt Brace and World, 1964, originally published in 1936).

23. *Business Week*, Oct. 26, 1929. p. 48

24. Alec Nove, *An Economic History of the USSR 1917–1991:* 3rd ed. (New York: Penguin, 1993).

25. Theodore Van Laue, *Why Lenin? Why Stalin? Why Gorbachev?: The Rise and Fall of the Soviet System* (White Plains, NY: Longman, 1997).

26. *Business Week*, Sept. 14, 1929: 35.

27. *Business Week*, Oct. 5, 1929.

28. *Business Week*, Nov. 20, 1929.

29. B.H. Liddell Hart, *Strategy*, 2nd rev. ed. (New York: Plume, 1991).

30. Alexander Gerschenkron, *Economic Backwardness in Historical Perspective: A Book of Essays* (Cambridge, MA: Belknap, 1962).

31. Ralf Dahrendorf, *Society and Democracy in Germany* (New York & London: W. W. Norton, 1967).

32. Linda Weiss, "War, the state, and the origins of the Japanese employment system," *Politics and Society* 21, vol. 3 (1993): 325—54.

33. Andrew Shonfield, *Modern Capitalism* (Oxford: Oxford University Press, 1968).

34. W.R. Smyser, *The German Economy: Colossus at the Crossroads* (Houndmills, UK: Palgrave Macmillan, 1993).

CHAPTER 7

1. Charles Kindleberger, *The World in Depression, 1929–1939*, rev. ed. (Berkeley: University of California Press, 1986).

2. Christopher Tassava, "The American Economy during World War II," *EH.Net Encyclopedia*, edited by Robert Whaples. February 10, 2008. http://eh.net/ency clopedia/article/tassava.WWII, accessed 1/23/2010.

3. Mark Harrison, "Resource Mobilization for World War II: The U.S.A., U.K., U.S.S.R., and Germany, 1938–1945," *Economic History Review* 41 (2nd series 1988): 171–191.

4. Kenneth T. Jackson, *Crabgrass Frontier: The Suburbanization of the United States* (Oxford: Oxford University Press, 1987).

5. Alan Milward, *The Reconstruction of Western Europe 1945–51* (London: Methuen, 1984).

6. Katie Alvord, *Divorce Your Car!: Ending the Love Affair with the Automobile* (Gabriola Island, BC: New Society Publishers, 2000), Chapter 2, "Other Suitors Drop by the Wayside: The Decline of Non-Car Transport."

7. Seymour Topping, *New York Times*, "Soviet Gaining in Machine Tools Over West, U.S. Expert Reports; Melman of Columbia Predicts Inroads in World Markets by Cheap Russian Items," p. 1, October 26, 1959.

8. Chalmers Johnson, *MITI and the Japanese Miracle: The Growth of Industrial Policy, 1925–1975* (Stanford: Stanford University Press, 1982).

9. Daniel Okimoto, *Between MITI and the Market: Japanese Industrial Policy for High Technology* (Stanford: Stanford University Press, 1990).

10. Bruce Cumings, "The Origins and Development of the Northeast Asian Political Economy: Industrial Sectors, Product Cycles, and Political Consequences," in *The Political Economy of New Asian Industrialism*, ed. Frederic Deyo (Ithaca: Cornell University Press, 1987).

11. Robert Wade, *Governing the Market* (Princeton: Princeton University Press, 1992).

12. Alice H. Amsden, *Asia's Next Giant: South Korea and Late Industrialization* (Oxford: Oxford University Press, 1989), p. 323.

13. Seymour Melman, *Our Depleted Society* (New York: Holt, Rinehart and Winston, 1965).

14. James Howard Kunstler, *The Long Emergency: Surviving the End of Oil, Climate Change, and Other Converging Catastrophes of the Twenty-First Century* (New York: Grove Press, 2006).

15. Jackson, *Crabgrass Frontier*, p. 241.

16. Robert Beauregard, *When America Became Suburban* (Minneapolis: University of Minnesota Press, 2006).

17. Franz Schurmann, *The Logic of World Power: An Inquiry into the Origins, Currents, and Contradictions of World Politics* (New York: Pantheon Books, 1974).

18. John Bates Clark, *The Distribution of Wealth: A Theory of Wages, Interest, and Profits* (New York: Macmillan, 1914), available at Google Books.

19. Paul Bairoch, "International Industrialization Levels from 1750 to 1980," *Journal of European Economic History* 11, nos. 1, 2 (Fall 1982).

20. Angus Maddison, *Dynamic Forces in Capitalist Development: A Long-Run Comparative View* (Oxford: Oxford University Press, 1991), Table 1.1, "Levels of GDP per Head of Population, 1820–1989."

21. Jonathan Temple, "The New Growth Evidence," *Journal of Economic Literature* 37 (March 1999): 112–56.

22. Nicholas Stern, "The Determinants of Growth," *Economic Journal* 101 (January 1991): 122.

23. Paul Samuelson, *Economics* (New York: McGraw-Hill, 1975), p. 747 (emphasis in original).

24. Robert Solow, "Technical Change and the Aggregate Production Function," *Review of Economics and Statistics* 39 (August 1957): 312–20.

25. Moses Abramovitz, "Resource and Output Trends in the United States Since 1870," *The American Economic Review* 46, no. 2, Papers and Proceedings of the Sixty-eighth Annual Meeting of the American Economic Association (May 1956): 5–23.

26. Avi J. Cohen, G. C. Harcourt, "Whatever Happened to the Cambridge Capital Theory Controversies?" *Journal of Economic Perspectives* 17, no. 1 (Winter 2003): 199–214.

27. Seymour Melman, "The Veblen-Commons Award: From Private to State Capitalism: How the Permanent War Economy Transformed the

Institutions of American Capitalism," *Journal of Economic Issues* 31, no. 2 (June 1997): 311–330

28. Jon Rynn, "The Rise and Decline of the Soviet Union," paper presented at the New York Political Science Association meeting, 1998. Available at http://www.manufacturinggreenprosperity.com.

29. Seymour Melman, *After Capitalism*, Chapter 6, "The Lesson of Soviet Russia: From Alienation to Production Collapse."

30. John Kenneth Galbraith, "The Second Imperial Requiem." *International Security* 7, no. 3 (Winter 1982–1983): 84–93.

31. Seymour Melman, *After Capitalism*, pp. 125–26.

32. *BusinessWeek*, Nov. 2, 1929. pp. 20–22

33. Paul Krugman, "Making Banking Boring," *New York Times*, April 9, 2009.

34. Bureau of Labor Statistics, Department of Labor, Occupational Employment Statistics, May 2008 National Occupational and Wage Estimates, available at http://www.bls.gov/oes/current/oes_nat.htm.

35. Ibid., May 1999, available at http://www.bls.gov/oes/1999/oes_51Pr.htm.

36. Statistical Abstract, Table 619, "Nonfarm Industries, Employees and Earnings, 1990 to 2008," available at http://www.census.gov/prod/2009pubs/10statab/labor.pdf.

37. American Society of Civil Engineers, "Report Card on America's Infrastructure," available at http://www.infrastructurereportcard.org/report-cards.

38. European Commission, Eurostat, Europe in Figures—*Eurostat Yearbook, 2006–2007*, chapter 8, "Industry and Services," available at http://epp.eurostat.ec.europa.eu/cache/ITY_OFFPUB/KS-CD-06-001-08/EN/KS-CD-06-001-08-EN.pdf.

39. United Nations Statistics Division, "GDP/Breakdown at Constant 1990 Prices in US Dollars (All Countries)" (Spreadsheet), *National Accounts Main Aggregates Database*, October 2009, available for download at http://unstats.un.org/unsd/snaama/dnllist.asp.

40. Keith Bradsher, "China Leading Race to Make Clean Energy," *New York Times*, Jan. 31, 2010, available at http://www.nytimes.com/2010/01/31/business/energy-environment/31renew.html.

CHAPTER 8

1. Paul Roberts, *The End of Oil: On the Edge of a Perilous New World* (New York: Mariners Press, 2004).

2. Jeff Rubin, *Why Your World Is about to Get a Whole Lot Smaller: Oil and the End of Globalization* (New York: Random House, 2009).

3. "China Overtakes US as World's Biggest Car Market," *The Guardian*, 1/8/2010, available at http://www.guardian.co.uk/business/2010/jan/08/china-us-car-sales-overtakes

4. Jeff Rubin and Benjamin Tal, "Will Soaring Transport Costs Reverse Globalization?" *CIBC World Markets StrategEcon* (May 27, 2008): 4–7, available at http://research.cibcwm.com/economic_public/download/smay08.pdf.

5. Christopher Steiner, *$20 per Gallon: How the Inevitable Rise in Price of Gasoline Will Change Our Lives for the Better* (New York: Grand Central Publishing, 2009), Chapter 8, p. 66.

6. Richard Heinberg, *Peak Everything: Waking Up to the Century of Declines* (Gabriola Island, BC: New Society Publishers, 2007).

7. D.L. DeAngelis, W.M. Post, and C.C. Travis, *Positive Feedback in Natural Systems* (Berlin: Springer-Verlag, 1986).

8. Fred Pearce, *With Speed and Violence: Why Scientists Fear Tipping Points in Climate Change* (Boston: Beacon Press, 2007), Chapter 14, "The Doomsday Device."

9. Ibid., Chapter 16, "The Winds of Change."

10. The data for sources of greenhouse gas emissions all come from the UN's International Panel on Climate Change (IPCC), and in particular, from the following:

B. Metz, O.R. Davidson, P.R. Bosch, R. Dave, L.A. Meyer, eds., *Contribution of Working Group III to the Fourth Assessment Report of the Intergovernmental Panel on Climate Change* (Cambridge: Cambridge University Press, 2007), available at http://www.ipcc.ch/publications_and_data/ar4/wg3/en/contents.html.

The IPCC uses data from the Netherlands Environmental Assessment Agency from a database called EDGAR, available at http://www.mnp.nl/edgar/model/v32ft2000edgar/edgv32ft-ghg/.

A detailed breakdown of the sources used by Jon Rynn, including a breakdown of the data, is available online at http://spreadsheets.google.com/ccc?key=pzrff2j0rl2wNrQfxOKkYYQ, and is also available at http://www.manufacturinggreenprosperity.com.

11. Metz et al., *Contribution of Working Group III*, Chapter 1, p. 105, available at http://www.ipcc.ch/pdf/assessment-report/ar4/wg3/ar4-wg3-chapter1.pdf.

12. Ibid., p. 259.

13. Metz et al., *Contribution of Working Group III*, Chapter 7, p. 460, available at http://www.ipcc.ch/pdf/assessment-report/ar4/wg3/ar4-wg3-chapter7.pdf.

14. Metz et al., *Contribution of Working Group III*, Chapter 8, available at http://www.ipcc.ch/pdf/assessment-report/ar4/wg3/ar4-wg3-chapter8.pdf

15. Julia Whitty, "The Fate of the Oceans," *Mother Jones* (March/April 2006). Available at http://motherjones.com/politics/2006/03/fate-ocean

16. Clive Ponting, *A New Green History of the World: The Environment and the Collapse of Civilizations* (New York: Penguin, 2007).

17. J.R. McNeill, *Something New under the Sun: An Environmental History of the 20th Century World* (New York: W. W. Norton, 2000).

18. Lester R. Brown, *Plan B 4.0: Mobilizing to Save Civilization* (New York: W. W. Norton, 2009).

19. David Montgomery, *Dirt: The Erosion of Civilizations* (Berkeley: University of California Press, 2008).

20. McNeill, *Something New under the Sun*, Chapter 9, "More People, Bigger Cities."

CHAPTER 9

1. Kenneth Jackson, *Crabgrass Frontier: The Suburbanization of the United States* (Oxford: Oxford University Press, 1987).

2. Alfred Chandler, *The Visible Hand: The Managerial Revolution in American Business* (Cambridge, MA: Belknap Harvard, 1977).

3. "Railroads: Green from the Start," Association of American Railways, December 2009, available at http://www.aar.org/InCongress/~/media/AAR/Background Papers/Green%20from%20the%20Start%20Dec%202009.ashx.

4. Alan Drake, "Multiple Birds–One Silver BB: A Synergistic Set of Solutions to Multiple Issues Focused on Electrified Railroads," *TheOilDrum.com*, July 15, 2008, available at http://www.theoildrum.com/node/4301.

5. Data on NYC subway electricity use from National Transit Database, Federal Transit Administration, Historical Data Files, Annual Databases, RY 2006 Database (Self-extracting xls). Online access: first go to http://www.ntdprogram. gov/ntdprogram/data.htm, then download RY 2006 Database (Self-extracting xls). Extract, then in Energy_Consumption.xls, agency number 2008 is the NYC MTA (according to agency_info.xls); in row 109, with column B as HR for heavy rail, there is 1,732,771 in column D, for kilowatt hours.

6. U.S. Energy Information Administration, U.S. Department of Energy, "Electric Power Industry 2008: Year in Review," available at http://www.eia.doe.gov/cneaf/electricity/epa/epa_sum.html.

7. National Highway Transportation Safety Administration, U.S. Department of Transportation, "Fatality Analysis Reporting System," National Statistics, 2008, available at http://www-fars.nhtsa.dot.gov/Main/index.aspx.

8. Traffic Safety Facts, Research Note DOT HS 810 936, "Motor Vehicle Traffic Crashes a Leading Cause of Death in the United States, 2005," April 2008, available at http://www-nrd.nhtsa.dot.gov/Pubs/810936.pdf.

9. National Highway Traffic Safety Administration, U.S. Department of Transportation, "The Economic Impact of Motor Vehicle Crashes, 2000," May 2002, available at http://www.nhtsa.gov/staticfiles/DOT/NHTSA/Communication%20&%20Consumer%20Information/Articles/Associated%20Files/EconomicImpact2000.pdf.

10. Bureau of Transportation Statistics, U.S. Department of Transportation, "Transportation Statistics Annual Report," Chapter 2, Table 2, available at http://www.bts.gov/publications/transportation_statistics_annual_report/2008/html/chapter_02/table_02_01_04.html.

11. Pat S. Hu and Timothy R. Reuscher, "Summary of Travel Trends: 2001 National Household Travel Survey" (U.S. Department of Transportation, December 2004): 30, available at http://nhts.ornl.gov/2001/pub/STT.pdf.

12. Referenced in Al Gore, *Our Choice: A Plan to Solve the Climate Crisis* (Emmaus, PA: Rodale, 2009), p. 260.

13. Michael Manville and Donald Shoup, "Parking, People, and Cities," *Journal of Urban Planning and Development* 131, no. 4 (December 1, 2005), available at http://shoup.bol.ucla.edu/People,Parking,CitiesJUPD.pdf.

14. National Highway Transportation Safety Administration, U.S. Department of Transportation, "Fatality Analysis Reporting System," National Statistics, 2008.

15. http://en.wikipedia.org/wiki/Jevons_paradox.

16. http://wheels.blogs.nytimes.com/2009/12/15/despite-qualms-toyota-will-bring-plug-in-hybrid-to-market/.

17. http://wheels.blogs.nytimes.com/2010/01/15/toyota-executive-sees-limits-to-electric-cars/

18. http://www.walkablestreets.com/speed.htm.

19. http://www.bts.gov/publications/highlights_of_the_2001_national_household_travel_survey/.

20. Annemarie Mannion, "Center Points: Urban Lifestyle Gains Foothold in Growing List of Suburbs," *Chicago Tribune*, business section, July 20, 2007.

21. Christopher Steiner, *$20 per Gallon*. Chapter 8, p. 66.

22. Garth Stapley, "High-Speed Rail Modesto Meeting Abuzz over Funds," *Sacramento Bee*, Jan. 29, 2010.

23. J.H. Crawford, author of *Car-Free Cities* (Nijmegen, Netherlands: International Books, 2002), has an interesting online article exploring the possibilities of a high-speed rail network that uses the Interstate Highway System, http://www.jhcrawford.com/energy/interstaterail.html.

34. Alexander Gerschenkron, "Economic Backwardness in Historical Perspective," in *Economic Backwardness in Historical Perspective: A Book of Essays* (Cambridge: Cambridge University Press, 1962).

25. Katie Alvord, *Divorce Your Car!: Ending the Love Affair with the Automobile* (Gabriola Island, BC: New Society Publishers, 2000), Chapter 2, "Other Suitors Drop by the Wayside: The Decline of Noncar Transport."

26. Jonathan M. Feldman, "From Mass Transit to Manufacturing," *The American Prospect*, April 2009, p. A12-A16. Available at http://www.prospect.org/cs/articles?article=from_mass_transit_to_new_manufacturing.

27. I have profited from the research of Jonathan M. Feldman, Professor of Economic History at Stockhom University, Sweden, in this section.

CHAPTER 10

1. Warren D. Devine, Jr., "From Shafts to Wires: Historical Perspective on Electrification," *The Journal of Economic History* 43, no. 2 (June 1983): 347–372.

2. Thomas Hughes, *American Genesis: A Century of Invention and Technological Enthusiasm, 1870–1970* (Chicago: University of Chicago Press, 2004).

3. H.E. Daly, "Toward Some Operational Principles of Sustainable Development," *Ecological Economics* 2 (1990): 1–6.

4. Keith Bradsher, "Earth-Friendly Elements, Mined Destructively," *New York Times*, Dec. 25, 2009.

5. Mike Sagrillo, "Putting Wind Power's Effect on Birds in Perspective," American Wind Energy Association, 2003, available at http://www.awea.org/faq/sagrillo/swbirds.html.

6. "Environmental Impacts of Coal Power: Water Use," Union of Concerned Scientists, available at http://www.ucsusa.org/clean_energy/coalvswind/c02b.html, accessed Jan. 17, 2010.

7. "External Costs: Research results on socio-environmental damages due to electricity and transport," European Commission, 2003, http://www.externe.info/externpr.pdf, accessed 1/17/2010.

8. The Menominee Nation, "Concept of Sustainable Forestry on the Menominee Reservation," available at http://www.mtewood.com/concept-sustainable-forestry.htm;

Scott Landis, "Seventh Generation Forestry: Wisconsin Menominee Indians Set the Standard for sustainable Forest Management," available at http://www.mtewood.com/seventh.htm; Marshall Pecore, "Menominee Woodland 141 Years of Sustained Yield Management," available at http://www.mtewood.com/sustained%20yield.htm.

9. George Weurthner, "Up in Smoke: Why Biomass Wood Energy Is Not the Answer," *Counterpunch*, http://counterpunch.com/wuerthner01122010.html, accessed Jan. 17, 2010.

10. Alice Friedemann, "Peak Soil: Why Cellulosic Ethanol, Biofuels Are Unsustainable and a Threat to America," *Culture Change*, April 10, 2007, available at http://culturechange.org/cms/index.php?option=com_content&task=view&id=107&Itemid=1.

11. http://www.stanford.edu/group/efmh/winds/.

12. Christina Archer and Mark Jacobson, "Supplying Baseload Power and Reducing Transmission Requirements by Interconnecting Wind Farms," *Journal of Applied Meteorology and Climatology* 46 (November 2007): 1701–17, available at http://www.stanford.edu/group/efmh/winds/aj07_jamc.pdf.

13. "Understanding Base Load Power. What It Is and Why It Matters" (October 7, 2008). Published by Dr. Matthew Cordaro in conjunction with New York Affordable Reliable Electricity Alliance (New York AREA), available at http://www.area-alliance.org/documents/base%20load%20power.pdf.

14. American Wind Energy Association, "The Economics of Wind Energy," available at http://www.awea.org/pubs/factsheets/EconomicsOfWind-Feb2005.pdf.

15. RenewableEnergyFocus.com, "Belgium inaugurates wind farm with largest wind turbines" (Nov. 30, 2009), available at http://www.renewableenergyfocus.com/view/5588/belgium-inaugurates-wind-farm-with-largest-wind-turbines/.

16. Dan Ancona and Jim McVeigh, "Wind Turbine—Materials and Manufacturing Fact Sheet," prepared for the Office of Industrial Technologies, U.S. Department of Energy, 2001, available at http://www.perihq.com/documents/WindTurbine-MaterialsandManufacturing_FactSheet.pdf.

17. "Supply Chain: The Race to Meet Demand," European Wind Energy Association, available at http://www.ewea.org/fileadmin/ewea_documents/documents/publications/WD/2007_january/0701-WD26-focus.pdf.

18. Jon Rynn, "How to Enter the Global Green Economy," *Foreign Policy in Focus* (June 2008), available at http://www.commondreams.org/archive/2008/06/17/9685.

19. American Society of Civil Engineers, "Report Card on U.S. Infrastructure," 2005, available at http://www.asce.org/reportcard/2005/page.cfm?id=25; an excellent overview is provided by "Gail the Actuary," "Will the U.S. Electric Grid Be Our Undoing?" http://www.theoildrum.com/node/4918.

20. Phillip Bane, "Laying the groundwork: Smart grid basics," available at http://www.ncsl.org/print/energy/Bane4-24-08.pdf.

21. Paul Davidson, "New Battery Packs Powerful Punch," *USA Today*, July 5, 2007, available at http://www.usatoday.com/money/industries/energy/2007-07-04-sodium-battery_N.htm.

22. National Energy Technology Laboratory, "Energy Storage: A Key Enabler of the Smart Grid" (September 2009), available at http://www.netl.doe.gov/moderngrid/referenceshelf/whitepapers/Energy%20Storage_2009_10_02.pdf.

23. "The Future of Geothermal Energy: Impact of Enhanced Geothermal Systems [EGS] on the United States in the 21st Century," Massachusetts Institute of

Technology, 2007, available at http://geothermal.inel.gov/publications/future_of_ geothermal_energy.pdf.

24. J. Lund, B. Sanner, L. Rybach, R. Curtis, G. Hellström, "Geothermal (Ground Source) Heat Pumps: A World Overview," *Oregon Institute of Technology GHC Bulletin* (September 2004), available at http://geoheat.oit.edu/bulletin/bull 25-3/art1.pdf.

25. *San Francisco Chronicle*, "From the Ground Up: Geoexchange Uses Earth's Energy to Efficiently Heat and Cool Homes," July 14, 2001, available at http:// www.sfgate.com/cgi-bin/article.cgi?file=/chronicle/archive/2001/07/14/HO121723. DTL.

26. "How to Buy an Energy-Efficient Ground Source Heat Pump," Energy Efficiency and Renewable Energy Federal Energy Management Program, U.S. Department of Energy, available at http://www1.eere.energy.gov/femp/pdfs/ground source_heatpumps.pdf.

27. "Solar Facts—Photovoltaics—The Basics," Energy Efficiency and Renewable Energy Federal Energy Management Program, U.S. Department of Energy, available at http://apps1.eere.energy.gov/solar/cfm/faqs/third_level.cfm/name=Photo voltaics/cat=The%20Basics.

28. Kenneth T. Jackson, *Crabgrass Frontier: The Suburbanization of the United States* (Oxford: Oxford University Press, 1987), Chapter 11, "Federal Subsidy and the American Dream: How Washington Changed the American Housing Market."

29. Van Jones, *The Green Collar Economy: How One Solution Can Fix Our Two Biggest Problems* (New York: HarperOne, 2009).

CHAPTER 11

1. Jane Jacobs, *Cities and the Wealth of Nations* (New York: Vintage Press, 1985).

2. Kenneth T. Jackson, *Crabgrass Frontier: The Suburbanization of the United States* (Oxford: Oxford University Press, 1987), p. 188.

3. Christopher B. Leinberger, "Footloose and Fancy Free: A Field Survey of Walkable Urban Places in the Top 30 U.S. Metropolitan Areas" (Paper of the Metropolitan Policy Program, Washington, DC: Brookings Institution, 12/04/2007). Available at http://www.brookings.edu/papers/2007/1128_walkableurbanism_ leinberger.aspx

4. Steve Belmont, *Cities in Full* (Chicago: APA Planners Press, 2002), referenced at http://greatergreaterwashington.org/post.cgi?id=1249

5. Laurence Aurbach, "Fun with Density and Transit Statistics," *Ped Shed*, 6/26/ 2007, available at http://pedshed.net/?p=131

6. Richard Register, *Ecocities: Rebuilding Cities in Balance with Nature* (New Society Publishers, 2006).

7. Robert Beauregard, *When America Became Suburban* (Minneapolis: University of Minnesota Press, 2006).

8. Jackson, *Crabgrass Frontier*, p. 203.

9. Ibid, p. 206.

10. James Howard Kunstler, *The Long Emergency: Surviving the End of Oil, Climate Change, and Other Converging Catastrophes of the Twenty-First Century* (New York: Grove Press, 2006).

11. 1963 Census of Manufactures, Volume III, Area Statistics, chart 9, p. 43 (Washington, DC: Government Printing Office, U.S. Department of Commerce, 1967).

12. Richard Florida, "How the Crash Will Reshape America," *The Atlantic Magazine* (March 2009), http://www.theatlantic.com/doc/200903/meltdown-geography.

13. Jacobs, *Cities and the Wealth of Nations*.

14. Eugene Ferguson, *Engineering in the Mind's Eye* (Cambridge, MA: MIT Press, 1994).

15. http://globalpublicmedia.com/richard_heinbergs_museletter_what_will_we_eat_as_the_oil_runs_out.

16. Ibid.

17. Ibid.

18. Amy Stewart, "The Man Who Would Feed the World: John Jeavons' Farming Methods Contain Lessons for Backyard Gardeners Too," *San Francisco Chronicle*, April 13, 2002. Available at http://www.sfgate.com/cgi-bin/article.cgi?file=/chronicle/archive/2002/04/13/HO126062.DTL.

19. Richard Heinberg, "Fifty Million Farmers," *EnergyBulletin.net* (Nov. 17, 2006), available at http://energybulletin.net/22584.html.

20. Dickson Despommier, "Growing Skyscrapers: The Rise of Vertical Farms," *Scientific American* (November 2009).

21. Michael Pollan, *The Omnivore's Dilemma: A Natural History of Four Meals* (New York: Penguin Press reprint, 2007), see section on Joel Salatin.

22. David Owen, *Green Metropolis: Why Living Smaller, Living Closer, and Driving Less Are the Keys to Sustainability* (New York: Riverhead Press, 2009), p. 40.

CHAPTER 12

1. Charles Montesquieu, *The Spirit of the Laws* Book 8, page 120 (New York and London: The Colonial Press, 1900), retrieved from Google Books at http://books.google.com/books?id=j6URLxeiwfIC.

2. W. R. Smyser, *The German Economy: Colossus at the Crossroads*, 2nd ed. (New York: St. Martin's Press, 1992).

3. Linda Weiss, "War, the State, and the Origins of the Japanese Employment System," *Politics and Society* 21, no. 3 (1993): 325–54.

4. Seymour Melman, *After Capitalism* (New York: Knopf, 2001), pp. 150–151.

5. John Zysman, *Governments, Markets and Growth: Financial Systems and the Politics of Industrial Change* (Ithaca: Cornell University Press, 1983).

6. Shoshanna Zuboff, *In the Age of the Smart Machine: The Future of Work and Power* (New York: Basic Books, 1989).

7. Naomi Klein, *The Shock Doctrine: The Rise of Disaster Capitalism* (New York: Picador, 2008).

8. William Foote Whyte and Kathleen King Whyte, *Making Mondragon: the Growth and Dynamics of the Worker Cooperative Complex*, 2nd rev. ed. (Ithaca, NY: ILR Press, 1991).

9. David Friedman, *The Misunderstood Miracle: Industrial Development and Political Change in Japan* (Ithaca: Cornell University Press, 1988).

10. I would like to thank Marshall Auerback for this suggestion.

11. James Galbraith, *The Predator State: Why Conservatives Abandoned the Free Market and Why Liberals Should Too* (New York: Free Press, 2009).

12. I'd like to thank Brian D'Agostino for this insight.

13. Mancur Olson, *The Rise and Decline of Nations* (New Haven: Yale University Press, 1982).

14. C. Wright Mills, *The Power Elite* (Oxford: Oxford University Press, 1957).

15. John Kenneth Galbraith, *American Capitalism: The Concept of Countervailing Power* (New York: Houghton Mifflin, 1956).

16. Statistical Abstract of the United States, 2010 (Washington, DC: United States Department of Commerce Census Bureau), Table 648, "Labor Union Membership by Sector: 1985 to 2008."

17. Bureau of Economic Analysis, "Gross-Domestic-Product-by-Industry Accounts, 1947–2008," available at http://198.76.170.20/industry/gpotables/gpo_list.cfm. Then, click on the "Value Added by Industry as a Percentage of Gross Domestic Product" interactive table link. Then pick "1970" in the "First Year" dropdown, then click "Refresh Table" button, and look at line 12, labeled "Manufacturing," for manufacturing as a percentage of GDP.

18. Russell Mardon, "The State and the Effective Control of Foreign Capital: The Case of South Korea," *World Politics* 43 (October 1990): 111–38.

19. Erick Reinert, *How Rich Countries Got Rich and Why Poor Countries Stay Poor* (New York: Public Affairs, 2007).

CHAPTER 13

1. John Kenneth Galbraith, *The Essential Galbraith* (New York: Houghton-Mifflin, 2001), pp. 21–22.

2. Ibid., p. 24.

3. Milton Friedman, *Capitalism and Freedom* (Chicago: University of Chicago Press, 1982), preface to 2nd edition, p. ix.

4. Matt Taibi, "The Great American Bubble Machine," *Rolling Stone* (July 2009), available at http://www.rollingstone.com/politics/story/29127316/the_great_american_bubble_machine.

5. Liz Walker, *EcoVillage at Ithaca: Pioneering a Sustainable Culture* (New Society Publishers, 2005). Also see, http://ena.ecovillage.org/eng/.

6. Thomas Paine, *Common Sense* (originally published 1776), available from Google Books at http://books.google.com/books?id=wVt7VxvFyegC.

Selected Bibliography

Abramovitz, Moses. "Resource and Output Trends in the United States Since 1870." *The American Economic Review* 46, no. 2, Papers and Proceedings of the Sixty-eighth Annual Meeting of the American Economic Association (May 1956): 5–23.

Abu-Lughod, Janet L. *Before European Hegemony: The World System A.D. 1250–1350*. Oxford: Oxford University Press, 1989.

Alvord, Katie. *Divorce Your Car!: Ending the Love Affair with the Automobile*. Gabriola Island, BC: New Society Publishers, 2000.

Amsden, Alice H. *Asia's Next Giant: South Korea and Late Industrialization*. Oxford: Oxford University Press, 1989.

Aristotle. *Physics*. Oxford: Oxford University Press, 1996.

Ashtor, Eliyahu. "Underdevelopment in the Pre-industrial Era: The Case of Declining Economies." *Journal of European Economic History* 7 (Fall 1978): 285–310.

Bairoch, Paul. "International Industrialization Levels from 1750 to 1980." *Journal of European Economic History* 11, nos. 1, 2 (Fall 1982).

Beauregard, Robert. *When America Became Suburban*. Minneapolis: University of Minnesota Press, 2006.

Belmont, Steve. *Cities in Full*. Chicago: APA Planners Press, 2002.

Brown, Ellen Hodgson. *The Web of Debt: The Shocking Truth about Our Money System and How We Can Break Free*. Baton Rouge: Third Millennium Press, 2008.

Brown, Lester R. *Plan B 4.0: Mobilizing to Save Civilization*. New York: W. W. Norton, 2009.

Calleo, David. *The German Problem Reconsidered: Germany and the World Order 1870 to the Present*. Cambridge: Cambridge University Press, 1980.

Catton, William. *Overshoot: The Ecological Basis of Revolutionary Change*. Urbana and Chicago: University of Illinois Press, 1982.

Chandler, Alfred D., Jr. *The Visible Hand: The Managerial Revolution in American Business*. Cambridge, MA: Belknap Harvard, 1977.

Clark, John Bates. *The Distribution of Wealth: A Theory of Wages, Interest, and Profits*. New York: Macmillan, 1914, available at Google Books.

Cohen, Avi J., and G. C. Harcourt. "Whatever Happened to the Cambridge Capital Theory Controversies?" *Journal of Economic Perspectives* 17, no.1 (Winter 2003): 199–214.

Crosby, Alfred. *Ecological Imperialism: The Ecological Expansion of Europe, 900–1900.* Cambridge: Cambridge University Press, 2004.

Cumings, Bruce. "The Origins and Development of the Northeast Asian Political Economy: Industrial Sectors, Product Cycles, and Political Consequences." In *The Political Economy of New Asian Industrialism*, edited by Frederic Deyo. Ithaca: Cornell University Press, 1987.

Dahrendorf, Ralf. *Society and Democracy in Germany.* New York & London: W. W. Norton, 1967.

Darwin, John. *After Tamerlane: The rise and fall of global empires, 1400–2000.* New York: Bloomsbury Press, 2008

DeAngelis, D.L., W.M. Post, and C.C. Travis. *Positive Feedback in Natural Systems.* Berlin: Springer-Verlag, 1986.

de Soto, Hernando. *The Mystery of Capital: Why Capitalism Triumphs in the West and Fails Everywhere Else.* New York: Basic Books, 2003.

De Tocqueville, Alexis. *Democracy in America.* New York: Penguin Classics, 2003.

Dehio, Ludwig. *The Precarious Balance: Four Centuries of the European Power Struggle.* Charles Fullman, trans. New York: Alfred A. Knopf, 1962.

Derry, T.K., and Trevor I. Williams, *A Short History of Technology: From the earliest times to A.D. 1900,* Oxford: Oxford University Press, 1960.

Devine, Warren D., Jr. "From Shafts to Wires: Historical Perspective on Electrification." *The Journal of Economic History* 43, no. 2 (June 1983): 347–372.

Deyo, Frederic, ed. *The Political Economy of New Asian Industrialism.* Ithaca: Cornell University Press, 1987.

Diamond, Jared. *Guns, Germs and Steel: The Fates of Human Societies.* New York: W.W. Norton, 2005.

Diderot, Denis. *A Diderot Pictorial Encyclopedia of Trades and Industry.* New York: Dover, 1959.

Doyle, Michael W. "Kant, Liberal Legacies and Foreign Affairs." *Philosophy and Public Affairs* 12 (1983): 205–235, 323–53.

Drake, Alan. "Multiple Birds—One Silver BB: A Synergistic Set of Solutions to Multiple Issues Focused on Electrified Railroads," *TheOilDrum.com*, July 15, 2008, available at http://www.theoildrum.com/node/4301.

Eisler, Riane. *The Chalice and the Blade: Our History, Our Future.* Gloucester, MA: Peter Smith Publishers, 1994.

Feldman, Jonathan M. "From Mass Transit to Manufacturing." *The American Prospect,* April 2009, A12-A16.

Fingleton, Eamonn. *In Praise of Hard Industries: Why Manufacturing, Not the Information Economy, Is the Key to Future Prosperity.* New York: Houghton Mifflin, 1999, 32.

Friedman, David. *The Misunderstood Miracle: Industrial Development and Political Change in Japan.* Ithaca: Cornell University Press. 1988.

Galbraith, James. *The Predator State: Why Conservatives Abandoned the Free Market and Why Liberals Should Too,* New York: Free Press, 2009.

Galbraith, John Kenneth. *The Great Crash of 1929.* New York: Mariner Books, 2009.

———. "The Second Imperial Requiem." *International Security* 7, no. 3 (Winter 1982–1983): 84–93.

———. *American Capitalism: The Concept of Countervailing Power*. New York: Houghton Mifflin, 1956.

Gerschenkron, Alexander. *Economic Backwardness in Historical Perspective: A Book of Essays*. Cambridge, MA: Belknap, 1962.

Gordon, David M. *Fat and Mean: The Corporate Squeeze of Working Americans and the Myth of Managerial "Downsizing."* New York: Free Press, 1996.

Gore, Al. *Our Choice: A Plan to Solve the Climate Crisis*. Emmaus, PA: Rodale, 2009.

Gunderson, Lance H., and C.S. Holling, eds. *Panarchy: Understanding Transformations in Human and Natural Systems*. Washington, DC: Island Press, 2002.

Habakkuk, H.J. *American and British Technology in the 19th Century: The Search for Labour-Saving Inventions*. Cambridge: Cambridge University Press, 1967.

Harrison, Mark. "Resource Mobilization for World War II: The U.S.A., U.K., U.S.S.R., and Germany, 1938–1945," *Economic History Review*, 2nd Series, 41, no.8 (1988): 171–191.

Hawken, Paul, Amory Lovins, and L. Hunter Lovins. *Natural Capitalism: Creating the next industrial revolution*, Boston: Back Bay Books, 2008

Hawken, Paul. *Blessed Unrest: How the largest social movement in history is restoring grace, justice and beauty to the world*. New York: Penguin, 2008

Heinberg, Richard. *Peak Everything: Waking Up to the Century of Declines*. Gabriola Island, BC: New Society Publishers, 2007.

Homer-Dixon, Thomas. *The Upside of Down: Catastrophe, Creativity, and the Renewal of Civilization*. Washington, DC: Island Press, 2006.

Jackson, Kenneth T. *Crabgrass Frontier: The Suburbanization of the United States*. Oxford: Oxford University Press, 1987.

Jacobs, Jane. *Cities and the Wealth of Nations*. New York: Vintage Press, 1985.

Jervis, Robert. *System Effects: Complexity in Political and Social Life*. Princeton: Princeton University Press, 1997.

Johnson, Chalmers. *MITI and the Japanese Miracle: The Growth of Industrial Policy, 1925–1975*. Stanford: Stanford University Press, 1982.

Jones, Van. *The Green Collar Economy: How one solution can fix our two biggest problems*. New York: HarperOne, 2009.

Kaiser, David. *Politics and War: European Conflict from Philip II to Hitler*. Cambridge, MA: Harvard University Press, 1990.

Keegan, John. *The Face of Battle*. New York: Penguin, 1983.

Kennedy, Paul. *The Rise and Fall of the Great Powers: Economic Change and Military Conflict from 1500 to 2000*. New York: Random House, 1987.

Keynes, John Maynard. *The General Theory of Employment, Interest and Money*. New York: Harcourt Brace and World, 1964, originally published in 1936.

Kindleberger, Charles. *The World in Depression, 1929–1939*. Rev. ed. Berkeley: University of California Press, 1986.

Klein, Naomi. *The Shock Doctrine: The Rise of Disaster Capitalism*. New York: Picador, 2008.

Kolchin, Peter. *Unfree Labor: American Slavery and Russian Serfdom*. Cambridge, MA: Belknap Press, 1990.

Komanoff, Charles. *Ending the Oil Age: A Plan to Kick the Saudi Habit*. New York: Komanoff Energy Associates, 2002.

Kuhn, Thomas S. *The Structure of Scientific Revolutions*. 2nd ed. Chicago: University of Chicago Press, 1970.

Kunstler, James Howard. *The Long Emergency: Surviving the End of Oil, Climate Change, and Other Converging Catastrophes of the Twenty-First Century*. New York: Grove Press, 2006.

Lakatos, Imre, and Alan Musgrave, eds. *Criticism and the Growth of Knowledge*. Cambridge: Cambridge University Press, 1970.

Landes, David S. *The Unbound Prometheus: Technological Change and Industrial Development in Western Europe from 1750 to the Present*. Cambridge: Cambridge University Press, 1969.

Liddell Hart, B.H. *Strategy*. 2nd ed. New York: Plume, 1991.

List, Friedrich. *The National System of Political Economy*. Translated by S.S. Lloyd. New York: Augustus M. Kelley, 1885.

McNeill, J. R. *Something New under the Sun: An Environmental History of the 20th Century World*. New York: W. W. Norton, 2001.

McNeill, William. *The Pursuit of Power: Technology, Armed Force and Society since A.D. 1000*. Chicago: University of Chicago Press, 1984.

———. *The Rise of the West: A History of the Human Community*. Chicago: The University of Chicago Press. 1963.

———. *Plagues and Peoples*. New York: Doubleday, 1976.

Maddison, Angus. *Dynamic Forces in Capitalist Development: A Long-Run Comparative View*. Oxford: Oxford University Press, 1991.

Manning, Richard. *Against the Grain: How Agriculture Has Hijacked Civilization*. New York: North Point Press, 2004.

Manville, Michael, and Donald Shoup. "Parking, People, and Cities," *Journal of Urban Planning and Development* 131, no. 4 (December 1, 2005): 233–45.

Meadows, Donella, Jorgen Randers, and Dennis Meadows. *The Limits to Growth: The 30-Year Update*. White River Junction, VT: Chelsea Green, 2004.

Melman, Seymour. *After Capitalism*. New York: Knopf, 2001.

———. "The Veblen-Commons Award: From Private to State Capitalism: How the Permanent War Economy Transformed the Institutions of American Capitalism." *Journal of Economic Issues* 31, no. 2 (June 1997), 311–30.

———. *Profits without Production*. New York: Knopf, 1983.

———. *Our Depleted Society*, New York: Holt, Rinehart and Winston, 1965.

Metz, B., O.R. Davidson, P.R. Bosch, R. Dave, L.A. Meyer, eds. *Contribution of Working Group III to the Fourth Assessment Report of the Intergovernmental Panel on Climate Change*, Cambridge: Cambridge University Press, 2007, available at http://www.ipcc.ch/publications_and_data/ar4/wg3/en/contents.html.

Mills, C. Wright. *The Power Elite*. Oxford: Oxford University Press, 1957.

Milward, Alan. *The Reconstruction of Western Europe 1945–51*. London: Methuen, 1984.

Mokyr, Joel. *The Lever of Riches: Technological Creativity and Economic Progress*. Oxford: Oxford University Press, 1990.

Montesquieu, Charles. *The Spirit of the Laws*. New York and London: The Colonial Press, 1900, retrieved from Google Books at http://books.google.com/books?id=j6URLxeiwfIC.

Montgomery, David. *Dirt: The Erosion of Civilizations.* Berkeley: University of California Press, 2008.

Moore, Barrington. *Social Origins of Dictatorship and Democracy: Lord and Peasant in the Making of the Modern World.* Boston: Beacon Press, 1993.

Morowski, Philip. *More Heat Than Light: Economics as Social Physics, Physics as Nature's Economics.* Cambridge: Cambridge University Press, 1991.

Nove, Alec. *An Economic History of the USSR 1917–1991.* 3rd ed. New York: Penguin, 1993.

Okimoto, Daniel. *Between MITI and the Market: Japanese Industrial Policy for High Technology.* Stanford: Stanford University Press, 1990.

O'Neill, R.V., D.L. DeAngelis, J.B. Waide, and T.F.H. Allen. *A Hierarchical Concept of Ecosystems.* Princeton: Princeton University Press, 1986.

Owen, David. *Green Metropolis: Why Living Smaller, Living Closer, and Driving Less Are the Keys to Sustainability.* New York: Riverhead Press, 2009.

Paine, Thomas. *Common Sense* (originally published 1776), available from Google Books at http://books.google.com/books?id=wVt7VxvFyegC.

Ponting, Clive. *A New Green History of the World: The Environment and the Collapse of Civilizations.* New York: Penguin, 2007.

Porter, Bruce. *War and the Rise of the State: The Military Foundations of Modern Politics.* New York: Free Press, 1994.

Prigogine, Ilya. *The End of Certainty.* New York: Free Press, 1997.

Putnam, Robert. *Bowling Alone: The Collapse and Revival of American Community.* New York: Simon and Schuster, 2001.

Register, Richard. *Ecocities: Rebuilding Cities in Balance with Nature.* Gabriola Island, BC: New Society Publishers, 2006.

Reinert, Erik S. *How Rich Countries Got Rich and Why Poor Countries Stay Poor.* New York: Public Affairs, 2007.

Ricardo, David. *The Works and Correspondence of David Ricardo.* Edited by P. Sraffa. Cambridge: Cambridge University Press, 1970.

———. *Principals of Political Economy and Taxation.* London: G. Bell and Sons, 1919. Available at Google Books.

Roberts, Paul. *The End of Oil: On the Edge of a Perilous New World.* New York: Mariners Press, 2004.

Rolt, L.T.C. *A Short History of Machine Tools.* Cambridge, MA: MIT Press, 1965.

Rosenberg, Nathan. "Technological Change in the Machine Tool Industry, 1840–1910." *The Journal of Economic History* 23, no. 4. (Dec. 1963): 414–43.

Rubin, Jeff. *Why Your World Is about to Get a Whole Lot Smaller: Oil and the End of Globalization.* New York: Random House, 2009.

Rubin, Jeff, and Benjamin Tal. "Will Soaring Transport Costs Reverse Globalization?" *CIBC World Markets StrategEcon* (May 27, 2008): 4–7, available at http://research.cibcwm.com/economic_public/download/smay08.pdf.

Rynn, Jon. "The Power to Create Wealth: A Systems-Based Theory of the Rise and Decline of Great Powers in the 20th Century." PhD Diss., City University of New York, 2001.

Samuelson, Paul. *Economics.* New York: McGraw-Hill, 1975.

Schurmann, Franz. *The Logic of World Power;: An Inquiry into the Origins, Currents, and Contradictions of World Politics.* New York: Pantheon Books, 1974.

Shonfield, Andrew. *Modern Capitalism*. Oxford: Oxford University Press, 1968.

Smith, Adam. *The Wealth of Nations*. Edwin Canaan Edition. London: The Modern Library, 1994.

Smyser, W.R. *The German Economy: Colossus at the Crossroads*. Houndmills, UK: Palgrave Macmillan, 1993.

Solow, Robert. "Technical Change and the Aggregate Production Function." *Review of Economics and Statistics* 39 (August 1957): 312–20.

Stern, Nicholas. "The Determinants of Growth." *Economic Journal* 101 (January 1991): 122–33.

Tassava, Christopher. "The American Economy during World War II." *EH.Net Encyclopedia*, edited by Robert Whaples. February 10, 2008. Available at http://eh.net/encyclopedia/article/tassava.WWII, accessed 1/23/2010.

Temple, Jonathan. "The New Growth Evidence." *Journal of Economic Literature* 37 (March 1999): 112–56.

Thucydides, *The Peloponnesian War*. New York: W.W. Norton, 1998.

United Nations International Development Organization. *International Yearbook of Industrial Statistics, 2009*. Vienna, 2009.

Van Laue, Theodore. *Why Lenin? Why Stalin? Why Gorbachev?: The Rise and Fall of the Soviet System*. White Plains, NY: Longman, 1997.

Wade, Robert. *Governing the Market*. Princeton: Princeton University Press, 1992.

Wallerstein, Immanuel. *The Modern World System I: Capitalist Agriculture and the Origins of the European World Economy in the Sixteenth Century*. New York: Academic Press, 1974.

Waltz, Kenneth N. *The Theory of International Politics*. New York: McGraw-Hill, 1979.

Weiss, Linda. "War, the State, and the Origins of the Japanese Employment System," *Politics and Society* 21, no. 3 (1993): 325–54.

Whitty, Julia. "The Fate of the Oceans." *Mother Jones* (March/April 2006), Available at http://motherjones.com/politics/2006/03/fate-ocean.

Whyte, William Foote, and Kathleen King Whyte. *Making Mondragon: The Growth and Dynamics of the Worker Cooperative Complex*. 2nd rev. ed. Ithaca, NY: ILR Press, 1991.

Zuboff, Shoshanna. *In the Age of the Smart Machine: The Future of Work and Power*. New York: Basic Books, 1989.

Zysman, John. *Governments, Markets and Growth: Financial Systems and the Politics of Industrial Change*. Ithaca: Cornell University Press, 1983.

Index

About the Author

JON RYNN is an environmental blogger for Grist.org and creator of Manu-facturingGreenProsperity.com. He has a PhD in international relations from the City University of New York and was an adjunct professor of political science at Baruch College. With help from the Institute for Policy Studies, he is working with experts from the City University of New York, Columbia University, and the steel industry to rebuild America's rail transit industries. For many years, he was a research assistant for the late Seymour Melman, one of America's greatest scholars of manufacturing.